D0709515

AUSTRALIA

History and Horizons

To My Very Special A.D.
Hope you enjoy the book and
had a very Merry Christmas.
(1973)

Love,
Sissy

AUSTRALIA

History and Horizons

Roderick Cameron

Weidenfeld and Nicolson
5 Winsley Street London W1

Hicks Smith & Sons
Sydney Melbourne Brisbane

© Roderick Cameron 1971
All rights reserved. No part of the publication may be
reproduced, stored in a retrieval system, or transmitted,
in any form or by any means, electronic, mechanical,
photocopying, recording or otherwise, without the prior
permission of the Copyright owner.
ISBN 0 297 00128 0
Designed by Sheila Sherwen for George Weidenfeld
and Nicolson Ltd, London
Printed by Sir Joseph Causton & Sons Ltd., London
and Eastleigh.

This book is for the Lindemans,
in particular my mother.

Acknowledgments

First and foremost I would like to thank Mr Richardson, Principal Librarian of the Mitchell Library and the Public Library of New South Wales in Sydney. I spent many months in their reading rooms and always found the staff most helpful and obliging. Amongst others I would also like to include Mr White, the Librarian of the National Library of Australia at Canberra, also Mrs Gibson and Mr Wallace, two curators who guided me through the invaluable material comprising the Nan Kivell Collection of Australiana now housed in the National Library. Mr Nan Kivell, Director of the Redfern Gallery in London, has spent a lifetime assembling the numerous paintings, drawings and engravings which form the bulk of this remarkable collection, and, being an old friend, I have often had recourse to his advice as to which of the many alternatives I should use for my illustrative material.

I should also like to thank the different State Libraries always so prompt in their replies, also the various State Galleries, their Curators doing everything in their power to make things easy for me. In particular I would single out Mr Daniel Thomas, the Curator of the Art Gallery of New South Wales and all members of the staff of the Art Gallery of South Australia, also those of the National Gallery of Victoria.

Amongst my friends I would like to thank Max Dupain who contributed generously to the book in giving me permission to reproduce his excellent photographs of colonial architecture, while Kerry Dundas, his associate, supplied most of the illustrations for the book. The charming Mrs Gregory Blaxland, Senior Vice-President of the National Trust of Australia (New South Wales) was also of great assistance, showing me round the buildings under the protection of her branch of the Trust. The National Trust in each state is doing an admirable job in helping to restore and preserve Australia's architectural past.

Last but not least comes Mr Walter Stone who advised me so wisely when starting on my researches. Himself an accomplished historian, he suggested that I purchase two indispensable works for anyone making a study of Australia; one, the *Australian Encyclopaedia* published by the Grolier Society of Australia and the other the *Australian Dictionary of Biography* published by the Melbourne University Press. The former was first published in 1965, the latter work appearing the following year. The Australian Department of Angus and Robertson, the Sydney publishers and booksellers, was also of much assistance to me.

Endpapers Grape picking at Lindeman's Hunter River vineyards in the turn of the century.

Contents

1 Perspective

Anthony Trollope, visiting Australia in 1871, complains of the ignorance of the English. One letter he saw had been addressed to 'Melbourne, New South Wales, South Australia'.[1] One wonders how much things have changed? People are certainly better informed. But how many, for instance, can name the state capitals, let alone place them correctly on the map? One remembers a passage in Oscar Wilde's play, *Lady Windemere's Fan*. The Duchess of Berwick is hoping to marry her daughter, Lady Agatha, to a rich young Australian called Hopper, whose father had made a fortune in tinned foods. The occasion is a ball in London in Lady Windemere's house; and Hopper is brought up to the Duchess.

'We all know', the Duchess greets him, 'how you are run after in London.'

'Capital place, London!' Hopper answers. 'They are not nearly so exclusive in London as they are in Sydney.'

The Duchess ignores this sally. 'Do you know, Mr Hopper, dear Agatha and I are so much interested in Australia … Agatha has found it on the map.'

Wilde's play was produced at the St James's Theatre in 1892; but even today his description of the Duchess's attitude does not seem completely far-fetched.

I am half Australian myself, though I was brought up in England and France. My mother, widowed when I was a year old, took me back to Australia during my early childhood: but of that visit I can, of course, remember nothing. I retain vivid memories, however, of stories she told me of her tomboy youth spent with her brothers on the family station, and of the fun they had while the grapes were being gathered. There were picnics on great empty beaches loud with the crashing of surf – and then, the terrible day when my mother's pet kangaroo, which followed her around like a dog, jumped through the glass of the drawing-room window, sliced his tail off at the stump and tragically bled to death.

A beautiful woman, and much spoilt by those who loved her, she would sometimes come to my nursery in a shimmer of beads, her hair closely cropped

Opposite Stairwell at Elizabeth Bay House, Sydney, built by John Verge in the 1830s for Alexander MacLeay, the Colonial Secretary.

to her head. If she had time before going down to dinner, she would sit on the end of my bed and tell me stories, or read me snatches out of books she had enjoyed as a child – Antipodean classics, such as *Seven Little Australians* by Ethel Turner, written in the Louisa Alcott tradition, or *Dot and the Kangaroo* by Ethel Pedley, a Sydney music teacher.

Australia was in my blood; and I grew up feeling that I almost knew the country. I was determined, as soon as I could to see it with my own eyes. My chance came at the end of the war in 1945; and the result was my first book. At that time the majority of my friends, travelled, sophisticated people, almost ignored the existence of the Antipodes. 'Just back from Australia?' they would say, and then slightly incredulous: 'Did you *really* enjoy it? Funny, there are so many other places I would rather go to.' I can, or rather could, understand their point of view. It's the furthest you can go on the map, and expensive to get there. The country's past is comparatively recent – nothing more venerable than a gum tree; and no name, as somebody snobbishly wrote, more ancient or sublime than has been inscribed over a shop board. There were no ruins, and presumably not very much of interest in the way of architecture. Nor are there any fierce animals to encounter, or unassailable peaks to climb. Is it different enough to warrant the effort, time and expense? These were some of the doubts that crossed my mind. There it lies, this great island, a remote European outpost on the fringe of a land mass that geographically belongs to Asia. Yet it remains stubbornly Anglo-Saxon. William Shaw, emigrating to Australia in 1853, found this an asset and wrote comfortingly that 'a person just landed from Europe need experience no violent transition of habit and ideas. A businessman has his muffin and morning paper at breakfast.'[2] I have twice returned to Australia in recent years and with each visit my enthusiasm grew. Here at last is a country that, the moment you land, gives you a feeling of immense enthusiasm; of faith in the future. There are no class hatreds, no violence, and much kindness.

Both my visits lasted for several months and much of my time was spent in museums and libraries. The country itself has a strange subtle beauty all of its own; and there is more good architecture than one might expect. As to the flora and fauna, it is full of surprises. The indigenous flora, together with that of South Africa, is the most varied in the world. Much of its fauna is unique. Mark Twain, who took the trouble to study the country at first hand, was also enthralled by its history. He found it immensely curious; 'that it is itself the chiefest novelty the country has to offer. It does not read like history, but like the most beautiful lies. And all of a fresh sort, no mouldy old stale ones.'[3]

On the face of it, it seems hard to explain how a country with so much to offer should remain comparatively so little known. A great deal was published on Australia during the nineteenth century; and a growing stream of books are again appearing, though the majority, it must be admitted, are sponsored by Australian publishers. Yet the northern hemisphere remains surprisingly indifferent. True, some excitement can be seen in the business world about Australia's recently discovered mineral deposits – for example, the iron El Dorado of the desolate, sunblistered Hamersley Ranges thrust out into the

Indian Ocean. These mountains, ignored for generations, contain enough iron to feed all the blast furnaces in the world for a good hundred years, and could well prove to contain half the known iron-ore reserves on earth. Japanese industrialists have signed contracts that involve gigantic deliveries of high-grade ore over the next twenty years. This, of course, had had an effect on the real estate values of western Australia; and astute operators are beginning to invest in land. There is also a slight stirring, especially among young parents concerned about their children's future in the western world. More and more people are seriously considering emigration. Certain families have already made the move; but, on the whole, the percentage of those fully conscious of Australia's growing importance is still fairly small.

Here, then, is my purpose: an attempt to project my mother's country, to interpret it as I myself discovered it. As I have mentioned already, some personal impressions of mine were published in a first book on Australia in 1950, and parts have subsequently appeared in various collections.

Now I intend to adopt a more historical approach, not one, however, that pretends to cover all phases of this vast continent's development.

For obvious reasons books have to be composed within given limits, more than a certain number of words or plates price them beyond reason; this necessarily imposes restrictions on the author. He must work within a fixed framework, a qualification which gives me a legitimate excuse to indulge in a certain choice. There are ample sources elsewhere that trace political and economic growth. I am more drawn to selecting events, atmospheres and personalities that emerge from the past to form, for me, the colour of this continent. But the past is as much the truth of a country as its present, and as revealing.

For these reasons, the text and pictures will dwell primarily with the discovery of Australia and those aspects that led up to the period of the First World War. This is not a systematic history, however, passages will occur when these self-imposed boundaries will be violated by excursions into the present.

Dutch seamen, employed by the East India Company, made the first shadowy hatchings on their globes to indicate Australia. Disjointed sections of the map were gradually combined; and, by the middle of the seventeenth century, a good three-quarters of Australia's vast coastline of 12,000 miles had taken shape. The Dutch, however, apart from christening their discoveries New Holland, put them to very little practical use; it fell to Great Britain, in the person of Captain Cook, to lay claim to the land the Dutch had spurned.

William Dampier, a buccaneer adventurer, was probably the first Englishman to land on the mainland of Australia. He visited it on two separate voyages and touched the north coast at four different places, the first in the *Cygnet* in January 1688. But Dampier, like the Dutch before him, found the shore he sighted impossibly bleak and barren. Captain Cook, eighty-two years later, striking the unknown, and comparatively fertile east coast, had quite a different impression. So also did Joseph Banks, the expedition's naturalist. Their landfall appeared full of promise; and the account of their voyage, published soon after their return, had an immediate success and completely changed the beliefs then current about Australia.

Cook returned from his voyage in 1771; five years later, the North American colonies declared their independence. The English, finding they could no longer send their convicts across the Atlantic, were forced to select a new place for transportation. Australia seemed the obvious choice. The First Fleet of eleven ships sailed in 1787 and, after a lumbering passage of eight months, eventually dropped anchor in one of the most beautiful natural harbours in the world – the future Sydney.

Accounts of the first years of settlement and the history of transportation make harrowing but absorbing reading; as do those of the lives and adventures of the men who opened up the country, a continent twenty-five times the area of Great Britain and Ireland and almost as great as that of the United States.

Pastoralists followed in the wake of the explorers. Drovers, with slouch hats turned back from their eyes, were to be seen herding vast mobs of cattle over the mountains to virgin pastures rolling out in endless plains. These pastoralists were divided into two groups: drovers and shepherds; and it was the shepherds, in the end, who became the kings of the land, turning Australia into the leading wool-growing country of the world.

The 1850s saw the discovery of gold, first in New South Wales, later in Victoria, and the results somewhat changed the appearance of the land. The population went sky-rocketing, as the great tide of fortune-seekers pressed forward. Lumps of gold were found, valued at £5 to £200. One nugget, the 'Welcome Stranger', measured twenty-one inches long; and the Holtermann nugget, or rather mass, weighed 3,000 ounces and was worth a small fortune. Dazzled by these glittering hoards, the bushrangers, Australia's equivalent of our highwaymen, became a serious menace. The police in the beginning were powerless. Too many of the farmers were on the side of the bushrangers, and regarded them as national heroes, Robin Hoods to be emulated in their games by every freckled tousle-haired youth in the country. It was only when Aboriginal trackers from northern Queensland were employed that these renegades were brought to bay and finally disbanded.

Meanwhile the country's political life developed. New South Wales, the original stake claimed by England, had control over a major part of the hinterland; but once the mountains that isolated the coast had been crossed, the area developed became too vast to be administered from one place. The island of Tasmania was the first to break away in 1825 from the central control. Western Australia was independently settled in 1829, and South Australia in 1834. Victoria seceded in 1851 after the discovery of gold, and Queensland in 1859. The last to become a separate state was the Northern Territory. Originally it had been administered by New South Wales, then South Australia; finally, in 1911, it was transferred to the Commonwealth.

Recognition of the need for some over-all co-ordinating machinery had come with the separation of New South Wales and Victoria. The suggestion, which originated in England, led to the appointment, in 1851, of a Governor-General of all the Australian possessions. The Governor of New South Wales, the premier State, was chosen to fulfil the role. The Governor's powers, both general and specific, were transmitted to him through the Secretary of State for the Colonies in distant London. Home-rule had been suited to a penal settlement; but it was hardly appropriate for a prosperous colony of free settlers with liberal ideas. A demand for self-government followed; and by 1856 most of the Australian colonies were governing themselves through their own elected parliaments.

With self-government came the real problem of defence. British troops were withdrawn in 1870; and thereafter small local forces were maintained by the separate colonies, or states. Under-populated, and far removed from its main sphere of interest, the Anglo-Saxon world, Australia was naturally very sensitive to colonising in the Pacific by other European powers, especially by Germany, which, when it occupied a part of New Guinea in the mid-1880s, was a leading military power in continental Europe. In 1874 Fiji had been annexed, mainly in the interests of the Australian colonists; but, when it came to the question of New Guinea, Britain appeared particularly obtuse. It was hardly wise to let the largest island in the world, lying within one hundred miles of Australia's shores, fall into other hands. Sir Thomas McIlwraith, Premier of Queensland, had warned Lord Derby, Secretary of State for the Colonies, of Germany's intentions; and Lord Derby had replied that he knew the Germans had no unfriendly intentions; they had told him so. Unconvinced, McIlwraith took the matter into his own hands and, on 4 April 1883, sent a Magistrate to plant the flag and take possession. Still Britain refused to recognise the action; and only when the other colonies sided emphatically with Queensland did Lord Derby proclaim a Protectorate over the south-eastern portion of the island, abandoning the north to Germany. During the First World War Germany was expelled from New Guinea; and the territory is now an Australian mandate.

This incident, as much as any other, impelled the country to seek Federation in order to be able to adopt a common system of defence. Compulsory military training was introduced in 1911; and in the same year the Royal Australian Navy was launched. As Professor Blainey[4] points out, while Australians have had to fight no war in defence of their own country, they nevertheless contributed willingly to Britain's squabbles in her outposts of Empire. Between 1845 and 1872, several Australian volunteers took part in the Maori Wars in New Zealand. An infantry battalion was shipped to the Red Sea to serve in the Sudan, and in 1900 an Australian naval force took part in quelling the Boxer Rebellion. The Boer War claimed a further 15,000 men with an equal quantity of horses. In the First World War more than 400,000 men voluntarily enlisted for overseas service and fought with distinction at Gallipoli, Palestine and in the terrible trench warfare of northern France. Her casualties, in proportion to their numbers, were higher than those of any other Allied Army. At Passchendaele alone she lost 30,000 men in three weeks of fighting, which put her losses at something like sixty-eight per cent of those engaged. In the Second World War Australia automatically followed Great Britain's declaration of war on Germany; and her forces saw fighting in Italian Cyrenaica, and in 1941, in Greece, Crete and the Western Desert. With the entry of Japan and the loss of nearly 30,000 prisoners in Malaya and Indonesia, Australia had very few troops left at home trained and equipped to fight. Obviously her primary duty now was the defence of her home territory; and, unable to turn to Britain for help, she decided to withdraw her divisions from the Middle East. Early in 1942 General Douglas MacArthur transferred his headquarters to Australia; and lend-lease supplies from the United States exceeded $1,000,000,000. The Japanese were halted at sea largely by United States Forces in the battles of the Coral Sea and Midway, and in New Guinea by Australians. The fact, however, that Australia ran a real risk of invasion did not stop her co-operating in the defence of Great Britain and in air attacks on Germany.

Since the last war Australia's position in world politics has changed considerably. She has been forced out of her isolation and been obliged to become an industrialised community. No longer able to depend on Britain for her defence, she has drifted into a new sphere of influence and responsibility. Facing her across the Pacific are two world powers – Japan and the United States. Fortunately, the stronger of the two is her ally and, for the moment, can assure her the protection she has lost through the relative decline of Britain. Japan, who if unchecked, might have swamped her completely, is now one of her most important markets. All is well in the present balance of things provided they stay that way; but with the great stirring of modern Asians, Australia cannot afford to take any chances and must build up her defences. This means a substantial increase of immigrants. China, across the way, has an annual population increase of roughly the total of Australia's population, which, for its size, is absurdly low, numbering some thirteen million, sixteen times less than the population of the United States. There is an abnormal concentration of people in the capital cities; Sydney and Melbourne between them contain about thirty-nine per cent of the total number. After Melbourne come Brisbane, Adelaide and Perth. The federal capital of Canberra houses a mere 100,000.

Soon after the discovery of gold in the 1850s, there were restrictions on the importation of coloured labour, laws designed to exclude mainly the Chinese. By the early 1900s it had become a definite ban. Australia isolated herself from Asia and Oceania with the policy known as White Australia. One per cent, I think, is the right assessment of Asian blood in the Australian population, the remaining ninety-nine per cent being of European stock. In 1947 out of 600,000 European-born residents of five years' standing, some 500,000 were natives of the British Isles, the remaining 100,000 being mostly Italians, Germans and Greeks, the Italians being in the lead.

Since the War, the Australian Government has done everything in its power to attract the emigrant. Even the White Australia policy is no longer enforced with quite the same ardour as formerly. There are some 12,000 young Asians studying in Australian universities; and some 30,000 Asians have become permanent residents, and in some cases even citizens. Free passages for British ex-servicemen and women and assisted passages for other British emigrants came into operation in 1947; by 1954 it had brought some 200,000 immigrants to the country. During the five years between 1947 and 1952, 170,000 refugees, mainly Poles and Yugoslavs, arrived from the displaced persons camps of Europe. In return for the shelter offered them by Australia, they assumed an obligation to work for two years in public construction or other works assigned to them. Further immigrants have arrived during more recent years; and optimism about the economic future of the country will certainly attract a fresh influx. But Australia has a long way to go yet, with an estimated population of four persons to the square mile. Europe, by constrast, can count over two hundred over the same area.

There are many things about Australia that catch the imagination: the vastness, for example, of the Northern Territory, ten times the size of England and two and a half times the size of Texas. Stations up there are called runs; and one of the oldest of them carries around 70,000 head of cattle. This particular station consists of some five million acres; and its fencing can be measured by hundreds of miles. Most of the water is supplied by bores drilled at vast expense. One station can count some fifty bores; and they are to be met with all over the country, since a fairly high percentage of Australia's cattle are wholly or partly dependent on artesian wells. Provisions for these large stations read like a list of army supplies, flour and sugar for the quarter being measured by the ton.

Bush fires are another particularly Australian phenomenon; and the really bad fires burn so fiercely that ashes have been known to fall like fine powder upon the decks of ships forty or fifty miles out to sea. First, as a terrible advance guard, come the shimmering waves of heat, like liquid fire; then the roaring flames, travelling quicker than the wind, huge tongues reaching upwards out of red clouds of billowing smoke. They sweep over the land, charred timber silhouetted against their angry glow, bringing huge hollow trees thundering down in explosions of sparks. The middle of a fire is indicated by clouds of birds. Then come the lizards and snakes that crawl over the blazing-hot ground, while kangaroos and emus keep breaking cover, hair singed and feathers hanging in shreads. It sometimes happens that men are also trapped in the blaze, and are obliged to abandon their cars or trucks and race for safety, lucky if they escape with only a burnt back. So frequent are these bush fires that even the country's flora has adapted itself to the ordeal. The seed pods of many species are not only fire-resistant, but rarely germinate freely unless a fire has passed over them – for example the different acacias, whose seedlings spring up by the hundred after the first rains that follow a forest fire.

Another feature of these conflagrations is the stupidity of the sheep. Of all the animals they are the only ones that do not have the instinct to run, but merely wait to be roasted alive. Their reaction to cold is equally imbecile. If by chance the temperature suddenly falls after the shearing, hundreds of them die helplessly in the frost. They just lie down and freeze. The only way to save them

'and there is more good architecture than one might expect.' *Above and opposite* Macquarie Field House, a late Regency house near Liverpool, New South Wales. The photograph above shows it before its restoration in 1962.

is to light a fire, or to set dogs chasing in amongst them to keep them moving. Rattles, clapping of hands and shouting can also work; but the station owner is not always aware of the drop in the temperature, with the result that he loses more than half of his flock.

The lambing season is another critical time. Vultures circles above, while blue-black crows with their sharp beaks sit, lined up on the fences, ever eager to pick out the eyes of the new-born lambs. To combat them, farm hands hang meat up in the trees and, when the crows gather thickly enough, blast at them with their guns. Sometimes they tether a captured crow to a length of cord; and the noise he makes keeps the others away.

Everywhere one turns one is greeted by some strange and unexpected detail. Take the State capitals. With the exception of the federal capital of Canberra,

16

Drawing by Hardy Wilson of the Burdekin House in Macquarie Street, Sydney.

St John's Church, Camden, New South Wales, is probably the finest example of the early Gothic Revival architecture in Australia. It was built by Mortimer Lewis who was appointed as official Colonial Architect in 1835.

they all lie next to the sea, astride large estuaries – beach-heads, as it were, for the invasion of the immense continent. As to their building styles, these vary considerably. The early colonial manner of building died out in the 1840s; and grandiose Victorianism reached its peak in the '80s. Melbourne, handsomely Victorian, has its streets laced over with an elegant tracery of cast-iron balconies, while Brisbane, the sub-tropical capital of Queensland, is almost exclusively Second Empire. Perth exhibits a decidedly Tudor air. But all this is by the way – let us turn back to the beginning, and approach the country methodically, trying to keep a certain continuity in the sequence of impressions.

19

2 The Dutch

Australia in the beginning was a matter of prediction. From earliest times, starting with Ptolemy, a succession of European cosmographers had conjectured that a great continent extended from the South Pole northwards to the tropics. Looking at the globe of the time one can readily understand why their reasoning appears perfectly logical. In front of them they saw the northern hemisphere tightly packed with land while the area south of Asia was awash with a frightening emptiness of water. There must be something missing: an antipodean counter-balance. A great unknown continent had to exist in the southern part of the Pacific. Without it the world would be top-heavy and unable to spin on its axis. This figment of the imagination was generally designated *Terra Australis Incognita* (the Unknown Southern Land), and it spread in a vague wandering line occupying the whole southern section of the globe. Australia or *Terra Australis* was the fabled South Land but not the great missing continent that had been anticipated, and it took a little over two centuries to convince the world that there was indeed nothing further to discover.

Rumours from the Viceroy's court at Lima were responsible for setting in motion the series of events which eventually led to the discovery of Australia. According to Indian tradition, one of the Incas had returned from a long sea voyage telling of rich lands to the westward of South America. Stirred by these tales the Viceroy financed an expedition, giving the leadership to his young nephew, Don Alvaro de Mendaña. Mendaña left Callao, the port of Lima, in 1567 with two vessels, and steering westward for about two thousand miles reached the Solomon Islands. It was a remarkable voyage but produced no profits.

In time news of Mendaña's discoveries reached England and in 1577 Drake left on his famous voyage of circumnavigation, which, as originally planned, might well have led him to Australia. Instead he was waylaid by the temptations offered by Chile and Peru. Raiding their ports he got no further than the American seaboard. Cavendish followed Drake in 1586, and Hawkins appeared

20

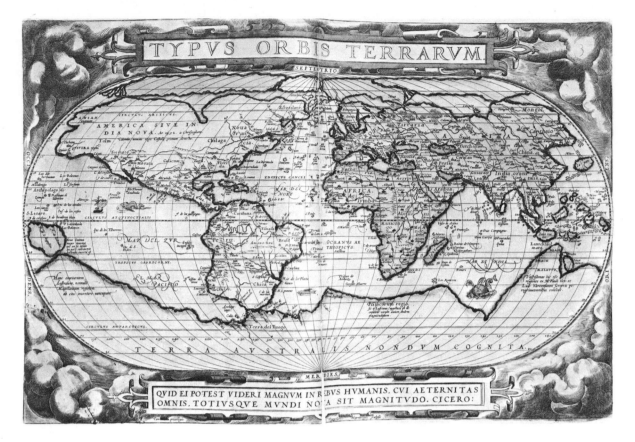

Map from an atlas published in 1587. The Great South Land is shown spread in a vague wandering line occupying the whole southern section of the globe.

in the same seas seven years later; both had as their objective the elusive *Terra Australis*. Hawkins and his men were captured off the South American coast and it is more than probable that the information gained from the captives spurred the new Viceroy on to further efforts. In 1595 Mendaña again set off, this time with four ships to form a settlement in the Solomons. From this outpost further voyages were to be made.

They left Callao in April and in July discovered the Marquesas. Due however to a miscalculation of the pilot, who underestimated the distances, they never reached the Solomons. Instead, Mendaña settled in the Santa Cruz group some two hundred miles to the east. The expedition had already lost one ship. More misfortunes were to follow; the natives proved hostile and Mendaña, worn out by worry, died of a remittent fever. Other members of the expedition died, another ship was wrecked and eventually, more dead than alive, the party, consisting notably of Doña Isabela, Mendaña's objectionable widow, and Pedro Fernández de Quiros the chief pilot, arrived at Manila.

Beyond the discoveries of three groups of islands, little had been added by Mendaña to the knowledge of the western Pacific. The Great South Land still beckoned, and Quiros, recovering from his ordeals, was to return to the search, this time heading his own expedition consisting of two ships, the second ship being under the command of Luis Vaez de Torres. They left Peru in December 1605; on 1 May, five months later, a large land-mass with high mountains was sighted. Quiros was convinced he had found the great southern continent, and amidst much rejoicing christened his landfall *Austrialia del Espiritu Santo*. Care must be taken here not to confuse *Australia* with *Austrialia*. Quiros was punning to flatter Philip III, his king, who was a Prince of the House of Austria.

Having secured his base Quiros, it seems, was preparing further expeditions but history becomes obscure at this point and one must suppose that mutiny broke out on the leader's ship. In any event Quiros abandoned his partner and sailed back to America leaving Torres to fend for himself. Torres, as it turned out, fared admirably. Exploring further he first found that what was believed to be a continent was only an island, the largest in a group which later Captain Cook was to re-name the New Hebrides. This accomplished, he caught the monsoon winds and set off in a south-westerly direction in search of the real Great South Land. He gave up the search in the vicinity of the Great Barrier Reef, a hundred and sixty miles off the Queensland coast, and instead headed northward, thus beginning his epic voyage along the south coast of New Guinea. Hugging the shores of this new discovery he became the first European to sail through the dangerous straits which long after were called by his name.

So far, of all the explorers who had set out in search of the *Terra Australis*, it was Torres who came the nearest to discovering it, or rather what the *Terra Australis* of the geographers finally turned out to be – the reality a mere shadow of the supposed bulk sprawled out across the bottom half of the globe.

In any event it was to be to the Dutch and not the Spanish to whom the prize eventually fell. Almost at the same time as Torres discovered his straits, Dutchmen from Java sighted Cape York Peninsula.

Dutch trading parties arrived at Djakarta in 1596 and by 1600 they had made contact with most of the islands of the Malay Archipelago, trading as far afield as the Moluccas and Banda way down to the south. It was only a matter of time before one of their ships, venturing a little further afield, struck a part of the Australian coast. This ship was to be the *Duyfken*, or *Little Dove*, under the command of Willem Jansz. He skirted the west side of Cape York Peninsula landing at the present Albatross Bay, and again at a point he named Cabo Keer-Werr, Cape Turnagain. The coast was very barren and scantily watered and the natives hostile. Contact was made with them, resulting in a serious clash in which a Dutchman was killed. The journal of the voyage has been lost but Jansz's report could not have been encouraging. 'No good to be done there', is briefly noted in the East India Company's books. It was a phrase that was to be often repeated over the next half century or so.

During the first years the Dutch used the old Portuguese seaway to India. They sailed north from the Cape of Good Hope to Madagascar, past the Seychelles and Maldive Islands, then south again skirting Sumatra to Java. But expert navigators that they were, it did not take them long to discover that a quicker route existed for their outward bound Indiamen. Already by 1611 Captain Hendrik Brouwer, commander of one of the ships, was experimenting

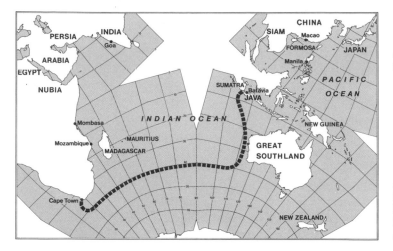

Left Route of the Dutch East Indiamen after 1616.

Below Print from *Licht da Zeevart* ('Light of Navigation') by Williem Blaeu, published in 1612, showing the Dutch plotting a new route for their outward bound Indiamen.

Replica of the Vlamingh Plate. The original of this plate is the oldest known relic of
European contact with Australia. In 1616 Dirck Hartog of Amsterdam landed on the island
that still bears his name. There he left nailed to a post a ship's pewter plate, flattened and
inscribed with a record of his visit. The plate was found in 1697 by another Dutchman,
Willem de Vlamingh, who removed the plate and substituted another on which he copied
Hartog's inscription and added a record of his own visit. In 1801 some members of a French
expedition, under the command of Captain Baudin, discovered Vlamingh's plate lying half
buried in the sand at the foot of the post to which it had been attached. The French had it
re-erected and also left a record of their own visit. On a later voyage Louis de Freycinet,
who had been a member of Baudin's expedition, called at Shark's Bay in 1818, and, fearing
that the plate would completely decay, removed it and sent it to the Institut de France in
Paris. It was presented by the French government to the Commonwealth in 1947 and is now
in the Perth Art Gallery. The replica shown here was presented to the Mitchell Library,
Sydney, by the Commonwealth government.

with the winds. Using the prevailing westerlies he sailed due east from Cape Town for about three thousand miles and then, catching the south-east trades, made swift passage northward. It worked perfectly and, on Brouwer's recommendation, the East India Company directors in Amsterdam adopted this as their official route. From 1616 on, all those sailing to the Indies were issued instructions prescribing the course to be followed. Naturally when plotting this course the Dutch were completely unaware of the proximity of Australia's western shore and since ships at this date had no way of accurately calculating longitude at sea before making their northings, it was no great time before one of them came by accident on land.

The Dutch had stumbled onto the north of Australia and they were now to make a series of landfalls on its western shores. To begin with they thought their sightings were islands and only time was to prove to them the compact nature of the terrain. Gradually the disjointed sections were welded together and briefly, in chronological order, these involuntary discoveries occurred as follows.

In 1616 Dirck Hartog, in the *Eendracht,* dropped anchor in what is now Shark Bay. Two years later the *Mauritius,* over-running its proper course, came in sight of land to the north, and the next year Jacob d'Edel landed approximately where Perth now stands. Three years later Australia's south-western extremity was passed by an unknown captain sailing in the *Leeuwin,* or *Lioness.* The point was named after the ship and juts out seaward, a great sandy stretch of land ringed round with rocks against which the Indian Ocean crashes in whirling eddies of foam; the equivalent of England's Land's End – a sentimental landmark for the homecoming Australian who travels by ship.

Other Dutchmen left their names on Australia's coast. In 1623 Jan Carstensz sailed completely around the great gulf in which Jansz had originally anchored. He christened it Carpentaria after Pieter de Carpenter, Governor-General of the Dutch East Indies. Carstensz's journal bears out the Company's earlier opinion of the land: no fruit-bearing trees 'nor anything that man could make use of. ... The Inhabitants, too, are the most wretched and poorest creatures that I have ever seen'.

In 1627 the *Gulden Seepaard* or *Golden Seahorse* with Pieter Nuijts, a member of the Council of the Indies on board, was blown so far off its course that it missed Cape Leeuwin and entering the Great Australian Bight, sailed along the coast for about a thousand miles until it reached a group of islands now known as the Nuijts (or Nuyts) Archipelago situated at the eastern extremity of the Bight.

Following the different charts one can assemble the fragments that eventually will begin to assume shape. It is too early, though, to be able to fill in much detail. Sightings were made, but most of the attempts at landing proved unsuccessful. In many cases the surf stopped the boats getting anywhere near the beach, and again and again monsoons chased the visitors off. Meanwhile the Dutch were puzzled by the extent of the land their seamen had discovered. How vast exactly was it? Could it possibly be part of the *Terra Australis* of

Anthony Van Diemen,
Governor General of
the Dutch East Indies.
Engraving by Jongman
after M. Balen.

geographers? To answer these questions the Governor-General and the
Council of the Indies at Djakarta decided to finance a lengthy expedition. It was
to discover the unknown South Land and explore the known South Land.
This, though, was not the sole purpose of the voyage. The Dutch in these early
days were not solely interested in defining geography, the thirst for gain rather
than the spirit of adventure prompted their initiations. The possibility of
plundering the wealth of Spain in South America was never far from their
minds, and, in this case, they hoped to find a short route from Java to Chile. The
command of the expedition was entrusted to Abel Janszoon Tasman, a seaman
of great experience who was bound to the East India Company's service for ten
years. Two ships were assigned to him: the small two hundred ton war-yacht
Heemskerck, and the *Zeehaen (Sea-cock).* They sailed from Djakarta on 14
August 1642 and a course was set for the Dutch settlement of Mauritius where
Tasman took aboard water and firewood; from there he sailed southward. In
November of the same year he sighted the west coast of Tasmania, which he
was to call Van Diemen's Land, after his patron, the Governor-General
Anthony Van Diemen. Proceeding south, Tasman skirted the southern end of
Tasmania and turned north-east until he was off Cape Frederick Henry. Several

landings were made but on the last, intended to be the official one, the surf was too high, so Tasman ordered the carpenter to swim ashore with a flag which was planted near some tall trees. Tasman notes in his log that he heard 'or at least fancied I heard, the sound of people upon the shore; but I saw nobody'. He also finds steps cut into the trunks of two large trees, 'a kind of step in the bark, in order to climb up to the birds' nests'. Not realising it was an island he drew it on his map as if it were a peninsula belonging to the mainland of Australia.

From Tasmania the ships sailed east to New Zealand which Tasman originally named Staten Landt, 'in honour of their High Mightinesses the States General'. Only later was it changed to Zeeland after a province of that name in Holland.

No landing was made in New Zealand and one of the *Zeehaen's* boats was attacked by Maoris in war canoes, resulting in the loss of four seamen.

From New Zealand the ships sailed north to Tonga and Fiji, and skirting New Guinea on its north side, finally regained the East Indies. Tasman had thus in effect circumnavigated Australia in a wide square without seeing more of it than the southernmost tip of Tasmania. His chart, incidentally, also shows New Guinea joined to the continent.

Tasman's voyage disappointed the Council. He had been ten months on the high seas without finding gold and spices. No trade connections had been made, and he had not explored the coast of the known South Land or charted its dangerous west coast. As to the unknown South Land, it still remained an unsolved mystery. He had shown that there was a route into the Pacific but had done nothing about establishing a revictualling base for ships embarked upon that route. The Council was equally unimpressed with his discoveries: the Dutch never bothered again about Van Diemen's Land which remained unvisited for a further hundred and thirty years. Marion de Fresne, a Frenchman, was the next to drop anchor there in 1772 within a mile of the bay where the *Heemskerck* and the *Zeehaen* had sheltered. New Zealand was totally ignored and was left for Captain Cook to chart.

Although Tasman's voyage was judged unsuccessful, it was apparent to the Council that an unknown land of such magnitude, within easy reach of their base in the east, could not be ignored. Another attempt had to be made to ascertain its real nature. It appeared to have a 'pleasant climate and attractive skies'. And its very size surely precluded it from not having benefits of some kind hidden away beyond its inhospitable shores. Comparison was made with the gold and silver-rich provinces of Peru and Chile. Surely, the Councillors speculated, the South Land, similarly situated in relation to the Equator, should prove equally fruitful.

Tasman was again summoned before the Council and this time was painstakingly briefed. It was not enough to just sail along the coast, some contact had to be made in order to establish the character of the lands and people he might encounter. One imagines Tasman's response to have been a demand for better equipment, more ships and more men. This second expedition, in any event, was to be much shorter than the first which was considered too lengthy for

practical purposes. Tasman's instructions limited him to exploring the north coast of the South Land. Apart from the hope of establishing trade connections, Tasman was expected to find a passage into the Pacific running somewhere between Carpentaria and the newly discovered Van Diemen's Land.

The second expedition lasted barely eight months and sailed from Djakarta early in 1644. A third boat had been added to the original two; and they were manned by a complement of over a hundred men. With them they carried an odd assortment of goods to be used for trade: elephants' teeth, porcelain,

Abel Tasman with his second wife and his daughter by his first wife. Painted in 1637, when Tasman was in Amsterdam, by Jacob Gerritsz Cuyp.

Tasman's discoveries were such a source of pride to the Dutch that they were inlaid in two marble maps on the floor of the town hall in Amsterdam, built by Jacob van Campen in 1655.

spices, ebony and gold, commodities that would have meant nothing to the Aborigines even if they had possessed the wherewithal to barter.

Tasman's journal, presuming he kept one, has been lost and the only surviving account is a letter. It gives an impression of a low shoreline with fires burning but seldom any sign of inhabitants. They caught great sharks and enormous turtles but there was little water. Digging in the sand a brackish, evil-smelling fluid was found. Never before had men sailed along a shore so desolate, barren and forbidding.

Tasman was a cautious navigator and his chart shows that much of the time he sailed a good distance from the land. Outlying islands are sometimes shown as peninsulas, and hills on the mainland are depicted as islands. But in spite of this defect his running survey of the coast remains a remarkable achievement. From the Gulf of Carpentaria he sailed clear down to the North West Cape and rounding this point set his course south to Dirck Hartog's Island, a distance of over a thousand miles. In point of fact he discovered a more extensive length of Australian coastline than any other navigator, greater even in linear distance than Cook's discovery over a hundred and fifty years later.

Remarkable as this was, the results of the voyage were a disappointment to those who had financed it. Neither the land nor its inhabitants produced anything of a marketable value – just a series of arid sightings : a bright world of aquamarine light, peopled by poor naked runners seen as black silhouettes, like so many ants, scurrying across the whiteness of endless beaches. It was a failure also from a strategic point of view – no passage leading into the Pacific ; just a solid unbroken coast of blasted desert, an indigestible mass of nothing. But this was hardly Tasman's fault ; his feats of seamanship were recognised and shortly after his return he was honoured by an appointment to the Council. A still greater honour awaited him at home. So proud were the people of Amsterdam of his accomplishments that his discoveries were inlaid in two marble maps on the floor of their new and splendid Town Hall.

The burghers might acclaim their citizen but not the Dutch East India Company ; they kept very quiet about Tasman's voyages and no official account was ever published. A private edition of his journal relating his discovery of Van Diemen's Land and New Zealand appeared in low Dutch and was translated into English in 1694, but no literature exists on Tasman's explorations of the north of Australia. The Company's policy was clearly one of deliberate discouragement. They had found nothing that could be turned to profit for themselves and they were determined not to excite the curiosity of others. They wanted no potential busybodies interfering with the rich trade they had built up in Dutch Indonesia. There was no question either, of settling these discoveries. It would be undertaking more than they, even the Republic of Holland, could manage. There was always the possibility, of course, that this mighty South Land would eventually turn out to be a source of untold riches, superior to any country yet known, surpassing even the treasures so recently found by Spain in South America. The only choice therefore that remained to the Dutch was to reserve the place until the time arrived when they could make use of it. So stories were circulated depicting an inhospitable coast, everywhere beset with rocks, absolutely devoid of water, and inhabited by a race of savages more barbarous, and, at the same time, more miserable, than any creatures in the world. As far as the Dutch were concerned this picture of desolation was the truth ; it was not very difficult to dampen the ardour of any enthusiastic would-be explorer. To the other nations of Europe, the southern continent was a chimera, as nebulous as a cloud ; or at least a country about which there were a thousand doubts and suspicions.

ACCORDING TO TRADITION
IN THE COOK FAMILY
MIDSHIPMAN ISAAC SMITH
COUSIN OF THE WIFE OF CAPTAIN JAMES COOK R.N.
AFTERWARDS AN ADMIRAL OF THE BRITISH FLEET
WAS THE FIRST ENGLISHMAN
TO LAND ON THIS ROCK AND ON THE SHORES OF
NEW SOUTH WALES
APRIL 29 1770

3 The English

William Dampier, the son of a Somerset farmer, was the man largely responsible for directing Englishmen's eyes to the Pacific. He wrote two books on his voyage and his life reads like an adventure story.

Born in 1652 and left an orphan at the age of sixteen, he took to the sea, made a voyage to Newfoundland, served on an East Indiaman bound for Java and for his coming of age found himself an able seaman on board a flagship engaged in fighting the Dutch. Leaving the navy he next tried a variety of occupations, becoming in turn an assistant manager of a plantation in Jamaica, a trader, and a logwood cutter in Yucatan. At twenty-six, brown, carefree and worldly-wise, he was back in England, a man of some means with a wife called Judith whom he describes as a young woman 'out of the family of the Duchess of Grafton'. The principal source for Dampier's life is his own writings, and in their clear, homely common-sense style, his books can almost be considered classics.

At one point he lived in the Caribbean, then he moved to Virginia: next he was sailing around the Horn. There are certain details, however, which he understandably glosses over. His years as a pirate are somewhat cursorily dealt with. One hears little of the years between 1679 and 1684 spent in the company of a heterogeneous collection of buccaneers, or 'privateers' as he prefers to call them. Roaming the Spanish Main in a variety of ships, for the most part commandeered, he and his companions seem to have spent most of their time sacking, plundering and burning. Finally in 1685 one finds him on board the *Cygnet*, the ship which carried him to Australia. Captain Swan, its commander, had originally intended to intercept one of the richly laden Manila galleons bound for Acapulco, but arriving too late he headed instead for the East Indies. Mindanão in the Philippines was their first anchorage, where time was spent in 'excessive drunkenness and debauchery'. Dampier disapproved but it did not stop him from remaining on board when the men decided to jettison their captain and sail off without him. Over a year went by cruising about the South China and Java seas, and, passing via Timor they eventually reached the west

Opposite Commemorative plaque marking the place where Captain Cook's crew first landed on the shores of New South Wales.

33

coast of Australia, or New Holland as Dampier referred to it. New Holland was now the generally accepted name for Australia and had been in use with the Dutch from quite some time already.

A landfall was made on 4 January 1688 in the vicinity of the present Pender Bay, about twenty-five miles south-west of Cape Leveque. The ship ran north-eastward along the coast, came to anchor next day, and there was careened, supposedly somewhere near the present Cygnet Bay in King Sound. The *Cygnet* was beached for about six weeks in a lonely inlet, and one can imagine Dampier, better educated than his companions, off on his own, exploring. He was the first man with any pretentions at being a naturalist to write about New Holland.

Not familiar with the knowledge acquired by the Dutch, Dampier gives us his impressions, and they must reflect the ideas current at the time. There are doubts as to the land's exact character, whether continent or island: 'but I am certain that it joins neither Asia, Africa, nor America. This part of it that we saw is all low with sandy banks against the sea, only the points are rocky.' They saw no animals, only the tracks 'of a beast as big as a great mastiff-dog'. No birds bigger than blackbirds; 'and but few sea-fowls. Neither is the sea very plentifully stocked...' but there were a lot of turtles. As to the Aborigines, Dampier refers to them as the miserablest people in the world. 'The Hodmadods of Monomatapa, though a nasty people, yet for wealth are gentlemen to these.' He has not a good word to say for them, for him they differed 'but little from brutes'. His reference to the flies strikes anyone familiar with Australia. They were so bad 'that no fanning would keep them from coming to one's face; and without the assistance of both hands to keep them off, they will creep into one's nostrils, and mouth too, if the lips are not shut very close'. So bad were they that the natives, on the rare occasions that they put in an appearance, had to keep their eyes half-closed with the result that they squinted at the strangers over the tops of their 'bottle noses'.

These descriptions of the north-west coast come in Dampier's first book on Australia called *New Voyage Around the World*. Joseph Banks had a copy of it with him on the *Endeavour* but had not much good to say about it and disagreed with Dampier's descriptions of the Aborigines. He was certainly wrong about their hair, which he described as 'short and curled like that of the negroes'. 'Dampier in general', writes Banks, 'seems to be a faithful relater.' But being 'in a ship of pirates', Banks imagines him to have been not a little 'tainted by their idle example'. He infers that Dampier wrote up the voyage from memory on his return to England in 1691. But Banks is mistaken; many of the original manuscripts are in the British Museum and, looking through them, it is obvious that they were spontaneous. Indeed, one of the remarkable things about Dampier was the dogged determination with which he kept his journal, no matter what the circumstances. One cannot help but admire him for it.

Dampier dedicated his *New Voyage Around the World* to his erudite patron, the President of the Royal Society, Charles Montague, the future Lord Halifax. The book was an immediate success, running into four editions in two years.

William Dampier.
Artist unknown.

Further editions appeared during the eighteenth century. There is no doubt
that Dampier's voyages set a new fashion in travel literature and at the same
time awakened a general interest in the Pacific. Dampier, probably the only
man in England to have been to New Holland and to have spent any length of
time in out-of-the-way places in the East Indies, immediately became the authority on the South Seas. The Admiralty, encouraged by Montague, proposed
some expeditions and consulted Dampier on the best method of exploring these
waters. The result was a proposed voyage to the unknown eastern coast of New
Holland. Had the plans gone as intended Dampier might have forestalled Cook
in his discoveries, but his departure was delayed, and in the end he sailed again
not by Cape Horn westwards across the Pacific, but by the Cape of Good Hope
to the western coast of New Holland.

HMS *Roebuck* sailed from the Downs on 14 January 1699. She carried
twelve guns, fifty men, some of them not more than boys, and provisions for
nearly two years. On 6 August she reached her destination and anchored at the
entrance to the inlet Dampier named Shark Bay. A week later, setting his course
north east, he starts on a coastal cruise in search of water. Failing to find it he
left Australia near Roebuck Bay and sailed off to Timor.

Nothing had been discovered, but at least Dampier gives us a picture that
reflects some aspects of the nature of Australia. In his second book, *A Voyage
to New Holland,* published in 1703, he writes what must be the first description
of an eucalyptus: 'leaves which were mostly long and narrow. The colour of the
leaves was on one side whitish and on the other green'. The trees were sweet-
scented. Dampier also notes the kangaroo, that he calls a sort of racoon. He
notes the short forelegs and mentions the jumping. Cutting open a guana he is
revolted by the smell; the flesh, however, appears to have made good eating.

He collects a variety of beautiful shells of every variety of colour and shape, and coasting along the shore they make land again 'and saw a great many smokes near the beach'. Dampier is more careful this time about details and Banks has no further criticism to make.

Dampier lands and takes with him 'a nimble young man' who runs off towards the natives gathered in a small group some way down the shore. He had a cutlass and they had wooden lances and outnumbered him. 'Fearing how it might be with the youth I discharged my gun to scare them.' The blast had some effect but it did not succeed in checking them. Waving their arms 'they came on again with a great noise. I thought it high time to charge again' – and one of the natives is shot. Among the band was a man 'who had the appearance and carriage' of a Chief. He was young, brisk, not very tall, 'nor so personable as some of the rest', but more courageous. His eyes were circled and his nose

'His eyes were circled and his nose streaked with some white pigment. His rib-case and his arms were also picked out, giving him the appearance of an animated skeleton.'
Painted by George French Angas in *South Australia Illustrated*.

streaked with some white pigment. His rib-case and his arms were also picked out, giving him the appearance of an animated skeleton. Dampier concluded that the purpose of this daubing was to frighten the enemy. He persevered also with the impressions gathered on the first voyage and maintains that they had the 'most unpleasant looks of any people that I ever met'. The country continues bleak and arid 'low, barricaded with a long chain of sand-hills to the sea, that lets nothing be seen of what is further inland'. Digging for water provides, at best, a liquid in which the men could boil their oatmeal. '... and thus having ranged about a considerable time upon this coast, without finding any good fresh water or any convenient place to clean the ship ... I resolved to leave.'

On the return voyage the *Roebuck* was in such poor condition that she foundered near Ascension Island in the South Atlantic. The crew and the captain, however, were all saved.

On the whole it was a disappointing voyage. As with Tasman, too much had been expected of it and, apart from the island of New Britain in the Bismarck Archipelago, off the east coast of New Guinea, nothing new had been discovered.

Dampier had been given his appointment solely on his literary and scientific merits.[5] He was an admirable observer but no good as a commander, being far too arbitrary with his men. It is possible also that the men, trained in the Royal Navy, resented being put under the orders of a one-time pirate. In any event the differences with his officers do not concern us here. When it came out, *A Voyage to New Holland* had only moderate success. It carried enough weight, however, to influence the British Government, convincing them that Australia was altogether unsuitable for settlement.

But not everyone felt this way. There were those who argued quite the opposite. A land of such magnitude, subject as it was to a variety of climatic changes, could not possibly be entirely devoid of interest. Foremost amongst those who believed this was Charles de Brosses, the French scholar and writer. In his *Histoire des Navigations aux Terres Australes,* published in 1756, he lays down certain geographical divisions, calling them Australasia and Polynesia (adopted by succeeding geographers) and indulges in a fantasy concerning a hypothetical continent. 'How can we doubt that such a vast expanse of land will supply objects of curiosity, opportunities for profit, perhaps as many as America furnished?' De Brosses still believes in a Great South Land, but how close his dream-picture and the reality of New Holland itself. He muses on the animals, plants, medicinal drugs, marbles, metals. 'In all these things there are doubtless thousands of species of which we do not even have a notion, since that world has never had any communication with our own, and is, so to speak, almost as strange to us as another planet could be.'

Ten years later, in 1766, John Callander brought out an English edition of de Brosses's work, calling it *Terra Australis Cognita*. He makes no mention of de Brosses and refers to him only as a 'learned French author'. These works were widely read and again turned contemporary thought and action to the Pacific. The next few years saw a succession of successful voyages; Byron, Carteret, Wallace and Cook representing the British. The French were represented by Bougainville, d'Urville, Marion de Fresne, and La Pérouse. Captain Cook, as everyone knows, was the man to discover New Holland's beckoning eastern shore-line. One wonders why it waited so long.

It was originally a matter of star-gazing that led James Cook to the shores of Australia. A rare occurrence called the 'Transit of Venus' was to take place in 1769. During a transit, Venus passes directly between the earth and the sun and is seen as a small black dot stealing its way across the gassy flames. Important deductions – such as the scale of the solar system and the distance of the earth from the sun – can be made from its passage. Astronomers' charts recorded only two previous transits, the first of which had occurred in 1639. The next had taken place in 1761, but the observation of the 1761 phenomenon had been unsuccessful, and it was therefore of particular importance that the 1769 event be properly charted.

The Royal Society, which was devoted to the cause of natural enlightment, took a lively interest in the coming transit and petitioned King George III not to neglect the chance of furthering the fame of British astronomy, 'a science', the members pointed out, 'on which navigation so much depends'. Several European nations, among them Russia, wanted to establish points of observation, and England, the Society argued, should certainly do the same. The Royal Society was considered the world's most distinguished scientific body and its petition carried weight with the King who was particularly interested in science and exploration. Because it was essential that the observers follow the transit from a point south of the equinoxial line, the recently discovered Island of Tahiti was suggested as a suitable place. The idea of sending an expedition to the Pacific appealed to the King. He promptly gave the project his approval, and the Royal Society approached the Admiralty for a ship and a competent man to sail it. James Cook, a forty-year-old naval officer who had already surveyed the coasts of Newfoundland and Labrador, was chosen to command HMS *Endeavour*.

In 1768 the expedition set out. Sailing with Cook were Charles Green, an astronomer, and various other scientific gentlemen; or simply 'the gentlemen' as Cook always referred to Banks and members of his party in his Journals. Joseph Banks, later knighted by the King, was a young naturalist of twenty-five with an independent fortune. With him was the slightly older Doctor Daniel Carl Solander, a Swede by origin and Linnaeus's favourite pupil, also two artists: the twenty-five-year-old Sydney Parkinson and Herman Dietrich Spöring, another Swede, who joined the ship at Cape Town and seems to have acted as Banks's secretary.

The transit of Venus was successfully observed from Tahiti, but it proved to be a task of secondary importance to the expedition, for Cook had been given secret instructions by the Admiralty. After exploring Tahiti and the neighbouring islands, he was to search for the Great South Land, that was believed might somehow still exist.

Cook and Banks between them had an extensive geographical library on board, and amongst the books de Brosses's useful *Histoire des Navigations aux*

Terres Australes. Accompanying the text were interesting maps by the celebrated French cartographer, Robert de Vaugondy. In one of the maps, Vaugondy marked out Tasman's discoveries – the southern part of Van Diemen's Land and the western coasts of New Zealand's North Island. The imaginary eastern coast of New Holland was shown by vague hatchings and was joined by the discoveries of Quiros, which were displaced westward. Van Diemen's Land, or Tasmania, was also shown connected to the mainland. No accurate chart existed of the straits between New Holland and New Guinea.

Joseph Banks as a young man, a seldom reproduced portrait by Daniel Chodowiecki.

These then were the geographical uncertainties which faced the crew of the *Endeavour* as the ship left Tahiti. Possibly New Holland and New Zealand formed the northern humps of the great mythical continent. Cook, however, doubted it. He sailed from the Society Islands in August, and by the end of March of the following year, 1770, he had already charted and had circumnavigated the two islands, thus disproving any continental connection. By April he had turned north-west towards Tasmania, but strong southerly gales drove the *Endeavour* north, so that the English arrived at the south-east corner of Australia itself. Had the weather been fair, Cook would almost certainly have discovered Bass Strait, which separates Australia from Tasmania. On Wednesday, 18 April, certain birds were sighted, a sure sign, Cook noted, of the nearness of land. The following day (20 April by modern computation) Lieutenant Hicks sighted a low hill and Cook named the point after him, though few maps now carry his name, their landfall being better known as Cape Everard. Sailing northwards the *Endeavour* hugged the shore looking for a safe anchorage. 'The face of the country is green and woody but the seashore is all white sand.' Dark figures can be distinguished against the glare. It is a calm, noble landscape with a certain haggard beauty all of its own. Smoke curls up through the dusty green hanging foliage of the eucalyptus, only to be lost against a pale sky. At night fires pricked the flat shoreland. One can imagine the intense curiosity of those on board the *Endeavour*. Cook, Banks, Solander and Tupaia, a Tahitian chief

Banks has persuaded to join the expedition, tried to land in a yawl, but were prevented by the surf. Banks noted the park-like aspect of the land, the trees separate from each other 'without the least underwood'. Passing within a quarter of a mile from the shore he is surprised at the total lack of interest shown by the natives. Deafened by the surf and concentrated on their occupation, they did not seem to notice the passing of the yawl; however, an old woman gathering sticks, followed by three children, 'often looked at the ship but expressed neither surprise nor concern'. It was Sunday 29 April that the *Endeavour* stood into Botany Bay, anchoring under the south shore.

According to traditions in the Cook family, Midshipman Isaac Smith, Mrs Cook's cousin, afterwards an Admiral of the British Fleet, was the first to land. Young Isaac, eighteen at the time, later recalled how Cook, on the point of stepping ashore, said 'Isaac, you shall land first'. Cook was forced to fire a musket loaded with small shot between two natives when a party of them threatened the explorers with spears.

Cook originally called their anchorage Sting Ray Harbour 'occasioned by the great quantity of these sort of fish found in this place'. The prodigious haul of new plants collected by Banks and Solander later provoked him to change the name to Botany Bay. The plants were kept fresh in tin chests, wrapped in wet cloths, while Parkinson and Spöring drew them. (Parkinson worked with such alacrity that he averaged seven meticulous drawings a day.) Afterwards, before pressing them, Banks spread the specimens out on sails to dry in the sun.

All the gentlemen remark on the loryquets and cockatoos in the trees and Banks, generalising, wrote that the Aborigines 'seemed never to be able to muster above fourteen or fifteen fighting men ...'. He seemed undecided about their actual colour – 'they were so completely covered with dirt, that seemed to have stuck to their bodies from the day of their birth'. On one occasion he spat on his fingers and tried to rub it off. His action altered the colour very little, and he judged their skin to be a kind of chocolate.

The *Endeavour* remained in Botany Bay just over a week. On 7 May Cook resumed his voyage and a few miles north passed present-day Sydney. He was aware that the bay or harbour was probably a good anchorage and named it Port Jackson in honour of one of the secretaries of the Admiralty.

Slowly Cook worked his way north, charting the coast. He frequently landed, climbing hills to take his bearings and never sailed very far without sending boats ahead to cast shoreward and seaward.

As they neared the northern end of the island continent, the voyage nearly came to an abrupt end when the ship grounded on a coral reef, twenty miles from the land. Cook's seamanship was, however, equal to the occasion: the

Opposite. above A bush fire. *Below* 'The country itself has a strange subtle beauty all of its own.' *The River*, by E. Buckmaster, 1928.

Overleaf A landscape with kangaroos, by the primitive painter Henri Bastin, once an opal miner.

Opposite, left Banksia spinulosa, from *A Specimen of the Botany of New Holland*, by Sir James Edward Smith, published in 1793. *Right* Flower of the New Zealand flax *(Phormium tenax)*.

Above 'All the gentlemen remark on the lory-quets and cockatoos in the trees...' Watercolour by Neville Cayley.

Right Banksia serrata, one of the plants discovered by Banks.

Endeavour was freed and, much damaged and leaking severely, was guided up the estuary of a small nearby river where she was banked and careened. There the men saw their first kangaroo which Cook described as 'an animal something less than a greyhound, of a mouse colour, very slender made and swift of foot'. Kangaroo, we learn, is an Aboriginal word. During Cook's stay, natives came to the camp, but they always left their women on the opposite banks of the river. Banks, busy with his glasses, commented on their nudity, noting that they 'did not even bother to copy our mother Eve in the fig-leaf'.

Although repairs on the ship finally were finished, a strong wind further delayed Cook's departure. Eventually he managed to creep out, and slowly threaded his way through the tortuous mazes of the Great Barrier Reef. Inch by inch, with suppressed anguish, the group advanced to the northern point of Australia which Cook names Cape York in honour of the King's late brother. Sailing west they rediscover Torres Strait, and before departing for Batavia and England they land on a small island (Possession Island) off the coast of Cape York. Cook made no claim regarding the strait, but he did claim the land. Accompanied by Banks and Solander he made for the island and climbed the highest hill from which he saw nothing but islands lying to the north-west.

Cook admitted that to the west he could make no new discoveries 'the honour of which belongs to the Dutch navigators; but the east coast I am confident was never seen or visited by any Europeans before us'. He had already claimed several places along the coast: now he 'once more hoisted the English colours and in the name of His Majesty King George III took possession of the whole eastern coast', christening it New South Wales. Three volleys of small arms were fired, and they were answered by a like number from the ship. Why, one asks, did Cook pick on so improbable a name? It has been suggested that since there already was a New Britain and a Nova Scotia, and since Cook wanted to associate the recent discoveries with his own country, he decided on New South Wales.

Cook had proved that New Zealand was an island group and had closed off Australia's missing coastline. The voyage had also thrust back any southern

The repairing of the *Endeavour* after it was wrecked on the Great Barrier Reef. Plate from Moore's *Voyages and Travels.*

continent, but it had not proved that one did not exist. A second voyage made in 1772 did, however, settle this question once and for all. In the three years Cook was absent, during this second voyage, he sailed between sixty and seventy thousand miles and made vast sweeps in parts of the Pacific not hitherto explored. He travelled down and up in a giant, irregular zig-zag penetrating as far south as 70° 10′ latitude, a record not bettered until 1823 by James Weddell in the *Jane of Leith* while on a sealing expedition. During this voyage Cook made numerous major geographical discoveries, one of them being New Caledonia, the largest island in the South Pacific after New Zealand. But ironically it was what he did not discover that was to count as his most important contribution on the second voyage. His conclusive proof that there was no Great South Land put our knowledge of the South Pacific on a sound basis. Indeed the maps of this part of the world still remain essentially as he left them.

Cook described the kangaroo as 'an animal something less than a greyhound, of a mouse colour, very slender made and swift of foot'. Joseph Banks was puzzled: 'What to liken him to I could not tell, nothing certainly that I have seen at all resembles him.'

47

4 Transportation

The first suggestion for establishing a Pacific Colony in Australia was made by Joseph Banks before a Committee in the House of Commons in 1779. In 1776 the United States had declared its independence, and the loss of her American Colonies meant that England could no longer send her convicts across the Atlantic. Nevertheless judges continued sentencing convicted persons to transportation, and jails were overcrowded; a new outlet for offenders had to be found. It was at this point that Banks enthusiastically recommended Botany Bay.

Prior to transportation 'rogues, vagabonds and beggars' had been sentenced to the galleys, or banished, being first branded on the left shoulder with a large R, the R standing for rogue. Use of galley slaves was a practice inherited from the ancients, but with the rapid progress being made in ship-building their use had become obsolete.

1619 seems to be the earliest actual recording of transportation to a Colony, 'a hundred dissolute persons' being sent to Virginia by order of James I. The first settlers were greatly in want of labourers and it seemed a logical conclusion. The mother country was relieved of undesirable characters and the Colony received the wanted assistance. Contractors were put in charge of the shipping and it proved a highly lucrative trade. They possessed a proprietary interest in their charges and were allowed to sell their interest in each convict to the highest bidder. Financial consideration also provided a powerful incentive to contractors to land their prisoners in as healthy a state as possible. Blacksmiths and carpenters got from £15 to £25, an ordinary male about £10 and a woman from £8 to £9. One shipment recorded cleared £40,000, and all told about 30,000 convicts were transported to the Colonies in America from the British Isles. Over the period of years this represented a fairly conservative figure but crime was on the increase and at the beginning of the War of Independence the number of convicts sentenced to transportation averaged some thousand a year. To cope with the overflow in the prisons, an experiment of housing convicts in

old hulks was tried. Hulks were warships, or old merchantmen due to be scrapped and were moored on the Thames or at Portsmouth and Plymouth and the large Irish ports. Conditions on board were appalling; by day the prisoners were detailed to labour on public works, dredging silt or mud in the harbours. By night they lay two to a bed with a blanket if lucky, but more often just shivering in their wet clothes on piles of straw. The hulks were supposed to have been a purely temporary measure, but the years dragged on while the Government seemed incapable of dealing with the projected penal reform for properly constructed and well organised penitentiaries. From 1775 to the end of the century 8,000 were lodged in these rotting hulks, each prisoner costing the country about £30 per annum. In addition to the expense, the hulks were rapidly becoming nests of pestilence, infecting the cities near which they were anchored. A census taken at about this time showed that there were some 4,000 persons in the country who would be better out of it. Obviously some action had to be taken. First the West Indies and then Canada were considered as possible

Convicts were housed in hulks, rotten warships or merchantmen which were due to be scrapped. Conditions on board these floating prisons were appalling.

49

places to which these unfortunates could be sent. The West Indies were ruled
out since this would interfere with the lucrative slave trade enjoyed by British
ship-owners and Gambia on the west coast of Africa was tried as a substitute to
Canada. The *Nautilus* sailed with 746 convicts on board, and of these unfortunate victims of experiment 334 died of plague, 271 deserted or disappeared, and
of the remainder no account could be given. The result stirred even the sluggish
to action and the Lord Mayor of London petitioned King George III.

Again Botany Bay was submitted and Banks's recommendation remembered.
He had said that 'the proportion of rich soil was small in comparison to the
barren, but sufficient to support a very large number of people. ... The country
was well supplied with water. There were no beasts of prey' and the natives
were comparatively peaceful when compared to those of New Zealand. Banks
did make the proviso that any body of settlers going to the country must take a
full year's allowance of such things as victuals, raiment, tools, seeds and stock.
Cook, in his Journals, had stated similar views. 'We are to consider that we see
this country in a pure state of nature, the industry of man has nothing to do with
any part of it and yet we find such things as nature hath bestow'd upon it in a
flourishing state. In this extensive country it can never be doubted but what
most sorts of grain, fruit, roots etc. would flourish were they once brought
hither.'

It is an interesting point that de Brosses, already in 1756, was advising France
to settle Dampier's discovery of New Britain with her foundling beggars and
criminals. '*Il faut*', he writes, '*déporter annuellement d'un grand état un certain
nombre de gens qui ne s'occupent qu'à nuire aux autres.*' 'The body politic,' he
goes on, 'like the human body has vicious fluids which must often be evacuated.'
Callander, copying de Brosses, suggests that England herself should settle New
Britain. De Brosses reasons so well it is difficult not to go on quoting him. 'When
the subject is wholly bad, the penal laws destroy him by the death penalty. ... If
the case is not dangerous enough to demand this necessary example, or if the
subject is not corrupted enough to leave no hope, the laws restrain him by
forced labour, or they expel him from society.' De Brosses then wisely advocates
caution. 'Nevertheless, I would not think it proper to undertake the proposed
deportation in the first moments of settlement in an unknown land. At that
time it is important not to put bad examples before the eyes of strangers whom
you want to win over, and you have too much to do with them to have also to be
on guard against your own people.'

James Matra[6], who had sailed with Cook on the *Endeavour*, also came forward
with a suggestion. Of an American loyalist family, his patrimony lost in the
War, he had a scheme for colonising New South Wales 'with those unfortunates
to whom Great Britain is bound by every tie of honour and gratitude to support'.
He advocates that the convicts go with the loyalists as servants. Matra makes
these points in a long glowing report to Lord Sydney, Secretary of Colonial
Affairs. New South Wales, he argued, would also make a convenient base for
Britain. 'If we were at war with Holland or Spain, we might very powerfully
annoy either State from our new settlement.' In his scheme of things the

deficiency in women was to be made up by importing natives from New Caledonia and Tahiti. He also suggested Australia as a possible source of flax which had been found growing prolifically by the men of the *Endeavour* in New Zealand. He writes that a cable made of New Zealand flax 'of the circumference of ten inches would be equal in strength to one of eighteen inches of European hemp'. Of all Matra's different suggestions the question of flax was the only one to really interest Lord Sydney. Captain Cook on his second voyage had discovered Norfolk Island lying off the east coast of Australia about a thousand miles north-east of Sydney. Its flora and fauna had distinct affinities with those of New Zealand, and flax was found growing in profusion in all the moist hollows. They also found stands of the tall *Araucaria excelsa*, or Norfolk Island pine which has now become a decorative coastal feature in Australia. Professor Blainey in his excellent book *The Tyranny of Distance* explained Lord Sydney's interest. 'Britain's military strength and an increasing part of her commerce', he writes, 'relied on seapower, and flax and ship's timber were as vital to seapower as steel and oil are today.' He writes further that during the eighteenth century flax came from the Baltic ports to England. 'England spent about £500,000 on importing flax, mostly from St Petersburg in Russia.' Flax not only was a source of sailcloth but also a substitute for hemp in the making of ropes for ships' rigging.

The question of timber was equally important and Norfolk Island was covered with tall, straight pines. 'England relied heavily on foreign timber for the building and repairing of ships. Most British ships of the line had Baltic planking and spars, North American mainmasts, Ukranian topmasts, and a hull framework of Sussex oak. When the American Colonies rebelled against England, the white pine forests of Maine and New Hampshire ceased to send their mainmasts to England and the English ships of war had no adequate substitute. As masts had to keep their resin in order to remain springy and storm-proof and as the resin vanished after ten or twenty years, the masts had to be replaced regularly.'[7]

There was another point to be considered. French sea power also depended on the same sources for its supplies and an expedition under Jean de la Pérouse was already hunting up specimens of the South Pacific flax.

There were, then, several counts why Australia should be given serious thought but the overruling factor was the question of the convicts. The problem could no longer be postponed and the Government was forced to take action. The need to empty the jails and hulks was even greater than the sense of obligation to the loyalists who in the end, kept waiting so long, settled themselves in Nova Scotia.

By August 1786 Lord Sydney had outlined a plan and the Lord Commissioners of the Treasury were petitioned to provide a proper number of vessels for the conveyance of convicts to Botany Bay. Arthur Phillip, RN, a man with a fine naval record, was appointed to lead this First Fleet which consisted of six transports, three storeships and two ships of war carrying a total of 1,138 people of whom 821 were convicts.

5 The First Fleet

Despite his stature – he was only five feet eight inches tall – Phillip's slight figure dominated all those around him, his subordinate officers, even some of his superiors in London. History does not actually relate how he came to be chosen as commander of what is now known as the First Fleet and subsequently Governor of New South Wales. He was born on 11 October 1738 in Bread Street, in the heart of the City. His father, Jacob, probably of Jewish origin, was a native of Frankfurt, who had settled in England as a language teacher. His mother, through her first marriage to a sea captain called Herbert, was related to the Pembrokes of Wilton and it was probably through her influence that he chose a sea-faring career. Educated at Greenwich, he was a midshipman by seventeen and saw active service the following year. Promoted lieutenant at twenty-four, he was married shortly afterwards to the widow of a prosperous London merchant. Semi-retiring from the Navy he lived the life of a country squire on a farm by Lyndhurst. But the marriage could not have been a great success for he was separated four years later and back again in the Navy, serving with the Admiralty's permission, as a Captain in the Portuguese fleet. While in foreign service he was given the assignment of transporting convicts from Lisbon to Brazil. This experience, backed by a sound naval training and at least a familiarity with the rudiments of farming, were surely recommendations enough for his appointment. In any event, Lord Sydney, faced with the need of finding someone in a hurry for the mediocre post of establishing a convict settlement in an unknown country the other end of the world, must have been relieved when a man of his qualities was brought to his attention.

Phillip was forty-eight when given command of the Fleet and not particularly prepossessing to look at; a small narrow face, a thin aquiline nose and full lips, and with a sharp powerful voice. He was intelligent, active, kind but firm enough to make his authority respected; no sense of humour but above all intensely humane. It was clear from the very beginning that the Government intended to devote the very minimum in money and materials on this settle-

Opposite Convicts embarking for Botany Bay. Watercolour and pen drawing by Thomas Rowlandson.

53

ment scheme and Phillip was obliged to heckle with the authorities for adequate stores and equipment. He was fairly successful with regard to the rations, obtaining two-thirds of the regular naval rations, their daily fare including bread, salt pork, salt beef, peas, oatmeal, butter, cheese and vinegar. When in port fresh meat, vegetables and fish were obtained. The sick were granted special compensations. Each convict was issued with what, under the circumstances, must have been considered an adequate wardrobe, but typical of the mismanagement prevalent at the time, much of the female convicts' clothing was unfinished and consequently left behind. What they had was so defective that it fell to pieces, and as no needles and thread had been provided one gathers from various reports that they arrived the other end almost naked. It was Phillip, also, who suggested the careful grading of the convicts. 'All the greatest villains', he writes in a memo now in the Public Records Office, 'should be stowed away in one ship.' He asks that all those suffering from venereal diseases should be precluded. 'During the passage when light airs or calm permit I shall visit and inspect all the ships of the Fleet.' He also proposed that the war ship should precede the transports by some two or three months to prepare for the arrival of the convicts. Even at the onset he was not convinced that Botany Bay would prove to be the best place for settlement. He wanted to get huts ready for the women and for those who were sick 'as the scurvy must make a great ravage amongst people voluntarily indolent and not cleanly'. Phillip appears to have been remarkably broad-minded. 'The women in general I should suppose possess neither virtue nor honesty.' He felt the better class should be segregated. The others, 'the most abandoned', he suggests should be permitted to receive the visits of convicts. He had plans to import women from Tonga for his officers, and himself took a mistress when he arrived in Australia, a convict girl called Elizabeth Evans who bore him a son. Not all Phillip's propositions were acted on and the more's the pity, for the first months of settlement would have been a great deal easier had some responsible person in the Government listened to him.

Various sources of references exist for the First Fleet and John Stockdale, a contemporary publisher, produced what can be considered the official account of the voyage. His work was published in London in 1789 under the title *The Voyage of Governor Phillip to Botany Bay* and consisted of an ably edited collection of Phillip's letters and various papers, along with the journals of other officers. It is a useful basic guide, but it is to Captain Watkin Tench of the Marine Corps to whom we must turn for a more immediate picture. He wrote two excellent books[8] on the expedition and the actual settlement. They were both published before the turn of the century and give a vivid, immediate impression of the proceedings.

Tench's father, a dancing master, kept a respectable boarding school in Chester which probably explains Tench's erudition. He was also a natural born writer and his descriptions of the voyage are 'without rival'. Another is John White, the Chief Surgeon, a sympathetic fellow of thirty and it is to him that we turn for a glimpse of the fleet assembling at Spithead. It is May and some of the

Opposite Arthur Phillip, painted by Francis Weatley after Phillip had been promoted to Rear-Admiral.

convicts had embarked already in January. 'They had been nearly four months on board and during that time had been kept upon salt provisions.' White saw to it that they got fresh food, he insisted also that they came on deck to breathe the fresh air and made what arrangements he could for the sanitation, 'white-washing with quick-lime the parts of the ships where the convicts were confined … thus correcting and preventing the unwholesome dampness which usually appeared on the beams and the sides of the ship occasioned by the breath of the people'. The burning of oil tar was considered another sweetener.

The Navy Board had picked a roomy three-master store ship called the *Berwick* to act as flagship, renaming her HMS *Sirius* after the bright star of that name in the southern constellation. To police the expedition Phillip had been allotted four companies of Marines; over two hundred men, some of them with their wives and children. The Marines were parcelled out to the different ships, the manner in which they were actually allotted depending on the size of the ship. The authorities had shown good sense in employing Marines. Sea-sickness would have incapacitated half the men had the regular army been used. Many of the officers and men of the Marine Corps were volunteers and had been lured to apply by promise of a discharge on their return home, or the permission to remain as settlers if they so wished.

Phillip joined the *Sirius* on 7 May at Portsmouth. On board with him were Captain John Hunter, second in command, also Philip Gidley King, appointed Second Lieutenant, both close friends of Phillip, and both men destined to succeed him as eventual Governors.

Before sailing, a guard-boat circled round the transports at night to make sure that no last minute escapes were attempted. Eventually at day-break on 13 May 1787, the signal was given to weigh anchor. They were away and His Majesty's Frigate *Hyena* was ordered to attend the Fleet until well clear of the Channel. It was thought that Phillip might have wanted to despatch a last message but 'the sea ran so high that the Governor found it difficult to even sit and write'. Tench, on the transport *Charlotte* with eighty-eight male and twenty female convicts on board, went below deck when clear of the Isle of Wight and notes that 'most seemed glad to be leaving though in some, the pain of being severed, perhaps for ever, from their native land, could not be wholly suppressed. In general, marks of distress were more perceptible among the men than the women.'

The public seemed to have been fairly apathetic and the papers made little fuss over the Fleet's departure. As Mr Mackaness writes the 'press found much more excitement and entertaining news in the trial of Warren Hastings and the morganatic marriage of the Prince of Wales'.[9]

The accepted route to Australia in the early days was a westerly route across the South Atlantic, stopping at the Canary Islands and Rio de Janeiro to revictual before making the run for the Cape of Good Hope. It appears a long way round but it was a question of winds and, above all, a way of avoiding the calms so frequent on the African side.

The ships must have presented a strange appearance for the officers had stowed away all kinds of luxuries; the surgeon of the *Sirius* had his own piano on board, while the decks were cluttered with pens crammed with every animal in the farmyard: sheep, goats, turkeys, geese, chickens, pigeons and cats. Dogs were not allowed, but according to an unpublished journal in the Mitchell Library, Phillip had smuggled between thirty and forty on board.

They had been a week at sea when orders came through from Phillip that 'using their discretion the officers were at liberty to release their convicts from their fetters'. Only the men were in irons. In this way they were able to strip off at night when they bunked down and, more important still, were able to wash themselves. There was an abortive attempt at mutiny on the *Scarborough* but otherwise Tench tells us that the convicts' behaviour was 'gentle, humble and submissive'. Phillip with a more over-all picture bears him out 'though', he writes, 'there are among them some complete villains'. Captain Clark, writing from the *Friendship*, seems to have had trouble with the women under his charge. 'Those damn troublesome whores', he explodes. 'I would rather have a hundred men than have a single woman.' They were put in irons and gagged. 'In all the course of my days I never heard such expressions come from the mouth of a human being.' Clark writes that he would have had them flogged had he been in command. Dousing with cold water was the usual punishment used and only exceptional cases were whipped.

Even with a humane Commander and sympathetic doctors there was little anyone could do to mitigate the hell endured by the poor wretches tethered between decks on a convict ship. Next to the hatchway was a cleared strip eight feet deep running the width of the ship and this, with a narrow passage between the rows of bunks, served from fifty to a hundred men with what room they needed for eating and recreation. In some ships, bunks or compartments were separated from each other by bulkheads and from the gangway down the centre by iron bars giving the impression of a menagerie. A lucky few were given hammocks, but the majority were put to bed in sixteen inches of space per man, stowed away as one convict writes, 'in a disgraceful indiscreet manner'.[10]

Narrow boxes were kept on deck for punishment. In these convicts were forced to stand erect for stated periods. On later convoys this box used to be suspended from the yard-arm in such a position that the box was submerged temporarily whenever the ship keeled. If the seas were running high the unfortunate man was, more often than not, drowned.

Guards were on constant duty and hardly ten minutes elapsed without an officer in charge going down between decks. He would have had to stoop for the convicts' cages were about five foot ten inches high. Coming in from the upper air the place must have seemed to be in inky darkness. Only the men accustomed to this sinister twilight would have been able to discern their surroundings. The ships were infested with rats, cockroaches, bugs and other vermin and the whole place smelt of unwashed humanity. The stench was appalling for, cutting across the rank atmosphere, was the acrid smell of stale bilge-water. The sea seeped through the ships' seams and in very heavy seas the port-holes had to be battened down, but even then it was not uncommon

The punishment of convicts during transportation was often horrific. *Above, left* An iron cage for refractory men in the prison hulk *Success. Right* A 'ducking box'. It should be pointed out that this was not a form of punishment used by Phillip in the First Fleet.

for the prisoners to find themselves washed from their bunks by a swirling mass of water.

John White, who had been apprenticed as Surgeon General to the settlement, had been signalled for on one of the ships where the convicts were suddenly taken ill. It was found to be the bilge water 'when the hatches were taken off, the stench was so powerful that it was scarcely possible to stand over it ... and the buttons on the clothes of the officers were turned nearly black by the obnoxious effluvia'.

Despite these horrors Phillip was able to write to Lord Sydney that his charges 'were much healthier than when we left England'.

On 3 June the Fleet arrived off Teneriffe in the Canary Islands. They remained on the island a week, watering and loading. The markets were full of poultry, pumpkins, onions, figs and excellent mulberries. White was shocked by the women's behaviour, 'some of them are so abandoned and shameless, that it would be doing an injustice to the prostitutes met with in the streets of London to say that they are like them'. Phillip, accompanied by twenty officers, paid his respects to the Marquess de Brancifort, the Governor of the Islands. The Marquess received him 'with the dignity of a Grandee of Spain', and fed them sherberts made from ice brought down from caves in the mountains. A prisoner tried to escape in a small boat but was caught, and the next day they were off. The equator was crossed on the evening of 14 July; it rained heavily and was intolerably hot, and Phillip was apprehensive for the health of the Fleet, but there were surprisingly few sick. Tench wrote that 'frequent explosions of gunpowder, lighting fires between decks and a liberal use of oil of tar' kept the air pure. At Rio the Fleet anchored about three quarters of a mile from the shore. The Viceroy who had already met Phillip when he was serving in the Portuguese navy made much of him, treating him far better than his predecessor had treated Cook. White, who had been so censorious about the women of

58

Teneriffe, tells us of a flirtation he had with a nun 'as tender an intercourse as the bolts and bars between would admit'.

The Fleet anchored at Rio nearly a month and spent another month at Cape Town, or more accurately Kaapstadt, for it was still Dutch. During the run from Rio they had met some rough weather. Orders were signalled from the *Sirius* and relayed from ship to ship; the convoy was told to keep near their commanding officer. A man fell off the top-sail yard and drowned, but the ship was going too fast even to try and save him. William Brown 'a very well-behaved convict' suffered the same fate while pegging out some washing. Mortlock, a convict on a subsequent convoy, adds a sinister note and writes that huge albatrosses have the habit of diving at a man overboard, stunning him with their strong beaks.

Once anchored at Table Bay, they began loading the cattle, a nucleus with which Phillip planned to stock the new Colony – two bulls, seven cows, an equal number of horses, forty-four sheep and twenty-eight boars and breeding sows. The Master's Mate on the *Sirius* describes his ship as resembling 'a livery stable ... partitions all along and between decks'. Eight cannon had been removed from the gun deck and stowed in the lower hold to make room for these stalls. All the women convicts were transferred from the *Friendship* to other vessels to make room for the sheep and Ralph Clark is of the opinion that they were certain to make 'more agreeable shipmates'. Besides the animals a whole forest of trees was moved on board; bananas, oranges, lemons, quinces, apples, pears, bamboo, figs, oaks and myrtle, and all the different grains.

This fleet of embowered Noah's Arks got under way on 13 November and twelve days later Phillip transferred his broad pendant to the *Supply*. With him went the three fastest ships in the Fleet; the *Scarborough, Alexander* and *Friendship*. He went ahead to make preparations for the landing, leaving Hunter in charge of the other ships.

Early in the morning of 7 January 1788, this advance guard sighted land, the South Cape of Tasmania, at that time believed to be the southernmost point of the Australian Continent. A few days later Tench notes that 'the wind was now fair, the sky serene, though a little hazy, and the temperature of the air delightfully pleasant'. On the 18th they came to anchor in Botany Bay. 'Joy sparkled in every countenance', and Tench, thoroughly carried away, relates to the classics. 'Ithaca itself was scarcely more longed for by Ulysses, than Botany Bay by the adventurers who had traversed so many thousand miles to take possession of it.' Much to Phillip's surprise, Hunter arrived on the 20th with the remaining vessels.

It was a remarkable achievement for a voyage of eight months' duration. They had sailed fifteen thousand miles over unknown waters and not once, except by design, had the ships been separated. Between embarkation and landing only forty had died out of a total of nearly fifteen hundred, and most of them it must be remembered, were the most depraved and unhealthy passengers already in a sickly state before leaving England.

Judged on the voyage alone, Phillip emerges as a man of exceptional ability and an excellent organiser. The following years were to bring out still further qualities. Trollope, writing about him, calls him 'one of the world's heroes of whom the world hears little – stubborn, just, self-denying, long-suffering, brave man when despair was all round him.'[11] Immediately on arrival at Botany Bay, he had an important decision to make. Not many would have shown his decision, and, had he not made it, the plan of colonising New South Wales might well have been written off as another failure. It was found that Cook's anchorage was exposed to the prevailing south-east winds which, when they blew, whipped up a dangerous swell. The Bay itself was too shallow to afford any protection, which meant that even ships of a moderate draught would always be obliged to anchor within the entrance and be exposed to a heaving sea. Added to this the surrounding country was very poor, being marshy and low-lying with an inadequate water supply.[12] Within two days of his arrival Phillip set out on an expedition to examine Port Jackson, a few miles to the northward, which had been named but not investigated by Cook. Ross, the Lieutenant-Governor, was left in charge of the fleet while Phillip and Hunter, two Masters with a party of Marines, set off in a rigged longboat. They were back on the evening of the third day with reports of an excellent harbour reached through great protective heads and stretching far to the west in sheets of still water, dotted with islands. The coastline was thickly wooded and fringed with strips of golden sands which spread in aprons across charming little bays. Phillip had investigated every inner reach and hidden arm of the harbour, and had finally picked on a little cove with a fresh stream. Later Phillip describes it in a letter to Lord Sydney as 'the finest harbour in the world in which a thousand sail of the line may ride in the most perfect security'. He adds that it is possible to 'anchor so close to the shore that at a very small expense quays may be made at which the great ships may unload'.

Phillip named the cove after Lord Sydney and hurried back to his fleet. It must have astonished him on rounding Cape Banks to find two ships under French colours struggling to get into the Bay. The wind was blowing too hard and, unable to advance, they disappeared out to sea in a thick haze. As Phillip had supposed, they were *La Boussole* and *L'Astrolabe* on a voyage of exploration of the Pacific. La Pérouse was their Commander and the expedition was under the direct patronage of Louis XVI. Phillip must surely have wanted to wait on their return but, anxious about the safety of his Fleet, left the visitors to be dealt with by his subordinates and himself went aboard the *Supply* and sailed for Port Jackson (the new Sydney), with instructions to Captain Hunter to follow him with all transport and victuallers as soon as the wind and the weather would permit. On the following day, 26 January, the French ships were again sighted, this time standing in for the Bay. White tells us that Hunter 'sent his First Lieutenant on board the Commanding Officer's ship to assist them in coming in'.

A few miles to the north of this scene Phillip had landed in Sydney Cove and unfurled the Union Jack.[13] Volleys were fired and toasts drunk – it was the beginning of settlement, and 26 January is now celebrated as Australia Day.

Above The First Fleet anchored in Botany Bay.
Engraving by T. Medland after a painting by Robert
Cleveley. Plate from *The Voyage of Governor Phillip to
Botany Bay*.

Right Inscribed copper plate unearthed in 1899 on the
corner of Phillip and Bridge Streets, Sydney. The plate
records Phillip's landing and was embedded in a
corner stone of the first Government House, laid on
15 May 1788.

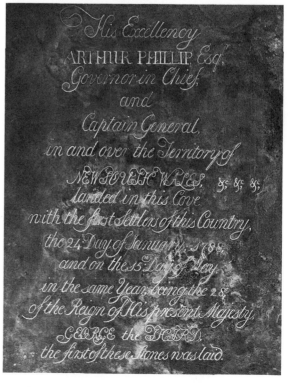

6 The foundation of Sydney

In the beginning Great Britain did not lay claim to the whole of Australia. People were still unsure as to the exact extent of the country and whether or not the part the Dutch called New Holland was separated from Cook's New South Wales. Phillip's commission gave him command over an area embracing roughly the eastern half of Australia, together with the adjacent Pacific Islands. When La Pérouse put in his appearance, and before the flag showing the Golden Lilies of France had been recognised, there were those with Phillip who immediately supposed that they were the Dutch 'coming after us to oppose our landing'. Holland, however, remained supremely indifferent and Phillip left to himself went ahead as instructed.

The harbour discovered by Phillip was indeed very beautiful; almost completely land-locked with spectacular cliffs and an opening between them less than two miles across giving abruptly on to the sea. The harbour runs chiefly in a westerly direction, about thirteen miles into the country, and contains numberless bays and coves. They indent the land and seen on a map the water lies something like an oak leaf. Sydney Cove, the place chosen for settlement, is situated on the south side of the harbour between five and six miles from the entrance. All round, the ground slopes gently down to the sea, and despite the rocks, is entirely covered with trees, new trees to the stranger's eye, that shed their bark and retain their leaves. Beautiful trees for those who have grown accustomed to them; grey-green with polished leaves that catch the light, the sun burnishing them on the hilltops and the shadows dimming them in the valleys.

From the very beginning the different explorers had called the eucalyptus 'gum'. Dampier wrote about gum seeping from 'the knots and cracks'. Cook also mentions it. They all complained about the impossible hardness of the wood, too hard and heavy for the ordinary axe. It was, in fact, with aboriginal trees, not tribes, that the settlers struggled so long and persistently. They are still struggling in certain parts of the country. John White, the surgeon general

Opposite Phillip had been ordered to deal with the natives in a friendly fashion and the first contacts were encouraging. Plate from François Péron's *Voyage de Découvertes aux Terres Australes,* engraved by B. Roger after a drawing by N. Petit.

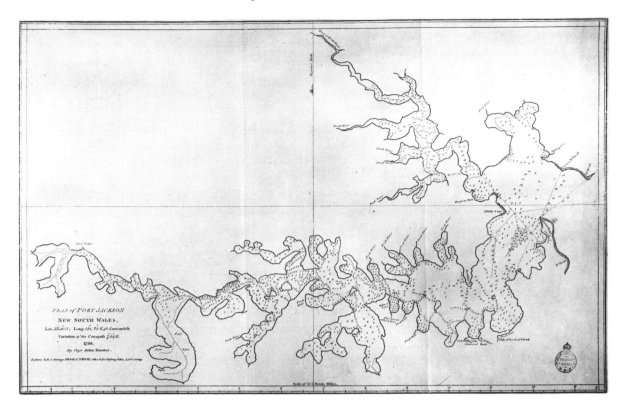

Port Jackson, the harbour of Sydney, with all the coves and bays, drawn by Captain John Hunter.

to the settlement, cites a case in which twelve men were employed for nearly a week in grubbing up a single tree. With the limited means at their disposal the settlers were unable to convert them into useful timber and the stumps were too numerous for them to remove.

However, there were more pressing details in the sequence of affairs, foremost, the natives of the country, strange, primitive people moving like spectres under the open shade of the eucalyptus. What were their reactions? Cook wrote sensitively about them; 'they may appear to some to be the most wretched people upon earth, but in reality they are far happier than we Europeans.' He envies them their ignorance of what we consider the necessities of life, and living in an equitable climate 'they have very little need of clothing ... Many to whom we gave cloth left it carelessly upon the sea beach and in the woods as a thing they have no manner of use for. In short, they seemed to set no value upon anything we gave them, nor would they ever part with anything of their own.' Phillip had been given strict instructions regarding the natives, and his own policy was, if possible, 'to cultivate an acquaintance with them without their having an idea of our great superiority over them'. He took great trouble to gain their confidence and friendship, and the first contacts were encouraging. Tench writes that, though timorous, 'the natives showed no sign of resentment of their going ashore. The people seemed at a loss to know (probably from our want of beards) of what sex we were, which having understood, they burst into the most immoderate fits of laughter.' Phillip always showed great courage in his relationship with them, advancing generally alone, holding his hands above his head as a sign of friendship. One of the first evenings on shore the English were eating their dinner on the beach and the natives came over to them. They would appear to have been in a troublesome mood and Phillip drew a circle round the place where they were sitting and without much difficulty made the natives understand that they were not to pass that line. One wonders how the war-like Maoris would have reacted had the picnic been set in New Zealand. But chance as well as courage and common sense seems to have favoured Phillip in his relationship with the natives. As luck would have it he had one of his front teeth missing, and this, apparently, had symbolic value for them, adding considerably to his prestige, for the knocking out of the front tooth was an important part of the Aboriginal's initiation ceremony.

It was a laborious job establishing the first camp; when a sufficient number of tents had been pitched, the convicts and the Marines started going ashore. The female convicts followed twelve days later. Tench tells us that while on board they had been carefully segregated (not, however, from the sailors), but that once landed 'licentiousness was the unavoidable sequence'. Another officer puts it more bluntly and writes that 'the scenes of debauchery and riot that ensued during the night may be better conceived than expressed'.

Calm returned in the morning. It was 7 February, another auspicious date in Australian history – the day formal possession was taken of the Colony. Government and law were established, at any rate nominally. Captain David Collins, the Judge-Advocate, read the Proclamation appointing Phillip as Captain-General and Governor-in-Chief of New South Wales, which gave him almost unlimited powers, civil as well as military. After the investiture, he made a short speech which White says 'was extremely well adapted to the people he had to govern'. Justice was promised to the convicts but they were warned that if they didn't work they wouldn't eat – and with the recent bacchanal in mind he advised his wards 'to consider seriously the holy state of matrimony'.

After the ceremony Phillip invited the officers to a cold collation served in his canvas house which he had brought out with him from England at the cost of £125. It was actually more a tent than a real house and had a rigid timbered frame with canvas walls and roof. At the time Phillip was still sleeping on board the *Sirius* and did not move into the temporary and far from weather-proof Government House until about the middle of the month.

The first concern of those responsible was the question of lodging. Hospital tents were given priority. More elaborate plans were to follow and Phillip with his optimistic nature looked to the future. Enlisting the help of William Dawes, a young Lieutenant of the Marines, the Colony's official astronomer, he traced out a network of streets, the main avenues measuring two hundred feet wide. Tench, echoing his Governor's sentiments, writes that 'to proceed on a narrow, confined space in a country of the extensive limits we possess, would be unpardonable'. One can almost see his chest swell as he pens the last words – 'the extent of Empire demands grandeur of design'.

All very well, but how to proceed with a limited number of carpenters; a few from the ship and no more than twelve among the convicts, and some of these sick, or not very experienced. The convicts were feckless workers unless forced to the job, and by some oversight no superintendents had been sent out. The Marine officers stubbornly maintaining that their duties did not extend beyond the voyage out, refused to act any longer. Phillip consequently was obliged to select his overseers from the ranks of the convicts themselves; not a very satisfactory solution. On top of this was the actual physical task of clearing the ground, which was very rocky. The timber, we know, was like iron, particularly the heavy-limbed *Angophora,* or red gum, which predominates round Sydney. To make matters even more difficult there was a scarcity of tools. 'Most of those we had', White informs us, 'being either worn-out by the hardness of the timber or lost in the woods among the grass through the carelessness of the convicts.' An excellent sandstone abounds in the area, indeed much of present Sydney is built of it, but in Phillip's day there was a shortage of mortar with which to bind the stone. With no obvious building material to hand it became a question of improvising, and what amazes one here is the ingeniousness displayed by a handful of men set down in a country seemingly destitute of help of any kind. 'No country', Phillip writes to Lord Sydney, 'offers less assistance to first settlers.' Not even the Aborigines could point the way, for their shelters were little better than card houses made out of slabs of bark, propped one against the other.

Experimenting, the settlers finally evolved a building pattern; the houses were little better than huts but had timber frames and wall panels of cabbage-tree trunks which were soft and easily cut. The spaces between were wattled over with twigs and plastered up with clay and daubed over with whitewash. The floors were made of packed mud and grass or reeds provided thatching for the roofs. Enough timber had been produced to build a hospital, barracks and warehouses, and in order to render them more durable these buildings were roofed with shingles. Government House was the only building in stone, the lime for the mortar being made from oyster shells collected by women convicts in the neighbouring coves. The convicts were in their huts before the officers, and it was nearly six months before a general move was made from the tents. White tells us living under canvas in the rainy season 'was a severe trial for the most robust constitution'.

On reading the different accounts relating to these early days, one is struck with Phillip's total disregard of the Frenchman camped across the dunes at Botany Bay. Strange indeed that he and La Pérouse never met, especially since La Pérouse's enforced sojourn lasted six weeks. Humanitarians, both accomplished, they would have had much in common. What in fact kept them apart? Certainly a reason of some kind existed, for the distance between their camps was negligible, but half a day's journey by boat for Phillip. Could it, perhaps, have been a question of protocol? But knowing their characters one must rule out so mundane a consideration. There must have been a more serious motive. Was it that Phillip mistrusted the Frenchman? Officially La Pérouse had put

into port to replenish his supplies of water and wood, and to refit and assemble new long boats to replace those he had lost in the massacre of his men at Tutuila in the Samoan Islands. These were perfectly valid reasons, but might they not have come also to spy on the English? There is little doubt that had the Revolution not cut short Louis XVI's reign, France was intending to annex those parts of Australia not already claimed by Cook and taken possession of by Phillip. La Pérouse's instructions had been to explore the north-west and south coast of Australia, and in his stores he carried plates bearing the Royal Arms – objects to be used in the ceremony of taking possession in the King's name. Certainly La Pérouse had no thought of contesting Phillip in his right of settlement, but at best it was an ambiguous situation and one Phillip must have judged better left well alone.

As mentioned already, an officer from Hunter's ship had boarded *La Boussole*, and La Pérouse writing in his Journal – the last entry he was to make – admits that 'the English Lieutenant appears to make a great mystery of Commander Phillip's plan, and', adds La Pérouse, 'we did not take the liberty of asking him any questions on the subject'. The French had guessed anyway about the projected establishment at Port Jackson and the English sailors, La Pérouse notes with a twinkle, had been less cautious than their officers. They had, anyhow, ample opportunities of hearing news of the English settlement 'from characters who caused us a great deal of trouble and embar-

The Aborigines' shelters 'were little better than card houses made out of slabs of bark, propped one against the other'. Engraving by T. Medland after R. Cleveley; from *The Voyage of Governor Phillip to Botany Bay*.

67

rassment'. Convicts were constantly trying to escape, hoping the French would smuggle them on board.

Apart from Phillip's strange silence, relations between the two camps were very cordial. Hunter paid a visit, and spent the night. 'After dinner I attended on Pérouse and his officers on shore, where I found him quite established, he had thrown round his tents a stockade which was guarded by two small guns.' One of the tents served as an observatory and Hunter was impressed by the equipment, also the astronomer, a member of the Academy of Science in Paris. The Frenchmen, in their turn, were generous in their praise of the English, especially the great Cook. They admitted that they had always found his reckoning 'so exact and true'. '*Enfin*' says La Pérouse, '*Monsieur Cook a tant fait qu'il ne m'a rien laissé à faire, que d'admirer ses oeuvres.*' That same evening Hunter returned on board the French flagship and was shown all the drawings that had been made during the voyage. Douché de Vancy, the landscape and figure draughtsman, and the Prévosts–uncle and nephew–the natural history painters, were first-rate artists and Hunter, himself adept with a pencil, must have enjoyed the visit. One regrets that Hunter did not record the drawings for they were to perish in the subsequent wreck of *La Boussole* and *L'Astrolabe* at Vanikoro.

Tench describes how they hear about La Pérouse's mysterious disappearance from the crew of the *Lady Juliana*, a transport ship that docked at Sydney Cove in the summer of 1790. 'No account of them', he writes 'has been received since they left Botany Bay in March 1788.' The French Government had equipped an expedition under Bruny d'Entrecasteaux to look for them, but the search proved fruitless. It was not until almost forty years later that the mystery was solved when Captain Dillon, an adventurer, reported finding relics in the New Hebrides. Dillon learned from the natives that the ships had been driven ashore in a storm. Some of the sailors had been massacred and others had built a boat from the wreckage and sailed away never to be heard of again.

But to return to the Colony, the next event of importance was to be the settling of Norfolk Island. Phillip's orders had been precise. He was to colonise the island immediately, first to prevent it being occupied by any other European power, and secondly 'to proceed to the cultivation of the flax plant which you will find growing on the island'. Phillip despatched the *Supply* with a small party of twenty-four under the command of Philip King. The party consisted of two Maoris who understood the dressing of the flax, nine male and six female convicts, one officer and six Marines. On the way there they discovered another island which they named after Lord Howe. They also describe the *Porphyrio albus*, a bird endemic to the island resembling a guinea-fowl, but all white with a red cockscomb. 'These not being birds of flight nor in the least wild, the sailors availed themselves of their gentleness and inability to take wing from their pursuers and easily struck them down with sticks.' The same fate awaited a species of dove, and both birds are now extinct. Only one skin of the *Porphyrio albus* is known and that is in the Vienna Museum.

King, in high spirits, is soon writing to Phillip about his new command. The

Père Receveur's grave at Botany Bay. Receveur was a Franciscan priest who sailed as naturalist and acting chaplain on board *L'Astrolabe* under the command of La Pérouse.

soil is a rich, black mould and he describes the island 'as one entire wood, or rather as a garden over-run with the noblest pines. ... The wood is said to be of the best quality almost as light as that of the best Norway masts.'[14] The flax, however, proved a disappointment and would not respond to propagation. They tried exporting it to New South Wales and there it failed altogether.

On hunting through the files, an interesting detail emerges in relation to King. One of the six convict girls becomes his mistress and produces two sons for him, christened Norfolk and Sydney. Nothing more is heard of them and one wonders how their father managed about their upbringing when he was appointed the third Governor of the new settlement in Australia.

The birds on Howe Island might appear intriguing but imagine the effect the bizarre, almost mythical creatures that lopped and shuffled about in the dappled shade of new clearings must have had on the settlers of the mainland. Already the clearings themselves were bordered by a completely new flora never seen before, clouds of powdered yellow mimosa with beyond, the stiff, wiry, thick-set flowers of the handsome *Banksia spinulosa* named after Banks by the young Linnaeus. Phillip in one of his many letters remarks on the prodigious variety of plants, and regrets that among all the people with him, 'there happened not to be one who has a tolerable knowledge of botany'. Exciting, all this, but I think of the animals ; the wombat, a strange burrowing marsupial, as impossible in appearance as its aboriginal name would suggest. Weirder still, a primitive egg-laying mammal with webbed feet named the duck-billed platypus, a combination of reptile, fish and bird ; a furred animal, that growls like a puppy when annoyed. Black swans had already been described by the Dutch and had been taken alive to Batavia. Emus, though, had never been seen and Tench shooting a bird is the first to supply us with details. White, who must have helped him eat it, said it was very good, 'and tasted not unlike young, tender beef'. The settlers, reduced by a failure in crops to eating what they could find, counted themselves lucky when it was emu. Hunter, obviously more particular than White, compares it with mutton 'but not as good as can be got in Leadenhall-Market'. Phillip on the other hand found the bird's flesh 'coarse and lean'. More details are supplied by Peter Cunningham, a surgeon serving on later convoys. At certain times of the year, he tells us, the emu was bedded around the rump with a prodigious quantity of fat 'which is melted down and much esteemed by the settlers'.[15] According to him the hindquarters are the only parts worth eating. He complains, however, about their 'dimensions' and writes that 'shouldering a couple of hind legs once proved as tiresome a task as I ever recollect'. Cunningham also passes comment on the Aboriginal manner of preparing the bird. They boiled it in a pit, covering it with stones with its neck sticking out. They considered it cooked when steam came puffing out of its beak, much like a kettle boiling.

The eggs, dark green and granulated, were also eaten by the early settlers and took about twenty minutes to cook. In the beginning the emu was known as the New Holland cassowary and the first skin cured was described as something between hair and feathers and was sent by Phillip to Lord Sydney who gave it to Banks. Alive, the bird stands nearly as high as a man, has a stride of almost ten feet and can do a fast sprint of anything up to thirty miles an hour. Causing considerable damage to crops, they were hunted by the settlers in much the same way as the kangaroo. Cunningham with his dogs chased a flock of five 'which had evidently never seen a white man on horseback before, from the degree of amazement with which they stared at me'. He was mounted on a swift blood mare which he kept at a hard gallop 'but they left me always with the most perfect ease'. As one might expect Banks was the first to receive a live specimen, and shortly afterwards Sir Walter Scott found himself encumbered with a pair of the great birds sent him by a naturalist friend. Scott's idea about emus must have been very hazy, and apparently he was appalled when they arrived, standing 'six feet in their stocking soles' and ready to swallow anything within sight.

Cunningham writes that 'a number of individuals in Sydney earn a good livelihood by collecting our beasts, birds, and insects ; stuffing, preparing, and arranging them in cases ; and disposing of them to individuals leaving the Colony'. Kangaroos were a very popular item and the first live one to reach

The wombat, 'a strange burrowing marsupial, as impossible in appearance as its aboriginal name would suggest'. About the size of a mastiff, it feeds on grass and roots.

Dr Shaw, a contemporary of Banks and the first man to describe this animal, named it the duck-billed platypus. It lays white, reptilian-like eggs. Watercolour by J. W. Lewin, 1810.

The black flying opossum, drawn and engraved by Peter Mazell; from *The Voyage of Governor Phillip to Botany Bay*.

England in 1790 caused quite a commotion when it was exhibited in the Lyceum Theatre in the Strand. Posters advertising it as *'the wonderful kangaroo from Botany Bay'*, the only one at that time to have been brought alive to Europe.

Australia's great marsupials are already too well known to add further literature on the subject. On one point only would I be allowed to enlarge – that being the subject of their birth. Many erroneous theories have been expounded as to how the newly born actually reaches the pouch. Few people have actually witnessed a birth and the journey of the mouse-sized embryo to the pouch. One man described what he thought was a small slug crawling on the kangaroo's tail. On closer examination he discovered it to be not unlike a small, stumpy-tail lizard, about the size of a man's thumb with a hint of a tail and four barely formed legs. The doe licked her tail to facilitate the passage; the whole procedure taking about twenty minutes. Once in the pouch the embryo clamps onto a nipple and does not move until it is about the size of a terrier.

It is touching to see a young kangaroo pop its head out of the pouch when its mother is grazing, and nibble too at the tender herbage. When hunted, the mother will stop suddenly, thrust her fore-paws into her pouch and drag the young one out and throw it away. She does this to make her own passage lighter, but to make this sacrifice they have to be very hard pressed 'and it is pitiful', Cunningham tells us, 'to see the tender sympathetic looks they will sometimes give at the poor little helpless creature they have been forced to oust'.

As it turned out, of Phillip's many tasks that of feeding the settlement proved to be by far the most arduous. Those who had planned the Colony had assumed that the soil was fertile and that it was regularly watered by a normal rainfall. It was quite the opposite. There was no land suitable for cultivation without extensive exploration, and the rainfall was highly capricious, either too much or too little, the first year producing a sequence of dry seasons. To aggravate matters all the wheat, and most of the other seeds brought from England, had heated on the voyage and very little of it germinated, while all the grain brought from the Cape was destroyed by weevils. Equally serious was the almost total lack of experienced labour. Hardly a man amongst them knew anything about farming. Edward Dodd, Phillip's personal servant, had a certain knowledge, but one alone could do little to instruct so many. The Marines were hopeless and the convicts would do no work unless an armed guard was standing behind them. The moment the guard turned his back they would deliberately destroy the utensils in their charge. Ploughs and other such implements were not in general use until the 1820s and furrows were consequently dug with the hoe.

As to the supplies the settlers had brought out with them, they were rapidly deteriorating; the rice was alive with weevils and the salt pork had become so old and dry that it shrank to nothing when boiled. By June the few sheep from the Cape had been killed for food while the rest of the cattle, carelessly husbanded by the convicts, had strayed off into the bush. The situation was becoming desperate and Phillip was forced to impose rationing, reducing the allowance by two-thirds. Worried by the lack of response from England he decided to send the *Sirius,* under the command of John Hunter, to Cape Town. She made a quick crossing via Cape Horn and was back again seven and a half months later, having sailed the whole way round the world.

In the meantime, weak and scorbutic (even Phillip was affected since he would make no distinction), the settlers improvised as best they could; soup of white cockatoos and crows, roasted wild duck stuffed with slices of salt beef. Possums made good eating but had to be soaked in water first to rid the meat of the strong aromatic flavour lent it by the gum leaves on which the animals fed. The bandicoot, a sharp-snouted, beady-eyed little creature of the rat family, tasted like sucking-pig, and made, we are told, a delicious dish with a well-prepared pudding in its belly. Both the possums and bandicoot are night-prowling animals and the settlers would hunt them on fine moonlit evenings when they came out to feed, the muzzle of their muskets chalked to enable them to take better aim.

To combat the scurvy, parties went out hunting for native plants; wild celery, spinach and parsley. Banks's considerate notes must have been of some help. 'I have been rather particular,' he writes, 'in mentioning the things we eat, hoping that such a remembrance might be of use to some others into whose hands these papers might fall.' Cook's party seem to have eaten almost every quadruped that came their way, and Banks lists the botanical names of the plants 'never eaten by Europeans before', the heart of the cabbage palm and fern roots being the most useful.

Fish are not always as plentiful as might be supposed, and Tench tells us that

A flock of emus. Pen sketch by George Hamilton from an original manuscript in the Nan Kivell Collection entitled *Journey in New South Wales and South Australia, 1836-45.*

everyone volunteered, in addition to their other duties, to go fishing alternately every night in their boats.

Watching the Aborigines eat, it is doubtful whether the settlers learned any new culinary possibilities. The natives' dietary habits could at best become but acquired tastes; large ghost-moths fluttering into the embers of a camp fire, and a drink made of crushed green ants. Kangaroo blood was fairly popular, also tadpoles fried on grass, and a kind of sausage made from pelican's entrails filled with fat heated to the consistency of oil. Picking up handfuls of ants they would sift the sand through their fingers and swallow the lot. Tench describes the carcass of a huge whale that was found rotting on a beach 'in the most disgusting state of putrefaction'. He writes that 'at least two hundred natives surrounded it, boiling the flesh on different fires, and feasting on it with the most extravagant mark of greediness and rapture'.

The months dragged by and still no news from England. The Colony were not to know that a store ship had been sent out but had been wrecked on an iceberg. The *Guardian* had been carrying fruit trees and livestock and a small group of specially selected convicts. She was, in fact, the answer to Phillip's request sent back by the First Fleet. Small wonder that a note of panic creeps into the different diaries. No word of any kind had been received from England since they left and there they were, completely isolated, with three thousand miles between themselves and the nearest white man. Before them stretched a great ocean and behind them an unknown continent, a vast uninhabited waste in which they formed but a tiny speck. Famine stared them in the face and the dread of want in a country destitute of natural resources must have been terrifying.

Further cuts were made in the rations and weekly parties would be sent to Botany Bay 'to see', as Tench puts it, 'whether any vessel, ignorant of our removal to Port Jackson might be arrived there'. One gets pathetic glimpses of soldiers mounting guard without shoes and of women convicts looking like gypsies. Few of the men had the strength to work, and Sunday services were attended by the 'most miserable beings in the shape of humanity I ever beheld'.

Tench never lets one down, for we do not only get details of the settlers' lives. Rivers, he noted, are a succession of stagnant pools, more sand than water, and one suffers with him when he describes a heat-wave; 'it is a still afternoon with the thermometer registering 109° [F]. Our dogs, pigs and fowls lay panting in the shade or were rushing into the water.' At Parramatta, a small settlement a few miles inland from Sydney, it was even hotter. An immense flight of flying foxes driven before a hot north-west wind 'covered all the trees around, whence they every moment dropped dead, or in a dying state, unable longer to endure the burning state of the atmosphere. Nor did the parakeets, though tropical birds, face it better' and the ground was strewn with their brilliant corpses.

One can imagine the excitement one morning when a sail was eventually sighted. Phillip had erected a flagpost on the South Head and stationed a party of Marines on permanent duty with instructions to run up a flag the moment a ship hove into sight. The joyful cry of 'the Flag's up' echoed through the settlement and a little later a large ship worked her way in between the heads. It was blowing and raining but nothing could keep the men back, a party rushed the Governor's boat, and pulling at the oars they made some leeway. 'At last', writes Tench, 'we read the word "London" on her stern. "Pull away, my lads! She is from old England! A few strokes more, and we shall be aboard! Hurrah for a belly-full, and news from our friends!"'.'

The ship turned out to be the *Lady Juliana*, another transport. She had left Plymouth in July 1789 and had taken nearly seven months in the passage. Old and leaking, she carried only a small stock of provisions and twenty casks of her precious flour were destroyed by sea water during the voyage. Ironically, her main freight was more mouths to feed – two hundred convicts, all women.

Fortunately the *Lady Juliana* was closely followed by another ship, the *Justinian*, entirely laden with provisions; at last this was what the settlement had been praying for. The famine was over and never to be repeated, though the Colony was on meagre rations many times during the next twenty-five years.

Though full of supplies, the *Justinian* was also the bearer of bad news. She represented the advance guard of what is known as the Second Fleet – a further consignment of convicts, also two Companies of the New South Wales Corps, arriving to replace the Marines. Phillip, expecting assistance rather than further responsibilities, was dismayed at the prospect. But dismay must have been the mildest of his reactions when the Fleet actually came to anchor. The Second Fleet was to be the worst blot on the history of transportation. Neglect, brutality and deliberate starvation had killed one in four of the convicts on board, more convicts died subsequently and were thrown overboard as the ships came into harbour. The Reverend Johnson, who boarded the transports on their arrival, paints a horrifying picture. Landed at the wharf, the poor wretches had to be lifted out of the boats. Most of them were unable to walk and crept on their hands and knees. Two-thirds of the convicts landed were hospital cases, fifty of whom died during the first month, with further deaths to follow.

As we know, Phillip had been entirely responsible for the low death rate in the First Fleet. This time the Government had handed the responsibility of transportation over to private contractors. They advertised for bids and the firm turning out the lowest estimates would be given the job. The contractor stood to gain by overcrowding the ships and by reducing supplies to make room for more freight. Once under way further paring went on with the rations, which meant that the men were reduced to a state of near starvation.

But not all was total degradation; a prefabricated hospital came over with the stores. It had been designed by Jeffrey Wyatville, a nephew and assistant to the famous James Wyatt who remodelled Windsor Castle. There was also a man on board destined to play an important role in Australian history, one of the officers of the newly-arrived regiment – his name: John Macarthur, the arrogant founder of Australia's wool industry, the only man, besides Phillip, with vision enough to see the potential of the pathetic, struggling colony to which he had been posted.

7 The Aborigines

The remarkable thing about Phillip was the optimism with which he handled the initial trying years. He had little support from his subordinates, who complained bitterly about the hardships they were obliged to endure. Most of them were for abandoning the settlement; never Phillip. He, alone, seemed sure of the future and he wrote prophetically to Lord Sydney asserting that 'this country will prove the most valuable acquisition Great Britain has ever made'. His attitude most certainly helped to keep the Colony alive for, without him, official circles in London might well have lost faith in the venture.

Of Phillip's many qualities, perhaps the most endearing was his concern for the natives. He appears to have been without apostolic zeal and was content to leave the Aborigines in peace, as far as their beliefs were concerned. Naturally, he could not be expected to have understood their customs, but as far as possible, he was anxious for a friendly relationship and should any difference arise, 'nothing less', Bradley the first lieutenant of the *Sirius* tells, 'than the most absolute necessity would ever compel him to fire upon them'.

The estimated native population of the whole country at the time of the settlement was in the neighbourhood of three hundred thousand, a total that was divided and sub-divided into about five hundred different tribes, each tribe numbering from between a hundred to six hundred natives. There were about an equal number of dialects and no *lingua franca*, and therefore little communication from one district to another. Having a total lack of political unity, and no common nationality, organised resistance to the invader was impossible, and, even had this been feasible, they had not the material goods with which to carry it through successfully.

No adequate records exist as to what the Aborigines themselves thought of the settlers. It would seem that they regarded the white men as returning spirits of the dead, and as two of the leading professors of anthropology wrote, 'perhaps frightening and even to some extent unpredictable, but at least beings who could be fitted into the local scheme of things'.[16]

Opposite Portrait of Bennelong, with 'armorial supporters', made at the time of his visit to England.

Allegorical medallion made from a sample of white clay sent by Governor Phillip to Lord Sydney in 1788. Sydney sent the clay to Sir Joseph Banks who forwarded it to Josiah Wedgwood. The female figure on the left represents Hope greeting Peace, Art and Labour. Webber sculptured the group for Wedgwood and Stockdale used it as a frontispiece to *The Voyage of Governor Phillip to Botany Bay*.

As we have seen, the first meeting passed off peaceably enough. Both sides must have been apprehensive but managed not to show it. White tells us that the Aborigines were quick to realise 'the nature of our military dress'. From the first they carefully avoided soldiers, or anyone wearing a red coat. An armed tribesman had stuck his shield into the sand as a target and was surprised when a shot from White's pistol perforated its bark surface. One can imagine with what interest strangers and inhabitants viewed each other. Tench tells us that they took a West Indian negro convict to be one of themselves. Rather naturally the natives were astonished at the white men's clothes, thinking every covering a different skin, and hats part of the head. The Europeans, in their turn, are amusing on the subject of the natives' fashion in dress. 'They may be said to go naked', writes a later visitor, 'both men and women, however, bind a small fillet round their head; the men also wear a narrow band about the waist, and the women sometimes throw a strip of kangaroo skin over their shoulders.' On the whole they were judged not bad looking; lively, well made and good humoured, their eyes a dark reddish hazel with very black lashes. They had good teeth but their noses were judged too flat and their nostrils too distended. Phillip remarks on the piece of bone which they habitually thrust through their noses. He judged them 'grotesque appendages' but concedes that they are probably 'marks of distinction'. 'Ambition', he goes on, 'must have its badges, and where clothes are not worn the body itself must be compelled to bear them.' One senses slight disapproval when it comes to the Aborigines' manner of dressing hair, 'in which they sometimes hang dogs' teeth, lobster claws and all kinds of small bones', trophies which were made fast with a paste of gum.

Tench tells us of an amusing episode that happened soon after their arrival. 'I was walking out near a place when I observed a party of Indians, busily employed in looking at some sheep in an enclosure, and repeatedly crying out "kangaroo, kangaroo!"'. Tench pointed out the difference and at the same time tried to explain the horses and cows 'but unluckily at that moment a party of female convicts made their appearance, and all our endeavours to divert their attention from the ladies became quite fruitless'. The natives did not try to approach them 'but stood at the distance of several paces, expressing very significantly the manner they were attracted'.

On one point the Englishmen were all agreed, what Hunter termed the Aborigines' 'abominable filth'. It appeared they never washed but just smeared themselves with fat to which everything stuck, ashes and sand and odd bits of flotsam. Small wonder that Joseph Banks found it hard to determine their colour and had to spit on his finger. Another disagreeable habit was that of covering themselves with shark or whale oil to keep away the mosquitoes. But apparently, even without this aid, they had a peculiar odour of their own. Cunningham describes how the cattle, whenever they meet with the natives 'run from them snorting and kicking up their heels'. Lady Franklin, wife of the Lieutenant Governor of Tasmania, had a similar experience, her horses always shying when they were around.

But what of the more significant facts? With no means of communication other than sign language, how could the two peoples possibly understand one another? The whites knew nothing of the Aborigines' subtle laws governing the tenure of land. By the nature of their country they were semi-nomadic and without permanent dwellings. Although ignorant of cultivation they were careful, nevertheless, as to the manner in which they garnered the meagre crop offered them by nature and when digging for yams, for instance, they would leave a residue of tubers for the next season's crop. The land, although not individually owned, was, just the same, considered as belonging to the different tribal units, one group of people occupying a recognised stretch of country over which they claimed hunting rights. There were also the sacred tribal areas, some water hole, or some perfectly undistinguishable plot of scrub which was considered pregnant with significance by the figures flitting in and out between the trees, their steps as light and soundless as those of a shadow.

The Aborigines were an intelligent, intuitive people and deeply religious, believing in a form of ancestor-worship. They worshipped Dawn Beings who inhabited the sacred past – the 'Eternal Dreamtime', or mythological era. They also had definite ideas about life after death and the survival of the dead person's spirit, which was supposed to ascend into the sky on the bright rays of the setting sun. The Milky Way was another road along which ghosts of the dead travelled; pathways echoing loudly with the screeching of white cockatoos, sacred birds that acted as guardians to the land of the dead, a nebulous place seen as a large camp with many people. The camp could be located almost anywhere, either in the sky, or possibly on some distant island.

The settlers, when they arrived, though well disposed towards the Aborigines, felt no scruples about helping themselves to land as it suited them. It appeared natural that the question of Aboriginal rights was never discussed. Considering the situation the Aborigines showed admirable restraint. They were, no doubt, suffering from shock and were further handicapped by their superstition. Protest on their part would, anyway, have been useless and in all fairness to the settlers one has to admit that, given the premise that they did not consider themselves poachers, they behaved decently. White's experience while watching some seamen hauling in a net illustrates the general attitude. The Aborigines were impressed by the size of the catch and 'no sooner were the fish out of the water than they began to lay hold of them, as if they had a right to them'. The officer in charge restrained them 'giving, however, to each of them a part. They did not at first seem very well pleased with this mode of procedure, but on observing with what justice the fish were distributed they appeared content.'

It is impossible, however, not to sympathise with the natives. What must their reaction have been, for instance, on 4 July when Phillip fêted King George III's Birthday. Three times the *Sirius* and the *Supply* fired a salute of twenty-one guns. The other ships followed suit, puffing out relays of five salutes each. On land the Marines under arms also demonstrated – three volleys followed by cheers. Not the least alarming must have been the band's rendering of *God Save the King*. Small wonder, really, that the Aborigines started avoiding the whites. More serious were the effects of the floggings meted out to the convicts. The native women were particularly affected, some of them crying, others losing their tempers; one of them went so far as to menace the executioner with a stick. What they saw of the conditions on board the ships of the Second Fleet must have horrified them.

In any event, the easy relationship of the first days had shown a marked deterioration long before this. Unfortunately La Pérouse had quarrelled with the natives and been obliged to fire on them, and this, coupled with the dishonesty of the convicts, who had started pilfering from them, produced what Tench refers to as 'a shyness'. But Tench minimises the situation for an unfortunate series of incidents occurred which aggravated matters considerably. Two of the sailors cutting rushes in one of the bays were speared and to make matters worse evidence seems to have proved the rush-cutters the aggressors. And then Phillip, who was always trying to mollify the Aborigines, was himself attacked, receiving a spear wound in the shoulder, near the collarbone. The wound was not serious and the offender was immediately set on by his compatriots. As it turned out the incident passed off better than might have been expected. Phillip appears to have borne no grudges and the natives, who were genuinely fond of him, seem to have regretted their act. No one can pretend, however, that it was an atmosphere conducive to friendly relations. Phillip decided that strong action on his part was the only way of dealing with the situation and he wrote off to Lord Sydney on the subject. 'Not succeeding in my endeavour to persuade some of the natives to come and live with us, I ordered one of them to be taken by force, which was what I would gladly have avoided, as I know it must alarm them; but not a native had come near the settlement for many months, and it was absolutely necessary that we should attain their language, or teach them ours, that the means of redress might be pointed out to them if they were injured, and to reconcile them by showing the many advantages they would enjoy by mixing with us.' Tench for once was less optimistic and thought 'they either fear, or despise us too much to be anxious for closer connections'.

Eventually a native was captured, a boy named Arabanoo. He lived in Government House with Phillip and just as he was becoming useful he caught small-pox and died.

Small-pox was not an endemic disease and no one can say for certain who first brought it into the country. Phillip asserts quite definitely that there were no signs of it amongst the people of the First Fleet. It could have come with the French ships, or Cook – even Dampier. But there is a theory now, equally accepted, that it might have been introduced by the Malay trepang fishers while prospecting on the north coast, and that, by chance, it had worked its way south to coincide with the arrival of the First Fleet. Hunter, who bears out the fact that it was entirely unknown to that part of Australia, describes its terrible ravages. 'It is truly shocking', he writes, 'to go round the coves of this harbour which used to shelter whole families' and find the 'men, women and children all lying dead.' Being a new affliction the natives had no idea how to treat it, and when it made its appearance the victim was immediately abandoned and left to die of hunger. Hunter found the bodies, 'some sitting on their haunches, with their heads between their knees; others leaning against the rock'. One is reminded of the pathetic remains unearthed in Pompeii.

Following Arabanoo's death, two more natives were taken; Colebee and Bennelong. Not much is known about Colebee. Bennelong, on the other hand, had a good deal written about him. He was about twenty-five at the time of his capture and from all accounts appears to have been quite a character – a good-looking young fellow with a lively disposition and an enormous appetite. Tench is obviously amused by him and says he took immediately to alcohol. 'He would drink the strongest liquor, not simply without reluctance, but with eager marks of enjoyment.' We are told that he towered above the majority of his country-men, but even at that, stood barely five foot eight inches high. Vain, he was continually asking for clothes, 'but he did not always condescend to wear them; one day he would appear in them; and the next you would see him carrying them in a net, slung around his neck'. Intelligent, quick-witted, he very soon picked up enough English to make himself understood; 'and willingly com-municated information; sang, danced and capered; told us all the customs of his country'. Love and war seemed his favourite pursuits; 'in both of which he had suffered severely'. His head, arms and legs were all scarred as well as the back of one hand. The wound on his hand, he admitted, had been inflicted by a girl from another tribe whom he had hit on the head and abducted.

With the advent of rationing, Bennelong became something of a problem. Were his compatriots to learn of the white man's plight they could conceivably have become troublesome. 'Every expedient', writes Tench, 'was used to keep him in ignorance. His allowance was regularly received by the Governor's servant like that of every other person; but the ration of a week was insufficient to have kept him for a day.' The difference was made up to Bennelong in fish and in any other game that could be caught. But it was not enough. 'Hunger made him furious and then put him in what might be called a decline, and in this melancholy state he made his escape.'

Bennelong was gone nearly six months and eventually, after much cajoling, he agreed to return on condition that he was not kept a prisoner. To do him justice Bennelong appears to have had a real affection for Phillip, and called him 'beanga' or father. Phillip from what one can gather treated him almost as a son and obviously spoilt him, building him a brick house on what is now known as Bennelong Point, where Sydney's splendid new Opera House now stands. Hunter, the future Governor, tells us that Bennelong was in the habit of holding court in his house, lording it over his companions, haranguing them in the harsh, strident voice common to all Aborigines when at all animated. They had taught him to pitch his voice differently, but having been away for some time, he had returned to his old habits. There were some who found Bennelong impossible. 'He had become a man of so much dignity and consequence', writes Tench, that it was not always easy to obtain his company. The inevitable was happening, Bennelong was being educated beyond his capacity of understanding. Worse was to follow.

Phillip's term of office, supposed to have been of five years' duration, was cut short by ill health. A serious pain in his side, probably gall stones, obliged him to seek medical attention. He sailed for England on 11 December 1792, and with him went Bennelong and another native called Yemmerrawannie. Phillip, the idealist, had hopes of educating the Aborigines, of integrating them. These charges of his were to become future ambassadors of goodwill returning to spread the good tidings. It would be their task to teach their compatriots the benefits to be gained by co-operation with the white strangers. In theory, of course, he was perfectly right, but he was expecting too much. A whole new way of life could not be so quickly assimilated, besides which the white people themselves had to be properly orientated. Subsequent settlers, with little or no conscience, regarded the Aborigines as of nuisance value only, with practically no importance in the general scheme of things; certainly not a people who could be regarded as having any claims. It was to take a generation or two for the new inhabitants to acknowledge a responsibility towards the displaced, and to work towards their complete Europeanisation; a slow process that is only now beginning to bear fruit.

The years between were a sad time for the Aborigines. They learned just enough to become aware of the low regard in which they were held, and comparing their lot with the newcomers, became discontented. What, for generations, had been considered natural living conditions, now appeared to them abject poverty.

To return to Bennelong; unfortunately little is known about his visit to England. He was taken to Court and presented to George III and certainly must have met Lord Sydney. One can see him doing the fashionable rounds in London: Vauxhall Gardens, and the different great houses. Joseph Banks had taken Omai, the Tahitian, to a shoot in his Yorkshire estate and he would, in all probability, have done the same for Bennelong.

Bennelong remained for nearly two years in England, his return to Australia having been planned to coincide with the sailing of Hunter, the future Governor. We get a glimpse of Bennelong on board the *Reliance*, cold and dispirited on account of long delays. The poor Yemmerrawannie had died of pneumonia and lies buried under a moss-grown stone in a little graveyard in Kent.

Once home, Bennelong assumed the most patronising airs and, according to Collins,[17] 'conducted himself with polished familiarity towards his sisters and their relations' but was distant and cold to his friends. The Aborigines are very good mimics and one can see Bennelong aping the supercilious young bloods who must have been his companions in England. Holding a silken handkerchief to his broad nose, 'he expressed his wish, that when his people visited him in Government House, they would contrive to be more cleanly in their person', stating quite bluntly in the meantime that their coarse manners bored him.

It was a sad picture. He had become a man without a real home, a stranger in his own tribe and not fully accepted anywhere else. References to him are scanty, but we know that he took to the bottle 'and while in a state of intoxication was so savage and violent as to be capable of any mischief'. He was twice dangerously wounded in tribal skirmishes, meeting his end in 1813; a censorious paragraph in the *Sydney Gazette* records his death.

As to Phillip, he had intended returning to New South Wales but his doctors compelled him to resign. By 1796, however, he had recovered sufficiently to resume active naval duties, having remarried in between times. By 1801, he had become a Rear-Admiral and was in command of the whole of the Sea Fensibles, with jurisdiction over the entire coastline of Great Britain; an important job at the time of the Napoleonic Wars. Further promotion followed, and he died on 31 August 1814 in Bath, three months after receiving his last promotion to Admiral of the Blue.

8 Growing pains

The next decade or so was a period of gradual expansion. The Colonists showed little interest in exploration, they knew the coast and were frightened of the interior which, in any event, appeared inaccessible, cut off from them by the Blue Mountains which reared in precipitous sandstone battlements about forty miles inland from Sydney.

The Blue Mountains form a section of the Great Dividing Range which runs roughly parallel to the east coast for virtually the entire two thousand miles of its trajectory. At no point are the mountains higher than five thousand feet, and viewed from a distance they take on the striking hue from which they are named; softly luminous masses of blue which Mark Twain described as smouldering 'as if lit by fires from within'.[18] So intense is the colour that it in fact makes the sky look almost pallid, and thus seen, in fine weather, they appear gentle and smoothly flowing, and easily negotiable. It is an illusion dispelled by a closer inspection. Their true character is something quite different, what Governor King referred to as a 'confused and barren assemblage of mountains with impassable chasms between'. He informed his superiors in London that the idea of crossing them 'was as chimerical as useless'. Indeed several had tried to force a passage, but had always been defeated by the towering cliffs and heartbreaking chasms. They were to be crossed eventually, but for the time being they confined the settlers to their cramped quarters next to the sea.

The trouble, of course, was the proximity of the mountains to the coast. When it rained, they acted as a watershed down which the rivers tumbled precipitously to the sea. This meant that the rivers, the usual means of access to the hinterland of a country, were too short and swift-flowing to be navigable except for a few miles from their estuary. The initial stages of exploration were thus painfully slow.

During the first five years only thirteen venturesome souls had dared to emigrate as free settlers, and who really can wonder? The distances involved were considerable and the conditions on arrival very uncertain. Tench's book,

Opposite The Blue Mountains; 'several had tried to force a passage, but had always been defeated by the towering cliffs and heartbreaking chasms.' Painted by W. C. Piguenit.

85

published with a view to encourage possible settlers, can hardly be considered as an unqualified paean of praise. He made it quite clear that only the rich should contemplate the move. The settler must have 'tools of every kind', clothes for himself and his servants – furniture! If really prepared to work hard for ten years, he might possibly break even. European commodities could be purchased at a price from the Masters of visiting ships, while cargoes from Bengal would supply him with most of his needs. He could buy Indian cotton for his wife and Bengal rum for those working for him. It was stronger than Jamaican rum and not so sweet, and had become Australia's national drink. 'But beyond this', Tench continued, 'the settler ought not to reckon.' Even if he had a success with his crops the distances he would have to send them would eat up all his profit.

A convict farmer called James Ruse was the first man actually to live off the land, making himself entirely self-supporting. Arriving in Australia in 1788 he served out his time and claimed his freedom. Being a diligent and sober character Phillip had made him a land grant of an acre at Rose Hill (near the present Parramatta) with a promise of thirty more if he made a success of his farm. Parramatta stands about fifteen miles west of Sydney on a river of the

Experiment Farm Cottage, Parramatta, built by John Harris in the early 1800s on the land given by Phillip to James Ruse.

same name, at the head of a tidal estuary forming part of Sydney Harbour. The soil is very rich here and had Phillip discovered it earlier, he probably would have made it the site of the principal settlement. Indeed for a time it looked almost as if Parramatta might eclipse Sydney in importance. A residence was built for the Governor, and people took up grants, foremost amongst them John Macarthur who obtained a grant of one hundred acres which he called Elizabeth Farm after his wife.

Ruse together with his convict wife, Elizabeth Perry, worked hard at cultivating his holding. The operations were primitive enough, but he knew more than the other men about husbandry. He burnt the fallen timber and dug the ashes into the ground. The rotation of crops was also taken into consideration, but without cattle for manure Ruse was uncertain of success. 'My straw, I mean to bury in pits, and throw with it everything which I think will rot and turn to manure.' His worst worry, however, or his 'greatest check' as he put it,

86

Floods in New South Wales come with fatal suddenness. Wood engraving from *The Illustrated Melbourne Post,* July 1867.

'was the dishonesty of the convicts, who, in spite of all my vigilance, rob me almost every night'. Phillip, as was the custom with settlers, had allowed Ruse convict labour and all those who were trying to farm had the same complaint to make. When Ruse was given his thirty acres, he moved to the Windsor district on the upper Hawkesbury, a particularly fertile stretch of country rich in alluvial deposits. But like all river sites in Australia, and especially those of New South Wales, the area was subject to heavy floods. These come with fatal suddenness and there have been times when the people of Sydney have been obliged to send aid to rescue the unfortunate settlers from the roofs and chimneys of their houses.

The Colony, then, must be seen as an isolated settlement, hemmed in by mountains and further restricted by short unnavigable rivers. If Australia was to be opened up the exploring would have to be done by sea. Fortunately for everyone concerned, the two men ideally suited to the work were conveniently at hand. They arrived with Governor Hunter in 1795, aboard the *Reliance;* two lively young men – George Bass, a tall ship's surgeon of twenty-four and a midshipman called Matthew Flinders, three years his junior. Enthusiasts, with a bent for exploring, Australia was to provide them with exactly the opportunity they needed. Bass had brought a small rowing boat with him, about eight feet long, which he had christened the *Tom Thumb* and within two months of their landing the two young men were off in it, tossed like a toy on the huge Pacific waves, to make an accurate charting of Botany Bay. Bass was also to attempt a crossing of the Blue Mountains, tackling their forbidding precipices with scaling irons. They defeated him, however, as they had done the others before him. The sea, anyway, was really Bass's element and it is for his remarkable thousand mile journey in an open whale-boat that he is best remembered.

John Hunter
Governor 1795-1800.

George Bass.

Matthew Flinders.

His exploration was completed in two journeys. The first probe south to investigate the possibility of a strait between New South Wales and Van Diemen's Land was a failure. The sea was too heavy for the size of his boat, and returning to Sydney he sailed again with Flinders in a twenty-five ton sloop; this time they passed through the straits – named after Bass on Flinders's recommendation–and returned by the south of Van Diemen's Land, thus being the first to circumnavigate the island.

Shortly after his return, Bass was invalided home where he married the sister of one of his captains. He became a trader in the South Pacific and sailing from Sydney on 5 February 1803, was never heard of again. Rumour has it that his ship was captured by the Spanish and that all aboard were sent to the silver mines, but no proof has ever been found to substantiate the story.

Remembered for the straits which are named after him, Bass must also be thanked for the impetus he gave to Australia's maritime exploration. Flinders carried on where he left off, and to Flinders fell the important role of mapping what remained of the coastline, thus proving to the few settlers in New South Wales that they were indeed sitting on the edge of a vast continent and not, as had been thought possible, on a land divided by inlets and channels. He was, in fact, the real founder of Australia's geography.

Remaining on in the Navy, Flinders first explored the coast to the north of Sydney, and returning to England in 1800 he took his detailed surveys with him. An excellent cartographer, his work interested the Admiralty and they had his maps published. Flinders, very appropriately, dedicated this first work of his to Banks, now become the portly Sir Joseph, President of the Royal Society. Following this up he wrote to Sir Joseph offering to explore the entire Australian coastline, providing the Government gave him a proper ship. Banks submitted the project to the Navy Board and they, wanting to fill in the gaps and aware at the same time that a French expedition was en route for Australia, accepted immediately.

Flinders was promoted and given command of a 334 ton sloop, the *Investigator,* while Sir Joseph was given a free hand in choosing the 'scientific gentlemen'. They included John Crossley the astronomer, Robert Brown, naturalist, and the Austrian Ferdinand Bauer, a natural-history painter. William Westall was chosen as topographical artist and landscapist. Crossley left the ship at Cape Town on account of illness and Samuel Flinders (the Commander's brother) took his place. Robert Brown, as a result of his voyage with Flinders, produced *Prodromus Florae Novae Hollandiae* which, according to the august Joseph Hooker, was the most extraordinary botanical work of its time. Sad to relate, Ferdinand Bauer's beautiful plates were never published in their complete form.[19] Bernard Smith, an authority on Australian painting,[20] considers Bauer one of the greatest of all botanical draughtsmen. William Westall also gets a very high rating.

Flinders received his sailing orders in July 1801 and reached Australia in December. Immediately, he began making a survey of the south coast and the map is now strewn with names of people associated with the expedition from the First Lord of the Admiralty downwards. While exploring the gulfs he sighted a sail in what he named Encounter Bay. The sail proved to be *Le Géographe,* under the command of Nicolas Baudin, part of the expedition sponsored by the Institut de France, and sent out under special orders of Napoleon. Baudin had been separated from his other ship *Le Naturaliste* in a storm and was to join up with her later in Sydney Harbour.

The French expedition was on a more elaborate scale than the English one and numbered twenty-three scientists. Among them were included François Péron, the naturalist, who, along with Louis de Freycinet, the cartographer-

François Péron, the naturalist, engraved by Lambert after a drawing by C. A. Lesueur, two weeks before Péron's death.

surveyor, were responsible for writing up the expedition after Baudin's death at Mauritius.

The French ships had been given a safe-conduct by the British Government, and on meeting them in Encounter Bay, Flinders called on the French captain. There could have been little doubt in Flinders's mind that the French were exploring with an eye to founding a settlement. They nevertheless had an amiable interview and breakfasted together the next morning. As it turned out, Péron and Freycinet laid claim to miles of Australian coast that had already been discovered. Completely ignoring the given Dutch names on the map, they had just stamped *Terre Napoléon* right across large sections of the land. Flinders is understandably very bitter about it in his book. 'My Kangaroo Island', he writes, a name which they openly adopted in the expedition, 'has been converted into "L'Ile Decrès". Spencer's Gulf is named Golfe Bonaparte; the Gulf of St Vincent, Golfe Joséphine; and so on, along the whole coast of Cape Nuyts, not even the smallest island being left without some similar stamp of French discovery.'[21]

Refitting the *Investigator* at Sydney, Flinders sailed north to complete Cook's chart of the east coast. No opening escaped his notice and land was followed so closely that they sometimes nearly got caught in the surf. Passing through Torres Strait he eventually regained Sydney, having completely circumnavigated Australia.

Flinders, his task accomplished, now planned his return to England. The *Investigator* was in no condition to undertake another long voyage and a change of ships was made. The change proved unfortunate for the *Porpoise* turned out as crank as the former vessel and, in fact, foundered on her voyage north of Sydney. There were not that many ships to choose from and Flinders was next obliged to embark on the *Cumberland*, a schooner of only twenty-nine tons. Fifteen thousand miles is a long cruise for a ship of this size, and the *Cumberland*, not used to heavy seas, needed almost constant pumping to keep her afloat. South-west of the Cape they ran into particularly heavy seas and Flinders decided that the only prudent course was to make for Mauritius. He arrived there on 17 December 1803, the day after *Le Géographe* had left for France.

Flinders, like Baudin, had been armed with a safe-conduct but his papers, unfortunately, did not make allowances for the change of ships and still carried the name of the *Investigator*. This, added to the fact that war had broken out again between Napoleon and England, was enough to arouse the suspicion of General Decaen, the Governor of the island. Flinders was put under guard and questioned, and resenting this treatment, haughtily refused a subsequent invitation to dinner at Government House. His lack of diplomacy cost him his freedom and for six long years he was obliged to remain under detention. Though well treated by the people of the island, the anxiety of being held captive worked on his nerves, and this, coupled with the hardships he had suffered during his previous voyages, had an effect on his health. His wife when she greeted him on his return hardly recognised him, and writes that at thirty-nine he looked like a man of seventy.

On condition he would not act in any capacity against France, Flinders was finally given his liberty and he arrived home in October 1810 after an absence of nine years. The sad part for Flinders was the time lost on his work. The account by Péron and Freycinet of Baudin's expedition came out well ahead of his own, the first volume appearing in 1807 under the title of *Voyage de Découvertes aux Terres Australes*. Accompanying Volume I was a handsome atlas of plates and views and two general maps of 'Terre Napoléon'. The French men of science had calmly taken credit for much of Flinders's work – a poor return for the hospitality they had enjoyed in Sydney.

Tragically, Flinders did not live to see his own work in print. It was published on 18 July 1814 while he lay dying. His wife brought the books to his room, but he was already unconscious.

In following Flinders we have projected ourselves into the future and must now return in time. After the meeting with Flinders in Encounter Bay, Baudin had sailed for Tasmania, but had been obliged instead, to make for Sydney to reprovision, and, above all, obtain medical aid for his men who were suffering severely from scurvy. He passed the Heads on 20 June 1802 and found his second ship *Le Naturaliste* already at anchor. Flinders had not yet sailed for his examination of the east coast and he describes Baudin's arrival. 'It was grievous to see the miserable condition to which the officers and crew were reduced by scurvy.' Out of the whole crew only about twelve were fit for service, and it was Flinders's men who assisted in bringing *Le Géographe* to anchor. The sick were sent to hospital; 'and both French ships furnished with everything in the power of the colony to supply.'

Baudin remained in Sydney nearly five months and scarcely were the ships out of port than rumour reached Governor King that the French intended to establish a colony in Van Diemen's Land. Some of Baudin's officers had bragged that they were an advance guard to spy out the land. King, although not convinced that this was the real purpose of Baudin's visit, could not afford to take any chances. Immediately Lieutenant Robins was sent post-haste after them and caught up with the French ships at King's Island, a few miles off the north-west coast of Tasmania. Robins, young, impressionable, and no doubt, indignant, could think of no better way of halting the intruders than by restating Britain's claim, which he did by hoisting the colours on a tree, but unfortunately, in his hurry, he ran them upside down. We have Baudin's views of Robins's flag waving in a letter to King. 'I was well convinced that the arrival of your ship had another motive than merely to bring me your letter; but I did not think it was for the purpose of hoisting the British flag precisely on the spot where our tent had been pitched a long time previous to her arrival. That childish ceremony', he continues, 'is ridiculous, and has become more so from the manner in which the flag was placed, the head being downwards, and the attitude not very majestic.' As a last dig Baudin added that he did not believe in 'annexing land already occupied by savage races'. Baudin was doubtless expressing what he really believed, but the same does not apply to some of his ambitious young officers, 'a fact', we are told, 'that contributed to the unhappy relations which marred the conduct of the expedition and caused Baudin serious worry'.

The colonising of Australia was making slow progress. By 1800 Britain had occupied a comparatively small area round Sydney and Norfolk Island in the Pacific. There were altogether some five thousand Europeans; about six men to every woman and of these forty-one per cent were convicts and fifty-nine per cent free or freed. They were restless times and people faced one another with suspicion. Gangs of convicts were to be met with on the roads, working in chains. These were the men whose behaviour precluded them from being employed by settlers. There were some desperate characters among the transportees. At first such men were flogged or hanged; but on the more hardened criminals flogging had little effect, and the numbers who had to be hanged increased at an alarming rate. Governor King felt that men of this class should not be left to contaminate the rest of the community but should be transported a second time to some lonely spot where they would have no one to corrupt. The founding of Tasmania was therefore not entirely due to King's need to thwart the French. It was a question also of establishing an isolated penal colony.

On Robins's return King sent out a further expedition under the command of the twenty-one-year-old Lieutenant John Bower, this time to the mainland. He arrived at Risdon, on the estuary of the Derwent, in September 1803, and with him went a number of the very lowest convicts, together with a powerful guard of soldiers. A few months later, another similar colony was founded in the north on the River Tamar. These settlements eventually became Hobart and Launceston respectively. On the mainland further penal establishments were settled at Macquarie Harbour, Maria Island and Port Arthur, all places difficult of access. 'There,' writes Mr Haskell, 'the convicts were made to work for the sake of work, even if it only consisted in opening cavities and filling them up again.'[22]

Gradually the country was beginning to expand. Free settlers followed in the wake of the convicts. Several families came out from England with Hunter and he gave them land near the Hawkesbury. Simultaneously the cows and the bulls, which had been brought from the Cape and had disappeared into the bush, were found again near the present Camden. From six beasts they had grown to a herd of sixty-one. Seventy miles north of Sydney a fine river had been discovered and named after the Governor. Signs of coal had been seen at its mouth, and convicts were sent up to open mines. They proved successful and the town of Newcastle rapidly formed. At Parramatta John Macarthur started using an ox-drawn plough on his farm and in 1796 was able to procure a few merino sheep that had been imported from the Cape. Keeping the strain pure, he succeeded in producing wool equal to that of the famous Spanish flocks, and it was samples of this wool that he showed to the English manufacturers when over in Europe at the turn of the century. They had told him that if he could produce enough of it, they would guarantee large orders and they might even be able to gain an ascendancy in the highly competitive wool market.

Fine wool in those days came only from Spain and merino sheep were a close preserve of those rocky slopes stretching to the south of the Pyrenees. A small flock existed in England, at Kew, owned by George III: a Royal Gift to him from the House of Bourbon. History does not relate the beginning of the flock at the Cape. Lord Camden, Secretary of State for the Colonies, impressed with Macarthur's project, and anxious for its success, interceded for him with the King and managed to procure a further nine merino rams and ewes. Encouraged by this success Macarthur sold his commission in the Army and, along with the sheep embarked in his own ship, the *Argo*, armed with a letter ordering Governor King to grant him five hundred acres of land of his own selection. He chose what was known as the 'Cow Pastures', the district in which the wandering herd had been found. Cunningham explained the reasons for the choice and complimented Macarthur on his astuteness. 'He conceived that cattle, being the best judge of their own feed, would naturally graze upon a land which produced it in greatest abundance.' Macarthur's contemporaries thought him crazy – 'forty miles from Sydney, no neighbours, it was counted such a piece of boldness, that some pitied, and almost laughed at him!' Not for long though. It was where lovely Camden Park now stands, so named by Macarthur in gratitude to the man who had set the seal of approval on his plans.

Already by October 1788 Tench was complaining about the tedium of life. The charm and novelty were wearing off. 'In Port Jackson all is quiet and stupid

Camden Park, built by John Verge for John Macarthur in 1831.

93

as could be wished.' Night, 'welcome as to a lover', allows him to dream himself into 'happier climes'. He would not have been so bored, however, at the turn of the century. By January 1796 the first play-house had been opened, with prisoners as the actors in a play called *The Revenge*. The previous year a printing press had begun operating, and day schools were founded to take care of the ragamuffins on the streets. A public clock chimed away in the tower of one of the windmills, and in 1803 Howe, an ex-convict, founded the *Sydney Gazette*, Australia's first newspaper. Important also was the fact that the Colony was beginning to trade. 'Slowly', writes Professor Blainey, 'Australia was becoming useful as a source of Britain's raw materials, wool from the land, and whale oil from the sea.'[23] By August 1800 London was unloading three hundred tons of sperm oil fished off the coast of New South Wales. By 1804 there were nine London whalers appearing in the Antipodes with cargoes with an estimated value of £121,000. The whales taken in Australian waters were enormous, the bull sperm whale sometimes measuring as much as seventy feet in length. Their blubber, when melted down, produced a fatty oil which was burnt in domestic lamps, and there were various other by-products. Another article of trade to draw ships from England and America were the fur-seals, their skins being sold as far afield as China. Phillip's optimistic views about the Colony he had been sent out to govern were perhaps not just wishful thinking, after all.

England, at war with Napoleonic France, could hardly be expected to show much interest in a small convict settlement on the other side of the world that cost her money. The fact that this colony might eventually become self-supporting, even a source of income, put quite another complexion on things. Lord Castlereagh, succeeding Liverpool as Secretary of State, re-assessed his Government's policy and began actively to encourage emigration, but among settlers of responsibility and capital only. As inducement the settler and his family were offered a free passage, a large grant of land and convicts to work his holding. The terms were generous and providing the settlers invested capital of up to £6,000, Government was further prepared to feed and clothe the convicts for a period of eighteen months.

Cunningham, writing about conditions in the Colony during the early years of the nineteenth century, has a good deal to say on the subject of emigration. His *Two Years in New South Wales* was published in 1827 and sold three editions within a year, an indication that the kind of people Castlereagh hoped to attract were, anyhow, enthusiastic. Cunningham recommends New South Wales, enumerates its advantages, and at the same time makes the comparison with the new South American Republics. These, he writes, 'can never be desirable as a permanent asylum to an Englishman, on account of the total diversity of language, religion and manners'. He dwells also on the insecurity which he rightly points out 'must for some time continue to exist'. North America he points out, Canada and the Colonies of Australia and Tasmania, 'must therefore long maintain a preference among all endowed with English feelings'. It was a question, really, of choosing between North America and

Right The Emigrant's Dream; coloured lithograph for a music cover.

Below News from Home; print by G. Baxter.

Australia. Cunningham had served in the English Army during the Revolutionary Wars and so was fully qualified to judge. 'In America and the Canadas', he tells us, 'you have to proceed some thousand miles inland before you can obtain unlocated grants.' And even then you are obliged to purchase the land and once you have started producing, transport your wares all the way back again to reach a point of exportation. 'In New South Wales, on the contrary, you may have abundance of land from fifty to a hundred and fifty miles from the coast' – the Blue Mountains had been crossed in 1813 – 'upon terms neither irksome nor burdensome' – in fact for the asking. Cunningham then paints an unflattering picture of America, covered with dense forests, 'the grass completely choked by fallen leaves'. Australia by comparison appears bright and shining; twenty to forty miles inland 'the country is generally so thinly timbered that you may drive a carriage over it'. This is a point that every newcomer remarks on, and there are, indeed, moments when the country does have a park-like aspect as if landscaped by Capability Brown for some great classical country seat. 'The trees', Cunningham continues, 'being but slightly clothed and never shedding their leaves, offered both a cool retreat for the cattle in the summer heat, and a tolerable protection for the native grass which everywhere abounds.' He extols the clement weather and compares the price of labour. In America labour is almost unobtainable, and, when found, prohibitive in price. In Australia labourers are plentiful and consequently cheap, besides which most farm labour was performed almost entirely by convicts whose only remuneration consisted of their keep. He admits that the passage to America is much cheaper; 'but when you come to add the expense of the inland journey to that of the voyage, I think the passage to this country will turn out to be fully as moderate.' Cunningham admits that the land in America is 'generally speaking richer,—but our more genial climate surely compensates this deficiency'. Cunningham fails only on one point, he does not emphasize the country's lack of natural resources, the only reason why Australia was not a serious rival to the United States.

In the meantime Sydney had undergone a considerable change. Tents and log huts were already things of the past and had been succeeded by brick and stucco houses of two or three storeys. The Colony had no trained architects, but this was not a serious drawback as might at first be supposed. Most officers in those days had at least a rudimentary knowledge of architecture and with the aid of a building manual, contributed to by all the leading designers, they were capable of planning almost anything demanded of them. There were bricklayers among the convicts and a brick-maker, as well as masons and plasterers. James Bloodsworth, a master bricklayer and the builder of Government House, had been emancipated in reward for his labour. In fact the Colony thought so highly of him that when he died he was given what amounted to a State funeral – troops with muffled drum and fife.

The typical settler's house was single-storeyed with brick walls; windows were shuttered and down to the ground, generally opening on to a wide, flagged verandah. The verandah in Australia came by way of India and was first

introduced by a military architect named John Watts. Once it was imported, Australia developed her own way of using them; they often completely surrounded the house and were formed by extending the roof well beyond the wall. Slender wooden posts supported these extended eaves.

A variety of engraved views exist showing Sydney in these early stages and the men responsible for them were mostly convicts transported for forgery, a few, like the architects, being members of His Majesty's Forces. Amongst the earliest of the convict artists was a coach-painter from Dumfries called Thomas Watling. He had been transported at the age of twenty-six for forging notes of the Bank of Scotland and a portfolio of his drawings exists in the Zoological Library of the British Museum. There are some five hundred drawings and water-colours showing landscapes and various nature studies of birds, animals, fish and shells. Amongst them are two views, one of Government House, and the other of Government Farm at Rose Hill. In the Rose Hill (Windsor) water-colour a collection of box-like houses with lean-to chimneys are set in rising fields seamed with young crops. Watling is a somewhat naive painter and in trying to represent the native flora he has produced clumps of unrecognisable cultural hybrids. There is nothing particularly distinctive about the painting and it could really be set anywhere, in any recently opened-up country. His view of Government House is interesting, however, for it fits exactly the contemporary description of it; a central doorway with a small circular pediment, plain windows and two sentry boxes at the corners. Cannon peep over the wall. For a long time it was the only house in Sydney to have glass windows. Phillip had brought the panes out with him in the *Sirius*.

Another set of views are those drawn by Captain Wallis and engraved by Walter Preston, a talented amateur, who had been sentenced to death for highway robbery. A reprieve had saved his life and instead he had been transported. In the introduction to the views we are told that Preston, unable to

The country is on the whole thin-timbered and, at times, has 'a park-like aspect as if landscaped by Capability Brown for some great classical country seat'. *Right* An old red gum which certainly must have been standing at the time of Captain Cook's discovery of the East Coast.

97

Government Farm, Parramatta, drawn by Thomas Watling, a convict.

Government House, Sydney, built by James Bloodsworth, a master bricklayer who had been transported. Drawing by Thomas Watling.

A panorama view of Sydney in 1820. Aquatint by Robert Havell from a drawing by Major James Taylor.

procure proper engraving material, was forced to work on ordinary sheet copper 'of the kind used on the bottom of ships'. The best of the engravings represents a native *corroboree*, an Aboriginal night fête which takes place at the time of a full moon. In it the natives are depicted daubed as skeletons dancing by the flames of a fire under a canopy of trees. The branches meet overhead lightly sketched in black and grey looking more like an anatomical rendering of nerve-ends than a forest scene.

John Eyre was another convict artist. Convicted of house-breaking, he was transported to Sydney in 1801, and after two years was granted a conditional pardon and employed in painting numbers on Sydney houses. A charming *View of the City* by him hangs in the Mitchell Library. John Lewin and Joseph Lycett are also names that one meets with; Lewin a naturalist, and Lycett another convict transported for forgery. Their paintings show us the fjord-like waters of Sydney Harbour, busy with shipping. Over the hills can be discerned the sparse sprinkling of a new settlement, square boxes set in straight rows like cabbages in a field. A windmill turns in the foreground and smoke mounts in straight plumes from the lean-to chimneys. To the left of the painting stands a naked group of Aborigines. They give a touch of local colour, but one suspects that the real reason for their being there is to balance the windmill on the other side of the canvas. No sophisticate our painter, and he dares not violate the canons of composition. Far superior in style are the aquatints by Robert Havell taken from drawings by Major James Taylor, a military surveyor who arrived in the Colony in 1817. They show a panorama of Sydney and depict a city of a slightly later period than the one we have been trying to evoke – but Governor Macquarie and the sweeping transformations he was to achieve must follow in a later chapter.

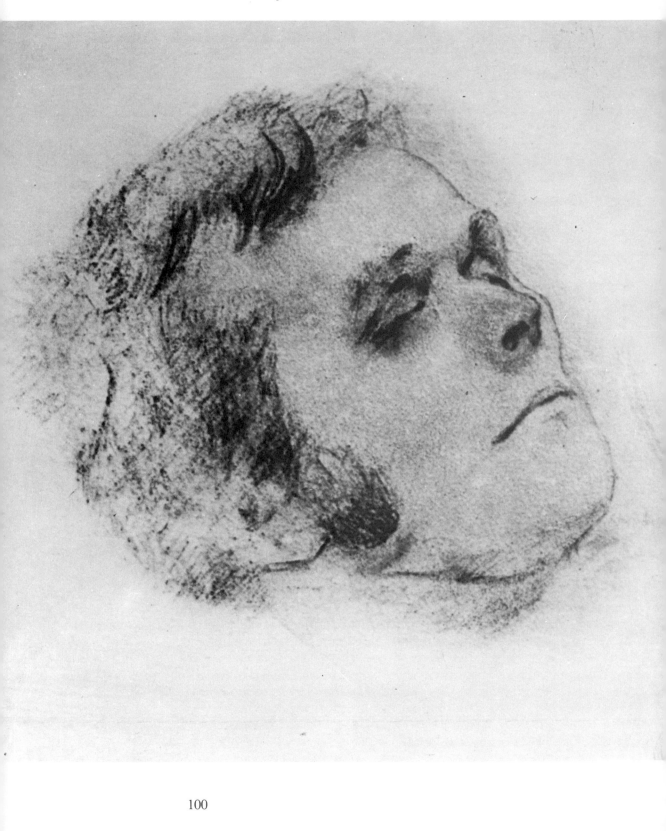

9 Old hands, or Government men

It is impossible to write about Australia at this period without constant references to the convicts. Most of its emigrants had come unwillingly – the transportation system, in fact, was the very essence of the country's being. Nine-tenths of the population had been convicts and for nearly half a century Australia was, primarily, an extensive jail. Convicts permeated the social and economic life, and New South Wales could not have been founded without them. It was convict labour that cleared and farmed the land, built the houses and constructed quays, jetties and dams. They laid hundreds of miles of road and built the bridges across what passed for rivers. It was a titanic job, for, as Trollope writes, 'the land was not a land of promise, overflowing with milk and honey'. It was a hard land, with much barren soil, often deficient in water. Pastures had to be reached across mountains which, for years, resisted all attempts to cross them. The men, individually, might have been bad workmen but this was compensated by the sheer force of numbers, and rigid, often cruel discipline.

These men and their lives demand attention. Whatever the defects of the convict system, it gave birth to a new and splendid country; the criminals of Great Britain had virtually carved out another world and founded a great city that people would proudly point to in the future.

Transportation to New South Wales ceased officially in 1840 and to Van Diemen's Land twelve years later. Western Australia, originally a free colony, had been obliged to petition for convicts in order to go on existing and it is, ironically enough, to her port on the Swan River that the last convict ship discharged her human freight in 1868. The generally accepted total number of convicts who went to Australia is 162,000, and of these the majority reached the country before 1840. No one can say exactly when they became integrated into normal society – at what point in history the convict really ceased to exist. It happened gradually. Their sentences terminating eventually, they imperceptibly faded into the background, and only one per cent of the population today in Australia can claim any convict ancestry.

Opposite Alexander Pearce, the Macquarie Harbour Man-Eater. A drawing made of him after he had been hanged at Hobart.

During the early days, the type of person transported was apt to be varied. It is difficult at times to know exactly for what crime the convict was sentenced. Very often he just had the vague term 'larceny' recorded after his name, which could imply almost any misdemeanour from sheep-stealing to highway robbery. The majority of offenders, however, were urban and could safely be categorised as either pickpockets, thieves or embezzlers. Whoring was another serious crime. Sometimes though, these unfortunates were convicted for the most paltry of reasons. What measure of guilt is there in someone poaching game? One poor young fellow was turned into a thief for pulling a turnip, and another was given fourteen years for stealing a kettle. A pair of stockings, or

George Barrington, known as the Prince of Pick-pockets. One of his most successful coups was carried out at a Royal Levee held at St James' on the occasion of the Queen's birthday. Disguised as a clergyman he managed to deprive Lord Mexborough of his diamond Order. He was eventually caught and condemned in 1777, being transported with the Fifth Fleet in 1791. Engraved portrait from the frontispiece to his *Voyage to New South Wales*, 1802.

five pounds of suet, warranted several years. These were all considered second-class crimes. First-class crimes were punished by death and of these there were endless lists. Trials were conducted with indecent rapidity and it was a common thing for prisoners to plead guilty in order to save time. Jorgenson, a Danish adventurer who had been transported to Tasmania, writes of such an occasion. 'I remember one day when five men appeared at the bar. The four most guilty, on being asked their plea by the Court answered promptly and with much seeming contrition "Guilty, my Lord", and were immediately sentenced to a few months' imprisonment, while the fifth, sensible to his comparative inno-cence, pleaded not guilty.' Three quarters of an hour was spent on his defence, and the judge, furious at the waste of time, sentenced him to seven years' transportation.

Throughout the era of transportation a large majority of the convicts were males (only twenty per cent of the total were women) and after 1817 the quality of the convicts seemed to have declined. Legal reforms in Britain made trans-portation the punishment only for serious crimes and this meant the very dregs of society. Between 1820 and 1850, most of the convicts were young, unmarried men between the ages of eighteen and twenty-five. Chiefly from the cities, they must have been a pretty desperate lot, but, even so, going through the records of their employment, it would appear that a comparatively high per-centage of those assigned to the settlers were considered reclaimable material.

Quite often, in fact, transportation proved beneficial to the prisoner. Certainly it did for the majority of the Irish. Living conditions in their own country were so wretched that even the hold of a convict ship could be considered a haven of luxury. Cunningham tells the story of an Irish girl who, after serving her seven years, returned to Dublin and immediately commited another crime for the express purpose of re-emigrating at Government expense. Cunningham, having served for two years on the transports as a surgeon, can be regarded as a reliable authority, and he even seems to have been of the opinion that the average English labourer at home lived no better than a convict servant on a farm in Australia. He tells us that they were accommodated in thatched huts, generally four to a hut. Saturday was a half-day off, and the day also on which they drew their rations which consisted of one pound of beef a day and sufficient flour to bake two or three loaves of bread. Tea, sugar and tobacco were also included, sometimes even milk, and the majority of settlers allowed them to raise their own vegetables. Wages were allowed at the option of the Master, who was obliged to supply them with clothes, mattresses, blankets and various household utensils for cooking. The working hours were also quite reasonable; ten hours for five days a week, and six hours on Saturdays. In later years the practice of working from sunrise until eight in the morning and from nine until three became general. 'You may say', Cunningham wrote, 'that these labourers are inferior to the free Englishmen, but individuals who have journeyed largely in England assure me that the convict labourers, with proper management and treatment, will do quite as much as the others, and they are generally more civil.' It was, of course, largely a question of humane and intelligent handling, and Cunningham's high opinion of the convict worker was not one generally shared by the other settlers.

What of the conditions on board the transports? On the whole they seem to have been fairly satisfactory. The appalling reports that circulated regarding the Second and Third Fleets had forced the Government to take action, and certain measures of control were put into practice. The contractors were paid for each convict embarked, receiving a further bonus for each prisoner landed alive, a sum total of about £25. Dead convicts were no longer more profitable than the living. A further check was practised after 1815, a surgeon superintendent being appointed to each ship to ensure that the rations were properly distributed, and that the men were well looked after. The surgeons also benefited by the bonus system, and Cunningham, who made five trips between 1819–28, only lost three of the 747 convicts in his care. The rations on board were, generally speaking, better than those issued to either the Army or the Navy. 'Each day the convicts sit down to dine off either beef, pork or plumpudding, having pea-soup four times a week, and a pot of gruel every morning, with sugar or butter in it. Vinegar is issued to the messes weekly; and as soon as the ship has been three weeks at sea, each man is served with an ounce of lime juice to guard against scurvy.' Wine was also served at stated intervals and three quarts of water issued daily. The regulation dress for the men consisted of dark blue jackets and waistcoat, check trousers and coarse linen shirts,

103

cotton stockings and woollen caps. The women were dressed in brown; a serge jacket and petticoat, linen shifts and caps and a kerchief to put round the neck. White jackets and checkered aprons were produced when the tropics were reached. Women were also allowed to bring their own clothing. Charles Bateson tells us that 'naval authorities objected on hygienic grounds to flannel and woollen garments, contending that these materials harboured diseases'. He also tells us that the clothing was generally of such poor quality 'that it was usually worn out by the time Australia was reached' an additional supply was taken along 'and the prisoners completely outfitted before being landed at their destination'.[24] Cunningham adds that they were shaved twice a week. When it was fine they were mustered 'with their shoes and stockings off, and trousers rolled over their knees, to see that their persons are clean, as many of them would not wash during the voyage if not compelled'.

A section of the ship was reserved for the young boys 'to cut off all intercourse between them and the men'. This was not for the reasons one might suppose. 'The young thieves are indeed generally the most troublesome and on this account a good purpose is answered by separating the boys from the men.' The convicts were allowed to choose their own mess-mates and dancing was encouraged, 'and they may sing all day if they please. I always admit all sorts of frolick to go on among them, so long as there is nothing obviously immoral; for it is better to let a little of the devilry out now and again.' If they were pent up Cunningham was anxious as to what might happen when 'it burst forth *en masse* at the end of the voyage'.

Cunningham had definite classifications for his charges; the English invariably turned out the strongest, the Irish the merriest, and the Scottish the keenest and best educated. The English convicts were divided into 'townies and yokels'; while the Irish divided themselves into three, namely the 'Cork boys', the 'Dublin boys' and the 'North boys'. The London Cockney was, of course, beyond all dispute the worst behaved: 'A leaven of a dozen of them is enough to infect a thousand of the country yokels, with whom peace is generally the order of the day. Such a number of these townees will keep a hundred of the others in subjugation.' Cunningham remarks that it was a waste of time to try and reform these people when crowded 'knave upon knave. Those who may be seriously inclined are jeered out of it by the rest'. He admits that religion sometimes helped and notes that Bibles and religious tracts were often distributed, especially among the women. The Bibles they took good care of since they knew that they would be reclaimed at the end of the voyage. Not so the tracts, these quickly vanished to reappear torn into shreds. Cunningham would pick them up 'on sunny mornings when coteries of these nymphs were unpapering their curls'.

From another source we learn that prisoners were allowed to air their complaints at the end of the voyage. A Board of Enquiry was appointed to interrogate them, and their reports were sent back to England. Obviously 'many convicts remained silent for fear of meeting with harsh treatment, but a sufficient number spoke up boldly and the system seems to have worked'.

Jorgenson, our Tasmanian informer, tells us that in his opinion the convicts were terrified of transportation, and regarded it in many instances as a punishment worse than death. 'The very remoteness of the scene and the uncertainty of the fate they are to meet with, affects them with a species of horror inconceivable.' On the other hand Cunningham, writing of conditions at a later period, tells us that of all who were shipped out with him, 'there were only two who went against their will'. And while on the subject, Cunningham has an amusing anecdote which can be regarded as the reverse side of the medal. Cunningham had retired and was living on his farm on the Upper Hunter River. A neighbour dining with him had brought his daughter along, a young girl born in the country, and, during the course of conversation, she had been asked how she felt about going to England. The idea appalled her. 'That country of thieves!' she exclaimed. To her England represented a hive of them 'that threw off its annual swarms to people the wilds of this colony'.

The voyage once over, the procedure on landing was more or less uniform. Considerably less than ten per cent of the prisoners ever saw the inside of a penal settlement, and many who did so were only there for a brief period. The main settlements in New South Wales were Newcastle, Port Macquarie and Moreton Bay. Tasmania had Port Arthur, Macquarie Harbour and Maria Island, and then lastly there was Norfolk Island, the Island of Hell, the most dreaded of all prison stations. Only refractory cases or reconvicted prisoners were sent to these places, dens of horror that made the chain-gangs appear like a Sunday outing in comparison.

On arrival the men were landed at daybreak and marched off under guard to the jail-yard, where their clothes were stencilled with broad arrows, and thus branded in either black or red paint they were despatched to the prisoners' barracks, to remain there until distributed by the local Board to farms or public works. The majority were assigned to private employment and this, of course, was a complete lottery. Very often the men were carelessly assigned; cooks being hired as woodcutters and poachers as cooks. 'Petty thieves, whose soft hands had touched nothing harder than a handkerchief, or a watch-chain were sent to grub roots or drive bullocks; while the accomplished valet whose skill in hairdressing was the boast of Portman Square was often condemned to the hardest labour.'[25] One settler describes the extraordinary mixture of assignees posted to his district as shepherds; three gentlemen's sons, a black fiddler, a dancing master, an apothecary, a lawyer, a clerk, several sailors, a tailor, a Jew and a Senegalese. William Shaw gives us the glimpse of a London thief clad in kangaroo skins reclining under the shade of a eucalyptus.[26]

From all reports the women prisoners were more quarrelsome and difficult to control than the men. It was not a question of dealing with attempted escapes, but since they were not allowed to be flogged, the authorities had the devil of a time keeping them in order. They nearly all slept with the sailors on the voyage out and with their guards when they were landed. Since women were very much of a minority (only one in ten amongst the convicts) they were a sore temptation for everybody. Distributing them to private houses virtually meant allotting the owner a mistress. Few ever married and most of the women during this early period had children by their employers. The dissolute behaviour of the servants was a constant topic of conversation among newcomers, and, one suspects also, among the ladies of the town. One woman told an English acquaintance of hers that it was 'almost impossible for these families who study the quiet and morality of their children to endure female convicts'. They were nearly all inveterate tipplers. Cunningham knew of one who never left the house without being 'overcome by the spirit, and requiring to be trundled home on a hand-barrow, shouldered like a sack of potatoes'. Professor Crowley tells us that 'if a female convict had been at all decent when convicted, in the United Kingdom, to transport her was in effect to give her a ticket to infamy'.[27] And to illustrate his point there is the pathetic story of a pretty Scotch girl who was embarked on the *Lady Juliana*, the first convict ship to leave England after Phillip sailed. The majority of the women prisoners were London prostitutes and the Scottish lass had just died of shame. John Nicol, a steward on board her ship, had trouble forgetting her. 'She was young and beautiful, even in her convict dress, but pale as death and her eyes red with weeping.'[28]

If not assigned as servants, the women were sent to the female factory at Parramatta, a kind of glorified marriage market. Suitors were never wanting, 'amorous youths, with a bloom of fifty-six summers on their cheeks'. The Mitchell Library in Sydney has an account of such a visit paid by a respectable farmer. At the entrance of the factory he was received by a dignified matron with a large bunch of keys, who conducted him to the central yard where fifty or sixty young women were lined up for inspection. They were dressed in grey duffle with white mob caps, under which protruded untidy wisps of short cropped hair. Not a word was spoken. From the yard he was taken to further courts and in one of them was shown the more troublesome and notorious characters. The visiting-surgeon of the establishment had just prescribed half rations and a gentle treatment of ipecacuanha to a ferocious giantess who had let fly at him with a fine display of Billingsgate oaths.

Continuing his round the farmer was finally escorted along the avenue of solitary cells. There was a great unlocking of massive doors and in one of the cells a woman was carding, while in another the inmate was combing wool. A third cell was opened and found to be in complete darkness. 'It seemed empty', writes the farmer, 'so I passed within the door better to examine its contents. It looked like the den of a wolf and I almost started back when, from the extreme end of the floor, I found a pair of bright flashing eyes fixed on mine. Their owner arose and took a step or two forward. It was a slight young girl – very beautiful in features and complexion – but it was the fierce beauty of the wildcat.' The honest fellow admits that he was terrified and writes that nothing on earth would have persuaded him to share the cell of that sleek little savage, 'for even half an hour'. As the heavy door was slammed shut in her face, the turnkey informed her visitor that this was one of the most refractory and unmanageable characters of the prison. The farmer does not tell us whether or not he found a wife, but one gets the impression that he did not much enjoy his visit.

But to return once again to the initial distribution centre and the newly arrived prisoners. The individual might not have been fully screened so far as concerns his capabilities, but his crime, however, was taken into account and those judged of a really serious nature were assigned accordingly either to the public works, or if really a hardened sinner, to the chain gangs. This meant pioneering work on the outer fringes of civilisation; a question of clearing the land and laying down roads, hard, gruelling work under rigid military discipline. Conversation was forbidden and the gangs were under close supervision twenty-four hours of the day. More often than not the men were chained in pairs to lessen the chances of escape. The guard unfortunate enough to permit such an escape was subject to a hundred lashes, while the prisoners themselves were flogged for the slightest offence, some of them receiving six to eight hundred lashes within the space of a year. As to the irons, they seemed to have varied in

A chain gang. 'A visitor to Port Arthur saw one of these gangs carrying a log and described it as a gigantic centipede.'

weight. One man who died shortly after being condemned to work in a gang, carried irons weighing thirteen pounds; and these were considered on the light side. Mortlock in his *Experiences of a Convict* tells us that when his irons were taken off and a smaller ring substituted, his feet would fly up in an odd manner for some time afterwards 'till the muscles grew accustomed to their lighter load'.[29] Cunningham remarks how curious it was 'to observe with what nonchalance some of these fellows will turn the jingling of their chains into music whereto they dance and sing', – but this could not have been in the chain gangs and is more likely to have been on board one of the transports.

These chain gangs must have presented a drastically oppressive sight. First one heard the noise of the shuffling chains, to be followed by a close packed mass of silent, grey-clad labourers. They straddled rather than walked and bent slightly forwards, an anonymous group of faceless men, their close cropped hair covered with leather caps, each marked with his number on his back. A visitor to Port Arthur saw one of these gangs carrying a log and described it as a gigantic centipede. Other teams, made up of ten to twenty men, would be harnessed to a great wooden plough which they dragged through fields; so many draught-horses kept moving by an overseer armed with a canvas ball at the end of a whip. The ball was not heavy enough to break any bones, but just bruised the convict 'horse' and would sometimes draw blood. These gangs were worked from dawn to dusk and the men were either lodged in stockades or in large vans which were trundled down the rough roads on wooden wheels.

Already the chain gangs provide one with enough harrowing literature and the special penal settlements are at times more than one can stand to read about. One is dealing now with the incorrigible and reconvicted prisoners, the very dregs of society. In those days the notion of reclaiming human beings by reason and kindness was completely unknown and what the prisoner might have been before his sentence was not even considered. Thrust into a suffocating barrack-room, herded with the foulest of mankind, he soon lost his self-respect, and became what his jailers took him to be – a wild beast to be locked under bolts and bars, lest he should break out and tear them to pieces.

Stories crowd in on one and it is hard to pick amongst them. Marcus Clarke is perhaps the writer who supplies us with the most material. Worn out by money worries, and overworked by the newspapers, Clarke had been ordered a change of air by his doctor. Melbourne, where the writer lived, could be oppressively humid and Tasmania was well known for its salubrious climate. To help defray expenses, *The Australian Journal* had commissioned stories from Clarke relating to the old convict days. The days, however, were hardly 'old' and Port Arthur, the largest of the penal settlements, was still operating when Clarke was there. In one of his articles he gives us a terrifying description of a lunatic, a man who had been arrested when thirteen years old for poaching. Endless flogging had driven him to the asylum. 'Criminal lunatics', write Clarke, 'were of but two dispositions – they cowered and crawled like whipped fox-hounds to the feet of their keepers, or they raged, howling blasphemous and hideous imprecations upon their jailers.' Later 'the warder drew aside a peep-hole in the

barred door, and I saw a grizzled, gaunt and half-naked old man coiled in the corner. The peculiar wild beast smell which belongs to some form of furious madness exhaled from his cell. The gibbering animal within turned, and his malignant eyes met mine. "Take care", said the jailer, "he has a habit of sticking his fingers through the peep-hole to try and poke someone's eye out!" I drew back, and a nail-bitten, hairy finger like the toe of an ape, was thrust with rapid and simian neatness through the aperture.'

Trollope, in Australia for his son's wedding, is another to give us his impressions of Port Arthur. He tells of an Irishman with one eye named Doherty. Enlisted in the Navy, he had been transported for mutiny and had been locked up for some forty years during which time he had received nearly three thousand lashes. A large man and still powerful, good-looking in spite of his eye, lost through the misery of prison life. He told Trollope that he was broken at last. If they would only treat him kindly, he would be like a lamb. The record of his prison life was frightful. 'He had always been escaping, always rebelling, always fighting against authority – and always being flogged. There had been a whole life of torment such as this; forty-two years of it; and there he stood, speaking softly, arguing his case well, and pleading while the tears ran down his face

The convict-built church at Port Arthur which, ironically enough, looks like a gentle English village church.

109

for some kindness, for some mercy in his old age. "I have tried to escape; always to escape", he said, "as a bird does out of a cage. Is that unnatural; is that a great crime?"

'I was assured that he was thoroughly bad, irredeemable, not to be reached by any kindness, a beast of prey.'

Trollope tells of another old Irishman called Barron, who lived on the Isle of the Dead, digging graves. He had lived on it for ten years. The island is dark and gloomy and, of course, now supposed to be haunted. There was also old Fisher who lay dying in the hospital. They had found sovereigns on him and it was known that he had others hidden away. Trollope asked why they didn't take them, and was told that Fisher had them in his mouth 'and he would swallow them if he was touched'.[30]

These impressions of Port Arthur are harrowing enough, but Macquarie Harbour, on the bleak west coast of the island, was even worse. Port Arthur at least lay in picturesque surroundings and looked, ironically enough, like a gentle English village. Not so Macquarie Harbour. Difficult of access, surrounded by thick scrub and hostile Aborigines (they were of a different strain from those of the mainland), anyone sent there must have felt entirely cut off from the rest of the world. The scrub is virtually impassable and even in present times this part of Tasmania has never been properly explored. One reads of scientific expeditions hacking their way through the forest and averaging not more than half a mile a day. The undergrowth is made up of a mat vegetation of fallen trees and Elspeth Huxley, who experienced it, describes it as horizontal and interlacing 'forming a sort of platform, sometimes as much as thirty feet above the ground, covered with moss and creepers, and rotten underneath. The traveller can walk, or lurch rather, over the top, but sooner or later is bound to sink down into a vegetable morass which may close behind him like a trap'.[31]

The Isle of the Dead, Port Arthur, Tasmania, 'The island is dark and gloomy and, of course, now supposed to be haunted.'

The only access to the place is by sea and this, according to Marcus Clarke, was equally hazardous. 'When the vessel, after a tedious voyage, had reached the entrance to the harbour, the main difficulty of the passage really commenced. A large rock or bar called Doom-Rock lay within the jaws of a sandy, barren bight, and the league-long rollers of the Southern Ocean broke unchecked upon it.' Hardly surprising that the place was known as 'Hell's Gates' and no doubt most of the poor creatures who negotiated the entrance safely wished later that they had been drowned.

So ghastly was the life in this dreadful place that absurd attempts of escape were constantly being made. Boats were stolen, and without sail, compass or water, the bolters, as they were called, took to the sea, eventually to die lingering deaths 'preceded in all probability by a loathsome banquet on each other'.

Here also, there was the celebrated case of Alexander Pearce, the Macquarie Harbour Man-Eater. Pearce had been a pie-seller in Hobart, and was convicted for using bad meat. Twice he escaped, both times killing and eating his companions. On his first escape there were seven of them, and striking off into the tangled bush they got hopelessly lost. Starving, they began eating their kangaroo skin jackets and then started on each other. One of them fell ill and was immediately hit on the head. The weakest was the next on the list. Finally only two were left; Pearce and a man called Greenhill. They neither of them dared to sleep and in the end Greenhill, unable to keep his eyes open any longer, dozed off. Within a matter of seconds he was dead. Pearce eventually gave himself up and confessed, but the authorities would not believe his story. On his second escape Pearce was accompanied by a convict named Cox, a farm labourer. Cox shared the fate of the previous companions, and Pearce, unable to face the ordeal alone, gave himself up, again confessing to his crime. This time the authorities paid more attention and on cross-questioning him found that he was wearing the murdered man's clothes. But what really puzzled his jailers was the fact that he was still plentifully supplied with food, his pockets being stuffed with bread and slabs of pork. Pearce, already conscience-stricken, eventually broke down and, horrified at his own conduct, blurted out that he preferred human flesh to any other form of food. It had become a craving with him.

He was hanged at Hobart and the priest attending him read his awful confession to the assembled crowd.

Escaping was not the only way of obtaining release practised in these dreadful settlements. More positive ways were put into practice, and incredible though it might sound, the convicts actually invented a desperate game of murder. Lots were drawn and the two winners were nominated murderer and victim. In full view of the officers and guards, the murderer slew his victim, thereby assuring his own execution. Reports also tell of those condemned to the gallows dropping to their knees as sentence was passed on them. They thanked God for their deliverance, while the others, the reprieved, 'remained standing mute and weeping'.

Mortlock in his *Experiences of a Convict* takes us to Norfolk Island. But first, since he is often quoted, let us note a few facts about the man himself: he was born of a well-to-do banking family in Cambridge and considered himself defrauded of his proper inheritance by an unscrupulous uncle; he was convicted for having threatened this gentleman with a knife and a loaded pistol. The pistol went off by mistake and slightly grazed the victim. *The Cambridge Advertiser,* reporting on the trial, describes the offender. Aged thirty-two 'he is of a fine open countenance, with a remarkably handsome profile, is about five and a half feet in height, and of an easy, gentlemanly appearance'. The paper admits that if one can judge by looks he certainly did not seem the type 'to commit the crime with which he stood charged'. That is as may be, for whatever his appearance at the trial it certainly had undergone a change by the time he arrived on the island. Mortlock describes himself 'as a strange looking object, who no one would recognise', and is grateful for the anonymity. As it happens, several writers remark on the change that takes place in the men's general appearance when serving a sentence. Suffering stamped them, seamed their faces, until they all looked hideously alike.

Mortlock complains of the vileness of the prison clothes; no linen, no drawers and a dirty, coarse threadbare cloth suit 'of yellow and black, called magpie'. These suits gave a kind of harlequin effect, one trouser leg black and the other yellow, the same with the jacket. The cloth was particularly thick and scratchy and must have been unbearable in the hot weather.

Landing on Norfolk Island was even more dangerous than Macquarie Harbour. 'The boat having received its living freight, we drew nigh the landing-place (always dangerous, on account of the heavy rollers), and were ordered to jump out and swim, which many did, getting safely to shore.' Skill and good management could not always prevent accidents and often people were drowned. Mortlock cites one particular officer 'justly detested for his unfeeling severity'. When seen to be 'struggling in the boiling surf' not a soul stirred to give him help, though 'they gallantly rescued his companion, the Honourable Captain Bent'.

Life there must have been hard to take for someone like Mortlock. The food, he tells us, was 'excessively meagre'; insipid hominy boiled with a hint of sugar for breakfast. 'A morsel of salt junk [salted beef], very like old saddle was served out for dinner.' There was no question of any fresh meat or flour, and it was quite usual for people to die of 'debility', or what really amounted to slow starvation. Medicine was non-existent, 'being too good for convicts, sea-water doing duty for epsom salts'. Mortlock was employed as wards-man with the job of sluicing out the dormitory 'of keeping it neat and clean, and of controlling as much as possible the men when locked up for the night – a difficult task in a dark room in which lights were forbidden'. 'What, anyway', Mortlock asks, 'could one person do with a hundred?' On his first night on duty 'a dour-looking fellow pointed out a hammock as the sleeping place of his predecessor, and enquired "where I thought his head was found one fine morning?" On my suggesting "perhaps upon his shoulders", he very quietly remarked that "it lay on the floor beneath his hammock, which, however, contained his body". I accepted this as a hint to mind my P's and Q's.'

Government buildings,
Norfolk Island.

Mortlock adopted a jaunty manner when writing his autobiography, but not the others. 'Knowing what I know', writes one man, 'of the customs of convicts, my heart sickened when I, in imagination, put myself in the place of a newly transported man, faced from six at night until day break to the fetid den of worse than wild beasts.'

From the very beginning of transportation the question of sodomy had been one of the problems confronting the authorities, a natural perversion under the circumstances, but one not often referred to in contemporary reports. As a visiting Anglican puts it 'the unrestrained indulgence of unnatural lust' is one of the first things to greet the prisoner, and one or two newspapers likened New South Wales to the cities of perdition in the Old Testament. Unexpected from someone so human, it was a topic that always upset Phillip. He regarded the death penalty as too mild a chastisement, and was of the opinion that those guilty of the practice would be best punished by being handed over to be eaten by the Maoris of New Zealand – an original turn of mind and one, fortunately, that remained but a threat.

Clarke in his novel *The Term of His Natural Life* paints a pathetic picture of a young Methodist prisoner of twenty-two called Kirkland. Kirkland is a fictional character, but was no doubt inspired by some case history. He had been a clerk in a banking house, and was transported for embezzlement–though grave doubts existed as to his actual guilt. To begin with Kirkland had been

113

employed as a batman by the Governor of the Settlement, a crusty bachelor of the old school called Burgess, whose every utterance was prefaced by a stream of oaths – sheer blasphemy to the over-sensitive Kirkland who 'one day so far forgot himself and his place as to raise his hands to his ears'. Kirkland was forthwith ordered to the chain gang for insubordination. With the white-handed young man came instructions to the jailer in charge to take the stuffing out of him. The jailer, a sadist named Troke, delighted in the project and that night after work, instead of placing Kirkland in a cell by himself which would have been the normal procedure, shut him into the yard with all the other hardened criminals, where he was discovered the next morning by North, the station chaplain. North in doing the rounds had been attracted by a dispute at the door of the dormitory. '"What's the matter here?" he asked.

'"A prisoner refractory, your reverence," said the watchman. "Wants to come out."'

It was Kirkland beating on the bars with sweaty hands. '"Mr North, Mr North! ... for the love of God let me out of this place!"'

Kirkland was ghastly pale, bleeding, with his woollen shirt torn, and his blue eyes wide open with terror.

'"Mr North!" screamed Kirkland, "would you see me perish, body and soul in this place."'

North tries to intervene with the Governor but is powerless. The next morning Kirkland, back in the chain gang, attempts suicide by throwing himself under a log. Failing in this he makes a dash for the river where he is stopped. The Governor, hearing of the episode, orders the boy fifty lashes. 'Kirkland was put into a separate cell that night; and Troke by way of assuring him of a good night's rest, told him that he was to have "fifty" in the morning.'

The morning sun, bright and fierce, shone down into a stone courtyard where they had led Kirkland. In the middle stood a form of triangle, three wooden stays, seven feet high, fastened together looking something like a painter's easel. 'To this structure Kirkland was bound. His feet were fastened with thongs to the base of the triangle; his wrists, bound above his head, at the apex. His body was thus extended to its full length and his white back shone in the sunlight.' During his tying up he had said nothing – only when Troke pulled off his shirt he shivered. A moment's hesitation and then the knotted cord whistled through the air. '"One!" cried Troke.'

'The white back was instantly striped with six crimson bars. Kirkland stifled a cry. It seemed to him that he had been cut in half.' With the next stroke blood beaded on the skin. The boy did not cry, his hands clutched the staves tightly and the muscles on his naked arm quivered.

'The third blow sounded as though it had been struck upon a piece of raw beef, and the crimson turned to purple.'

'"My God!" said Kirkland, faintly, and bit his lips.'

'The flogging proceeded in silence for ten strokes, and then Kirkland gave a screech like a wounded horse.'

All control gone, he shouted '"Oh! Captain Burgess ... Mr Troke ... Oh

my God! ... Oh! Oh! .... Mercy ... Oh! Oh! Oh!" the lad's back, swollen into
a hump now presented the appearance of a ripe peach which a wilful child had
scored with a pin.'

As the flogging progressed, Kirkland ceased to yell and merely moaned.
Eventually his head dropped on his shoulder and loosening the thongs, they
threw him off. A few minutes later he was dead.

The penal settlements were not the only places to administer floggings. 'The
fact is,' wrote Alexander Harris in 1847, 'flogging in this country is such a common thing that nobody thinks anything of it. I have seen young children
practising on a tree, as children in England play at horses.'[32] Statistics bear out
Harris's statement and show that it was a common form of punishment, but a
punishment, alas, that did not always have the desired effect. Cunningham
remarks that a flogging 'may serve effectively to check the poor cowardly,
pitiful thief, but only hardens the bold and courageous. Old hands display their
welts as an old serviceman might show off his medals. All agree that it is a
degrading, brutefying experience'. Harris, who wrote a treatise on the subject
when pioneering the abolishment of flogging, says that it is impossible to tell
how profound an effect it will make, depending as it does on the strength of the
giver and the 'thickness or thinness of the culprit's skin' and 'the vast difference
of nervous sensibility of the culprit'. He points out that you may be inflicting
punishment equal to a thousand lashes by the sentence of a hundred; and vice
versa. One boy sentenced to a thousand lashes collapsed after two hundred and
seventy and was given the remaining lashes in four instalments.

Harris further elaborates on the different methods of punishment and of the
horrors involved. Some magistrates had their victims' gashed flesh rubbed with
coarse salt, and there were floggers who were so adept that they could use the
cat so as to cross the cuts, defining small rectangles on the flesh with almost
mathematical exactitude. It hurt less if the tails were knotted and the blows
were showered in quick succession. The longer the interval between the cuts,
the more acute the agony. Harris, himself, once passing a triangle 'saw a man
walk across the sand with the blood running from his lacerated flesh and
squashing out of his shoes'. A dog was licking the blood off the triangles, and
the ants were carrying away great pieces of his back that the lash had scattered
about the ground.

Consulting men of the medical profession, Harris found that 'death is more
likely to have taken place by means of the first fifty lashes',[33] the nervous system
reacting more forcibly at the beginning than towards the end. It would also
seem that the cat was capable of reducing the flogged to a state of impotency.

Faced with some of the facts one realises to what extent the convicts could be
made to suffer. But incredible though it may appear it would seem that offenders
dreaded solitary confinement far more than any brief corporal punishment,
however brutal.

The cells reserved for this particular form of punishment were small and
dark and entered, more often than not, by a trap-door. If lucky, the occupant
had a small exercise yard. The ordinary terms were anything up to ninety days,

115

Above, left Solitary confinement. The prisoner 'loses all identity, his head being muffled in a cloth helmet pierced with eye holes'. *Right* 'If lucky, the occupant has a small exercise yard.'

though there are cases on record where the individual has been entombed for years. From the moment he enters his cell he is entirely alone. No one is allowed to speak to him and he loses all identity, his head being muffled in a cloth helmet pierced with eye holes. Unrecognisable, he faces day after day of nothingness and gradually becomes moronic. It is such a strain on the nerves that twelve months of solitary can seriously damage the mind.

But in these last pages we have been dealing with conditions prevalent in what were considered the hell holes of the convict system. They are the exception rather than the rule. More often than not the prisoner, if reasonable in his behaviour, or in any way useful with his hands, was immediately granted a ticket-of-leave. This also applied to those who possessed any personal property or social standing. Tickets-of-leave meant that the holder was, to a great extent, free. Although not allowed to quit a particular district without permission, he was at liberty to behave as if he had been pardoned; but with the slightest misdemeanour, the leave was revoked. Emancipation was the next step up the ladder – freedom granted when the prisoner's sentence had run out, or, a provisional pardon. No pardon, however, could be granted unless the wrongdoer had served at least a part of his sentence. An absolute pardon was supposed to restore the convict to all the rights and privileges of a free man, while a conditional one meant that he continued to live within limits for the remainder of the original sentence – in other words, he was not allowed to return to the

British Isles. The ease with which pardons were issued depended largely on the disposition of the various Governors. Most of them made it a practice to grant a certain number on the different public holidays, especially that of the King's Birthday. Macquarie, for instance, over a period of ten years, granted over three hundred absolute and about a thousand conditional pardons. Often the clause regulating the number of years a man had to serve before applying for any form of remittance was ignored. Macquarie himself was always making exceptions.

There were also laws governing the question of land tenure. The Government was generous with its grants in regard to emancipists and expirees, hoping in this way to encourage settlement. Each applicant got twenty acres, with twenty acres more for a married man, and ten acres for each child born in the colony. Help was also forthcoming in order to get the person established. Certain less tangible aids were also to be counted on. After about 1810, it was tacitly agreed by the free never to use the word 'convict'. '"They" considered it an insulting term and the expression therefore is, by all right-minded persons carefully avoided.'[34] The transportee was referred to as a 'pensioner of the Crown', an 'old hand', a 'Government man' or merely described as having been 'sent out'. These euphemisms were employed not so much for the benefit of the actual offenders as to spare the feelings of their descendants. It was not always easy for the 'old hands.' Free they might be but there were, nevertheless, rigid class barriers. Colonel Mundy, Deputy Adjutant-General, and author of *Our Antipodes,* sums up the situation as he knew it and writes that, 'in spite of the position they have attained to, and many of them live in very good style, they were just the same considered to be in a class apart from the "untainted". Their place on the social scale is assigned and circumscribed. They have, humanly speaking, expiated their crimes, whatever they may have been, and they belong, indeed to the common flock, but they are the black sheep of it.' The merchantmen and men of business generally met on equal terms but 'official juxtaposition does not bring with it any plea for social intimacy.'[35]

The brand was to wear off, but it took time. Now the 'old hands' are a thing of the past, of legend almost, a subject for humour. Australians today rarely speak of them. They have simply been forgotten and it is only the visitor who shows a certain curiosity.

10 Over the mountains

Up to this time the Colony was still dependent on the sea, ships rather than ploughs were the means of its existence. All its Governors had been naval men; first Phillip, then Hunter followed by King, and now the fourth, William Bligh, was also to be from the Navy. The map beyond the rapidly crowding coast, was still a blank; but things were about to change.

An insufficiency of coinage had led to the practice of barter and the most valued commodity in this thirst-making country had been liquor – rum. Rum also had the propensity of making men forget and, to judge from contemporary accounts, no people had ever absorbed more alcohol. Men would sit round a bucket of spirits and drink themselves into a stupor. Tippling houses were to be found at every corner and the country was overrun with illicit stills. Under these conditions trading in spirits became a highly lucrative pastime, and those who had the opportunity formed a monopoly, making profits of a hundred to two hundred per cent on their sales. Even wages were paid in rum and in most cases you could not get labour performed without it. Increase in demand led to a fresh evil – inflation.

The British Government, alarmed at the importance rum had assumed in the Colony, decided that it must curb this inflammatory traffic. It was deliberately demoralising the degraded population which it had been hoped transportation might help reform, and to make matters even worse the men foremost amongst the monopolists were the officers of the New South Wales Corps, the 102nd Regiment of the Line which had been sent out to replace Phillip's original Marines–the very men who should be setting the tone, not deranging it.

On Sir Joseph Banks's recommendation – Banks was always a man of influence where New South Wales was concerned – Captain William Bligh of *Bounty* fame had been selected for the post of Governor to succeed King. But unfortunately this able, though hot-tempered individual was not the right man for the job, and indeed perhaps no one person alone could have accomplished it. It was not only the officers who were implicated in the rum traffic, but all the

Opposite Hogsheads of rum. Old oak barrels in the Argyle Bond and Free Stores, Sydney.

119

According to the legend Governor Bligh was eventually found hiding under his bed. Facsimile of a painting exhibited at Sydney shortly after the Rum Rebellion.

free settlers and they resented any interference, especially when coming from a disciplinarian like Bligh, who was accustomed to using summary measures. Within a matter of months, Bligh and Johnston, the Commander of the New South Wales Corps, were at loggerheads. One thing led to another and eventually the responsible citizens, pushed mainly by Macarthur, having himself fallen out with the Governor, decided to take positive action. A petition was signed asking Major Johnston to depose Bligh and himself take charge of the Colony. A council was held, and the next morning some soldiers, fortified by tots of rum and the beating of drums, marched to the gates of Government House. Here they were met by Mrs Putland, Bligh's daughter, who did her best to dissuade them. Nothing, they declared, could deter them, and swaying slightly they marched on up the drive. Legend has it that the Governor was eventually found hiding under his bed, but this, considering Bligh's disposition, is hardly likely to have been the case.

Bligh was arrested in January 1808 and for more than a year after this date remained in confinement. He flatly refused to sign an agreement that if liberated he would immediately leave for England. One must admire his courage. When, at last, the news reached London, Major Johnston was dismissed and Lachlan Macquarie appointed as the new Governor to replace Bligh, who in the meantime had fled to Tasmania.

Bligh's successor was a man of exceptional calibre, a direct descendant of the last chieftain of the clan Macquarie. Being gentle born, albeit of impoverished descent, he had managed to get an ensigncy in a Highland Regiment, and from that moment on his career was made. Ambitious and able, and at the same time kind, with considerable charm, he achieved a rapid series of promotions. The Revolutionary War in America took him to New York and Charleston, following which came a successful army career in India, where he married a pretty

Governor Lachlan Macquarie, by John Opie.

West Indian heiress. The Battle of Seringapatan and the death of Tippoo Sahib allowed him a handsome share of prize money, and further promotion followed, a short Governorship in Ceylon, and then service in Egypt. Macquarie's 'good, amiable girl', as he referred to his pretty heiress, had, in the meantime, died of consumption. Affected by his widowhood – for he was a man of heart – he returned to England. Here, more honours were to accumulate and we must see the 'awkward, rusticated jungle-wallah' as he jocularly described himself, moving in the highest society. He was presented at Court, where he met the Queen and all the Princesses and found them 'a splendid sight – some of the finest women in all the world'. Equally flattering was his interview with Lord Castlereagh who consulted him on Indian affairs. A hurried visit to a dying uncle in the North brought him together with Elizabeth Campbell of Airds, an accomplished kinswoman, who eventually became the second Mrs Macquarie. Another brief spell in India was followed by Macquarie's appointment as Governor of New South Wales. He was paid the compliment of being ordered out as Commander of his own Regiment, which embarked with him. The picture is rather an impressive one and Macquarie knew full well how best to display his trappings. His arrival in Sydney with the new Mrs Macquarie is almost viceregal in its splendour. The *Hindustan* and the *Dromedary* sailing bravely through the Heads came to anchor, 'and with the entire population gathered, the Governor moves slowly off the quay closely guarded by a gilded staff; a suite composed of a Brigade Major, an Aide-de-Camp, a Private Secretary and an impressive Coachman, who had learned his art in the employment of the partly-royal Lord Harrington.'[36] There must have been a moment of hesitation as the cortège wound up in front of Government House. Phillip's humble building, though enlarged by Hunter, who had added a drawing room and a verandah, was hardly in keeping with all the splendour, and, ironically enough, with all the improvements Macquarie was to achieve, Government

121

House was to be the only building he was not allowed to touch – the Colonial Office would approve no other.

It has always been said that 'Lachlan Macquarie and architecture arrived in Australia together', and in a sense this is true. The Governor, much travelled, must have retained pleasant memories of Charleston, its elegant, early Georgian houses and its commodious, columned plantations on the Ashley and Cooper Rivers, not to mention the splendours of eighteenth-century India, a place where Governors thought nothing of running up princely residences, inspired by the grandiose seats planned by the brothers Adam. Indeed, Sydney must have appeared as a mean little place to this grand *nabob* from more spacious climes on the other side of the world.

In the city itself, Phillip's orderly planning had been encroached on, and during Johnston's régime the officers had been allowed to pick out the best sites regardless of the fact that the spot they had chosen might interrupt the sweep of an intended avenue. The streets, in consequence, needed straightening, while the trespassers themselves had to be evicted. Animals also came in for their share of attention, mostly the goats and the pigs. A solemn proclamation announced that any livestock found encumbering the city proper would be seized and sold at auction, the proceeds being promised to charity.

Once straightened, the streets were widened and pavements were added. With one sweep of the pen the Governor disposed of their plebeian nomenclature, a town with Sydney's future could not go through life supporting a Sergeant-Major's Row or a Windmill Alley. Sergeant-Major's Row became George Street after the King, with beyond George Street a whole nest of royal dukes; Clarence, York and Cambridge. There were, of course, several reminders of the Governor himself and his family, Macquarie Place being a point in question. It was here that the Governor erected the obelisk from which the mileage was to be measured of the new roads radiating out into the fast-developing hinterland.

It is amazing how much Macquarie was to accomplish during his twelve years of office. He put up something like two hundred main buildings, ranging in scale from cottages to guard-barracks large enough to accommodate eight hundred men. He built a hospital, founded churches and inaugurated new townships, laying down also something like three hundred miles of turnpikes and carriage roads. No Governor in any Colony of similar size and remoteness has ever come near to his achievement as a constructor. When Macquarie left, he had entirely rebuilt Sydney's main public edifices, all upon a grand scale. He had done the same at Parramatta and Windsor and had literally created some dozen other townships, carving them out of the wilderness. In Tasmania he replanned Hobart and Launceston, which were to become the island's major cities.

As Ellis writes, all building labours were carried through in a turmoil of protest. Bathurst, the Secretary of State for the Colonies, 'demanded at first that local projects must be paid for out of Colonial Funds; but when these funds were raised, the British Treasury turned a greedy eye upon them, with a view to reducing the expenses of the Mother Country'. It was not only Bathurst the Governor had to contend with, the free settlers 'railed at the extravagances involved in so much grandeur and adornment – especially the extravagance in cheap labour, which would they believe have been better devoted to their own enrichment and the promotion of their own comfort'. This reference to cheap labour refers, of course, to the convicts.

Fortunately Macquarie had two supporters to back him up, one his wife who 'had an interest in architecture that almost lifted her to amateur status'[37] and Francis Howard Greenway, a talented little architect from Bristol who had been found guilty of forging a contract.

Greenway had been sentenced to death but the penalty was later changed to transportation for fourteen years. He arrived in February 1814 on the transport

Francis Howard Greenway; self-portrait in crayon.

General Hewitt armed with a letter from Governor Phillip in which he is styled 'an architect of eminence'. Macquarie, an admirer of the Rear-Admiral, and wanting to attend 'to the first request he ever made of me', immediately gave Greenway a ticket-of-leave.

Phillip's letter would certainly have helped, but the very fact that Greenway was able to draw plans would have been enough to recommend him. Within a year Macquarie had appointed him Civil Architect, and this very much against the home Government's wish, who, when asked, had flatly refused such an office. This policy of adorning a convict Colony was entirely beyond their comprehension. 'No building!' stormed the Foreign Secretary, 'and therefore why a Public Architect?' Macquarie, ignoring both injunctions, went about his way and with Greenway's able pencil accomplished a greater part – besides his castellated dwelling – of what he had dreamed. It was sad about Government House but at least its stables were free of the Colonial Office's ban, and under Macquarie's direction these assumed such proportions that people sailing past their crenellated towers thought that they were indeed the Viceroy's seat. Whitehall already disapproving of the stables, one wonders what the effect would have been had Macquarie gone ahead with the dwelling that was supposed to complement them. Greenway's plans allowed for a two hundred foot

St Matthew's Church, Windsor, Greenway's masterpiece.

façade fronting a quadrangle incorporating a whole suite of reception rooms, magnificent stairs, a grand hall – even a museum! Macquarie himself might possibly have been embarrassed had it ever become an accomplished fact, but not Greenway who, in no way diminished by his experience as a convict, had still grander flights of fancy than his master.

Greenway must have been a tiresome little man to work with; conceited, tactless, always picking quarrels with people, and according to Macquarie, his supporter, habitually indolent and neglectful to duty. Yet, 'indispensable ... therefore I continued him in office from sheer necessity'. One forgives him, anyway, his dilatory habits for he produced some of the handsomest buildings in Australia; his masterpiece, St Matthew's Church at Windsor, followed very

Opposite Government House, Sydney, painted by G. E. Peacock the year of its opening.

Overleaf, left Lady Darling, wife of Sir Ralph Darling, Governor of New South Wales in 1825, and her two children. Painted by J. Linnell.

Overleaf, right A primrose could reduce people to tears with nostalgia.

Windsor Court House, designed by Greenway in 1819 and recently carefully restored.

closely by the delightful little court house in the same town, and his handsome Hyde Park Barracks in Sydney.

The South Head lighthouse was his first official work; 'a plump, classical column', as Robin Boyd describes it, sitting on a charming pavilion base. It so delighted Macquarie that he presented Greenway with a conditional emancipation, the morning he opened it, while the convict barracks finished later made his pardon absolute.

Poor Greenway, one cannot help but feel sorry for him. Despite his indolence his life must have been pretty hectic. One moment we see him, a prim little man

The South Head lighthouse, Greenway's first official work and one that gained him a conditional emancipation. After a painting by de Sainson who was with d'Urville on board *L'Astrolabe*.

Opposite Colonial Clowns. Lithograph by W. H. Fernyhough, 1836.

rampaging at the delay of the roofing of his Church at Windsor, the next he is back again in Sydney, the next again at Parramatta, long journeys accomplished on an old Government horse allowed him as part of his humble perquisites. On one occasion he is horsewhipped by an enraged officer who considered himself affronted by his insolence, at other times he forgets he is a convict and angrily admonishes a 'free' contractor and again gets into trouble. Needless to say, he had to contend with endless petty hindrances bred of jealousy. So misused was he that sometimes he was compelled to draw plans piecemeal, on bits of masonry, 'because upon paper, they were sure to be plagiarized'. But his arrogance was the real stumbling block and in the end, even his benefactor would have no more of him. He quarrelled also with Brisbane, Macquarie's successor, who had confirmed Greenway in his office. Stupidly he presented an enormous bill for fees and, at the same time, grumbled that the eight hundred acres he had been granted on the Hunter River was not enough, maintaining that he had also been promised building ground in the city. His dismissal followed and fifteen years later, in 1837, poor and neglected, he died on his farm with not even a tombstone to mark his grave.

Although building played a considerable role in Macquarie's years as Governor, he had other more important tasks to accomplish. Castlereagh had emphasized various points, and foremost amongst them had been the country's need to increase her arable land. The Colony must be made self-supporting. One of Macquarie's first acts as Governor had been a tour of inspection through the inundated areas laid waste by the disastrous floods which had occurred before his arrival, and it was yet another extreme of climate that allowed him to witness the crossing of the hitherto uncrossable mountains.

The situation was roughly as follows : the sheep and the cattle were actually prospering but they had not enough land on which to feed. If more could not be found, the stock would have to be exported, hardly the solution for a country struggling to support itself. All depended on what lay behind those mountains, but a kind of apathy had seized hold of the settlers and they just stared out over the blue distances of rock, accepting their impregnability. Floods there had been and now came a disastrous drought in which the flocks died like flies. The position was desperate when Blaxland, Lawson and the young Wentworth joined forces, with the idea of attempting yet another crossing. It seemed the only hope.

Gregory Blaxland, a free settler, had a farm at the foot of the mountains they hoped to cross, Lieutenant Lawson was an officer of the New South Wales Corps, and William Wentworth, barely twenty-three, was still a student. Of the three, Wentworth was by far the most interesting character. His father, D'Arcy Wentworth, a medical practitioner, of good Irish family, had twice been implicated with highway robberies. On the third charge he had judged it wiser to absent himself before he was arrested, applying for the appointment of surgeon on Norfolk Island, and it is here that young Wentworth was born of a convict girl, Catherine Crowley. Sent to England to be educated, Wentworth was already widely read by the time he joined the expedition ; in any event this

Gregory Blaxland.

tall auburn-haired figure with the Roman head wrote with far more feeling about his adventures than his fellow-explorers.

The mountains that faced the three men have already been described – canyoned plateaux almost as deep as they were high, enveloped entirely in thick timber. Given their peculiar character there was only one way of crossing them, it was a question of keeping to the crowning ridges and of spying a way down. It would appear that Blaxland was the first to suggest this plan of action. Perhaps local hunting expeditions had taught him the secret, or possibly he had learned it from the Aborigines; in any case, short of blasting a way clear through these rocky walls, it was the correct solution.

Early one May morning in the year 1813 the party left Blaxland's farm in a straggling little file, attended by servants, dogs and horses, laden with provisions. The first night they camped at the foot of the great ridges, preparing for the arduous climb the next day. On reaching the top they spent about three

Overleaf Blaxland and his party were lost for three weeks in the mountain fastnesses. Painting of Govett's Leap in the Blue Mountains, by Eugène von Guérard.

weeks grappling their way across the top of perpendicular walls, winding their tortuous way above terrific gulleys that plunged down sheer for hundreds of feet. Great waterfalls tumbled ominously near, feathering out into plumes of spray far down below – too far to look. It was a frightening world of echoing silences, cut across, at times, with the soughing crash of the wind. At last, towards dusk one evening, they came to a point where, peering over the precipitous sides, they could see the glinting of a stream, and beyond in the distance, what looked like acres of fertile land, 'enough', writes Wentworth, 'to support the stock of the Colony for the next thirty years'.

As it turned out the party had unwittingly diverged from the central ridge and the tantalizing glimpse was only a fertile valley. They had not truly crossed the mountains, but were certainly responsible for having found the way in which they could be traversed. The actual crossing was left to Evans, the Colony's assistant surveyor.

No sooner had Macquarie learned of the discovery, than he sent his surveyor and a small party to plot the trail. Keeping this time to the main ridge, Evans pushed on further until the rocky walls gradually subsided, flattening out to an infinity of plains, rolling away in soft undulations far into the distance.

Evans conveyed his enthusiasm to the Governor, and Macquarie immediately investigated the possibilities of building a road. On being advised of its feasibility, he put William Cox, the chief magistrate at Windsor, in charge of the undertaking. Cox, Mr Ellis[38] tells us, had the reputation both amongst the friendly natives and amongst the convicts of being humane and generous and was the perfect man for the job. Official pardons were offered to any convict who volunteered for the job, the only proviso being that the road had to be finished within a certain time. Thirty men were chosen from amongst those who presented themselves and were marched off under a guard of soldiers into the mountains. As can be imagined, it was no easy task. A highway, twenty feet wide (so that carriages could pass each other with ease) had to climb to more than four thousand feet, winding some seventy miles among sandstone cliffs, and then, bridging yawning chasms, ribbon down the far side. The road, which followed Blaxland's and Evans's route, was begun in July 1814 and finished in a remarkably short time, six months later. The following year Macquarie set out to see for himself and with him went Mrs Macquarie, Oxley, the surveyor-general, and Lewin, the botanist. Also included were numerous members of his staff. Again the true viceregal progress; comfortably equipped tents and simple but elaborately served meals. On reaching the far side there was the fascinating occupation of naming the suitable sites for future development; the Macquarie River and on its banks the town of Bathurst, in honour of the Secretary of State. Beyond were the waters of yet another river – the Lachlan. It was truly magnificent country and back in Sydney Macquarie widely acclaimed the newly won pastures, even punning in the *Sydney Gazette* by naming the discoveries 'County of West-More-Land'.[39]

The news was not without its effect in England. Perhaps, after all, there was more to New South Wales than just a penal Colony. The future Australia was gradually taking shape and Macquarie even advocated a change of name. He was not the first; Flinders had already wanted to call the country by a single word. New Holland was hardly applicable any longer and referred, really, only to the West Coast. Cook's New South Wales was equally limiting. *Terra Australis* was too long and in any event it was Latin. Flinders, searching for a title for his book, had wanted to incorporate the word 'Australia' but Sir Joseph Banks had discouraged him, arguing that the general public would find it strange. Flinders did not give up without a struggle and added a footnote to his work explaining his thwarted intentions. Australia, he argues, would have been 'more agreeable to the ear, and an assimilation to the names of other great portions of the earth'. Macquarie needed no sanction and just boldly stated in a despatch that he hoped that it would be authorized. It was, but we still have a few years left of the old order of things.

Blaxland and his companions were each awarded a thousand acres in the rich pastures they had helped reveal. Further discoveries were expected and with this in view the surveyor-general was again despatched by Macquarie to trace the course of the two rivers bearing his name. The result was a disappointment, for when the surveyor returned he declared that both the Lachlan and the Macquarie, instead of winding quietly through rich prairies, disappeared abruptly to be lost in desolate marshes; the shores, more than likely, of a vast inland sea, a brackish quagmire, 'unprofitable to both man and beast'. But Oxley, essentially a sailor, was not the best fitted for inland exploration. His was not the role to discover the great Murray and its massive tributaries – Australia's Mississippi. Other explorers, a decade later, were to have this satisfaction. In the meantime, the settlers, their ardours slightly cooled, turned their attention once more to the familiar coast, and the exotic and somewhat unusual charms of their fast-growing city.

11 The Sydney scene

The first thing probably that would have struck a visitor to Sydney during the early years of the nineteenth century would have been a certain look amongst the young that passed him by in the streets: the *currency* as they were called, a term applying to all those born in the country as opposed to the *sterling,* or those arrived from England. They were also known as *cornstalks* 'from the way they stood up'. Commissioner Bigge, appointed by the Home Government in 1819 to make a report on the Colony, also noticed them. 'They are generally tall in person, and slender in their limbs, of fair complexion and small featured.' Cunningham describes them as having a 'gothic' look and compares them to the American type. Their complexion is tanned. 'Cherry-cheeks', he says, 'are not accoutrements of our climate and a blooming complexion singles you out as having arrived from overseas.' John Harris, a surgeon, finds the youth 'almost animal-like in their force and crudity'. No doubt a daily diet of wheat bread, fresh meat and sunshine had had its effect. They looked tough and vigorous and their attitude had changed along with their physique. They had gained a certain confidence, a self-reliance that bordered at times on belligerency. Even in speech there was a difference, many of the native-born having adopted the 'flash' language of their parents – 'flash' being a London slang commonly used in the underworld.[40] There was something, too, about the voice. By degrees they were developing their own distinct pronunciation, but this, one imagines, was a slower process and for the moment depended more on a turn of phase than an actual accent. Later on, though, there was little doubt that a different intonation came into being and Mark Twain is one of the first of Australia's distinguished visitors to pass comment on it. 'Now and then.' he writes, 'one hears such words as *piper* for paper, *lydy* for lady, and *tyble* for table from lips whence one would not expect such pronunciations to come.'

Up until now we have been dealing with English people in Australia but

Opposite Aboriginal boy in European dress holding a cricket bat. Artist unknown.

from this moment on it is a case of real Australians, many of whom have never known the Old Country. By 1828 a quarter of the population had been born in the Colony ; they regarded it as their home.

Further revealing statistics can be made : by the early 1820s emancipists constituted the far greater majority of the free inhabitants and those who emigrated as free men were a marked minority. Rather naturally these latter considered themselves the élite of the Colony, thus causing a definite rift in polite society. 'We have the *legitimates*', writes Cunningham, 'those who have legal reasons for visiting this Colony and the *illegitimates*, those who are free from any stigma.' The *illegitimates*, also styled the *exclusives*, centred round the Macarthurs, the wool aristocracy at Camden Park, Australia's grandest country house, then in the process of building. It was a delicate situation made no easier by the splendid Macquarie, who insisted on inviting emancipist friends to Government House ; people like D'Arcy Wentworth and Simeon Lord, a pickpocket who had made a fortune in the sandalwood trade. William Redfern, a surgeon and valuable settler who had been tried by court martial for mutiny, was another of his habitués ; Henry Fulton, a worthy parson and school master implicated in the Irish rebellion, yet another. The talented but aggravating Greenway and his nice little wife would often have been greeted at the door by a respectful aide-de-camp waiting to bow them into the drawing room. Upstart officers of the mess were continually complaining of having to dine in Government House in the company of convicts, 'dubious characters that one would avoid in the street', and one young subaltern had the temerity to rise from the Governor's table 'rather than eat in such company'. Such behaviour explains Macquarie's angry retort when he asserted that the Colony consisted of those 'who had been transported and those who ought to have been'. Macquarie viewed the Colony as a settlement for convicts and acted accordingly. His humanitarian policy towards them laid him open to constant attacks from the *exclusives*, or the *pure Merinos* as they were derisively called by the emancipists. When he made two emancipists magistrates, the senior chaplain, Samuel Marsden, a narrow-minded little hypocrite, refused outright to serve with them. With feeling, Macquarie justified his emancipist policy in a letter to Bigge, who had sided with the *exclusives*. He writes that his first reactions were the same as those of any newcomer to the Colony. 'Certainly I did not anticipate any intercourse but that of control with men who were, or had been convicts. A short experience showed me, however, that some of the most meritorious men of the few to be found, and who were most capable and most willing to exert themselves in the public service, were men who had been convicts!' In a remarkable letter to Lord Sidmouth, he reveals himself still further. 'It would be better', he argues, 'not to hold out hope to a man if he is ever afterwards to be treated as infamous.' And later 'what can be so great a stimulus to a man of respectable family and education, who has fallen to the lowest state of degradation, as to know, that it is still in his power to recover what is lost, and not only to become a worthy member of society, but be treated as such ?' So vehemently does Macquarie feel on the subject that he actually underlines some of his phrases :

Opposite A dress designed by the artist Nicholas Chevalier for the wife of the Governor of Victoria in 1856-63, Sir Henry Barkly. The dress was for a fancy-dress ball and is decorated with emblems of Australia.

EC 9B

'This country', he writes, 'should be made the home *and a happy home* to every emancipated convict who *deserves it.*' In a lighter mood he laments 'that we are not all Moravians and Quakers', quite the contrary and 'it should be recollected that this settlement was formed, not for the purpose of depriving England of her virtuous subjects, but to relieve her of her vicious population'. To Lord Bathurst in answer to some further jibe, he flatly retorts that Australia was a convict country and people who were too proud or sensitive to consort with them had better go elsewhere.

Cunningham, in no way responsible and not obliged to justify his behaviour, can afford to write superficially on the same subject. Once returned to England, he notes wryly that Australia is the only country in the world 'which you are ashamed to confess having visited. I have made several slips of this kind before strangers and I have certainly never yet gained a friend by this disclosure'. He tells of being in a stagecoach with a voluble, much-travelled companion. 'You are naturally induced to repay him in kind' and impulsively 'burst forth perhaps in praise of the beauties of Botany; when lo! the smile which played upon his face at once vanishes.' Suspiciously the traveller questions Cunningham. '"What! Have *you* been there, Sir?" he asks.' Cunningham, realising he has alarmed his companion, hesitates for a reply. This only aggravates the situation. 'His *suspicions* are now converted into *certainties*', and he finds the man gradually edging himself into the furthest corner of the coach, where he ' ... under the pretence of fumbling after a penknife or toothpick assures himself that all his pockets are safe'. The rest of the journey passes in an exchange of the 'barest civilities'.

Cunningham is full of stories and cites the meetings between old friends who unexpectedly recognise one another in the streets of Sydney. Embarrassed, they approach 'with a confused, sheepish sort of smile. Uppermost in each of their minds is the reason for their presence in that country – their *legitimacy!*' Cautiously they sound each other out; 'and finding that there is no "jury question" they burst out laughing and join hands in a hearty congratulatory shake, walking merrily off arm-in-arm.'

Etiquette in such a restricted society would obviously have been very puncti-lious, 'more studied', as someone puts it, 'among our fashionable circles than in those of London itself'. Precedence was considered of such importance that the peace of the whole Colony was severely shaken one night by the opening of a ball before the leading lady of the *ton* made her appearance. Calm was only restored, Cunningham tells us, when the 'indignant fair' had been made to believe 'that it was nothing more than the experiment of a few couples trying the spring of the new floor, and that they were still awaiting her arrival to commence'.

The balls were largely Government House affairs to celebrate official holidays, His Majesty's Birthday being the most important occasion of the year. Sir Ralph and Lady Darling's ball in 1825 was the first gathering in which the women were not hopelessly outnumbered by the men. The Sydney papers reported it as a very splendid affair; some two hundred people 'a considerable portion of whom would qualify by wealth and respectability to move in the most

genteel society in England'. Cunningham has more to say on what he calls 'our *ultra* aristocracy', he scoffs at them and tells us that 'their pride and dignified *hauteur* far eclipses those of the nobility in England. Should you address someone you don't know in the street, more likely than not you will be rebuffed by a self-important "upon my word, I don't know you sir!"' Not all, however, were so haughty, and the guests at a ball given one evening by Captain John Piper, in his renowned Henrietta Villa, appear to have been in a more relaxed mood. John Piper had been the Collector of Customs Duties and had made a small fortune by clever investments in Sydney real estate. Henrietta Villa, on what is now known as Point Piper, was one of his developments, and engravings show it to have been an elegant, domed Regency pavilion furnished, one reads, 'in the most luxurious style'. In any event this is the setting for the ball described by Cunningham, and as to Piper himself, he does not, despite his army rank, appear to have belonged to the *exclusives* since he had a convict mistress who bore him numerous children and whom he subsequently married. But, to the ball. A somewhat extravagant figure, son of a noted London tailor, was visiting Sydney 'deeming his education incomplete', as Cunningham puts it, 'without a finishing trip to the fashionable shores of Botany'. He had come with an extensive wardrobe and was invited everywhere. In short no party was complete without him and the 'beau', of course, had received the 'usual pressing summons' to attend this ball. 'Never,' writes Cunningham, 'was this personification of bodkin chivalry seen to better advantage than on this eventful night.' The beau skimmed round and round 'in the magic mazes of the waltz with one of our pretty young currency *belles;* his head twirling awry, now this way, now that, in languishing dandied perfection, and his body bent stiffly forward into that twisted lumbago-like stoop, unattainable except by

141

Above, left Bungaree in naval coat and hat with Fort Dennison, Sydney Harbour, in the background. *Right* Gooseberry, drawn after Bungaree had died.

exquisites of the highest caste'. Certain that all eyes were on him, and lost in self-admiration, the beau was suddenly conscious 'of a boisterous peal of laughter from a crowded circle of gazers'. Looking around, he perceived 'to his inexpressible horror … a sort of goblin facsimile of his own person, in every particular except that of the white face'. An Aboriginal had borrowed a suit from one of the guests and was pirouetting at his elbow imitating his every gesture. The goblin, it turned out, was a native from the Parramatta River, a familiar figure in town called Bidjee-bidjee. Bidjee had been peeping through a hatch in the pantry and, unable to contain himself, had prevailed on some wag to lend him his clothes and thus was waltzing about 'in exact conformity to the movements of the dandy'.

The Aborigines are well known for being wonderful mimics, and another contemporary of Bidjee's was a man who went under the name of King Bungaree. He could imitate anybody and apparently affected the walk and mannerisms of every Governor from Hunter to Brisbane. Bungaree must have been quite a character and was used by Flinders as an interpreter on board the *Investigator* when he sailed round Australia. His favourite pastime seems to have been dressing up in old discarded uniforms and playing official host to the newly docked transports and trading vessels. He would arrive on board accompanied by a boat load of dingy retainers, himself resplendent in a cocked hat and a gold laced, blue coat, 'buttoned up to evade the extravagance of including a shirt'. Slowly he would advance along the decks 'his hat gracefully posed in his hands' ready to sweep a bow to the Captain 'to bid *massa* welcome to his country'. The leave-taking was equally ceremonious but would be accompanied by a request for some small remuneration 'as a pretence of treating his sick wife to a cup of tea, but in reality with a view to indulging himself' with a swig of rum 'to which his majesty was most royally devoted'.[41] Bungaree had several wives, all with whimsical names: Askabout, Boatman, Broomstick, Onion and Pincher. Subsequently he married Gooseberry who became his principal wife with the title of Queen.

Bungaree always wore a silver plate round his neck, a sort of identification tag which proclaimed him as Chief of the Broken Bay Tribe. In a sense he had a right to a title of a kind, although he actually no longer had any real tribal authority, as his friendly relationship with Governors and officials gave him a standing of kind with the Aborigines camping in and around the town; a pathetic remnant of their people who eked out a living giving exhibitions of boomerang throwing, doing odd jobs, and begging for anything they could get, particularly liquor. Most of the fish hawked around the streets were caught by these people, and excellent it must have been; lobsters and prawns and the most delicious oysters.

Bungaree died in November 1830 but Gooseberry, his wife, lived on to a ripe old age, and George French Angas, the artist novelist writing in 1847, remembers stories she told him about her father and the arrival of the First Fleet. Her father and the rest of the tribe had thought the ships huge sea monsters and had been so terrified 'that they ran into the bush, and did not stop running for about twenty miles'.[42]

Others give us pathetic pictures of the once proud Aborigines, their hunting grounds destroyed, wandering about the streets of the Australian capitals; vignettes, for instance, that tell of a man and his wife who appear attended by mangy curs. 'The male walks behind with a long wand in his hand with which he occasionally taps the head of his spouse when he wishes her to stop, or turn in any direction.' The women, it would seem, are nearly always dressed, wrapped

143

either in a possum cloak or a blanket 'but the men walk carelessly about quite naked with a pair of breeches probably dangling around their necks'.

With the years the attitude towards the natives had changed. Governors Hunter and King in the eighteenth century had depicted them as noble savages, striking out bravely, proud of themselves. They had now become distorted silhouettes shorn of their dignity and clad in European rags. Contact with the whites had degraded them and, as Mr Smith[43] writes, they were no longer seen as romantic figures performing their strange rituals under the light of the moon, but as colonial clowns; caricatures masquerading with ridiculous nicknames such as Long Jack, Pussy Cat or Hump Back'd Maria. There were several painters working at their period producing comical drawings, among them T. R. Browne, a convict stationed in Newcastle; William H. Fernyhough, a surveyor and architectural draughtsman, was another and he produced an album of twelve lithographed portraits, some of which are reproduced here.

Perhaps a slightly oppressive picture of Sydney emerges from all this. But it is certainly not my intention, nor would it be an accurate interpretation. Sydney must always have had a gay sparkling quality due to the light and to its splendid position. Built on undulating heights, it slopes down to the sea; a metallic choppiness of refracted sunshine that dances over the shore-line and is, itself, a mirror to the white buildings that mount up from its indented promontories. Bowling along in a varnished carriage, the views would have changed incessantly. The roads dip and turn, swerve and dip again, at one moment you would be facing due north over the harbour, the next due south with yet another exposure. The fashionable promenades of the time were Mrs Macquarie's Drive in the Government domain, and the South Head Road leading out to Greenway's lighthouse at the southern entrance to the harbour, overlooking a great expanse of ocean. Bellevue Hill was another popular district. These particular drives are still the most beautiful and they retain a certain air of distinction. South Head Road for a while lost its renown but is fast coming back into the fashion again. Cunningham tells us that the *beau-monde* of his day poured out *en masse* on gala days and that 'few individuals of any respectability are without their gigs or riding horses'. According to Shaw the crowd was not at all 'exclusive'. 'Almost every shop-keeper mounts a steed and caracoles among the fashionables.' There were bushmen, too, dressed in their tattered finery mounted on 'steeds worth eighty guineas at Tattersall's'. He found it difficult to believe that the ladies he saw placidly reclining in their silk-lined carriages 'had once incurred the law's displeasure'. The women's fashions must have been slightly behind the times and not at all in conformity with the mode set by the elegant Joséphine so lately dead at Malmaison. There was no sighing after China crepes and Indian muslins like the English beauties. Cunningham tells us that the Sydney ladies like nothing better than clothes with a London label in them. 'The products of the Eastern loom being here too common and too cheap for them to bedizen themselves with.'

Prints and water-colours show us what the city must have looked like; houses set in gardens along unpaved streets, sheltering behind picket fences or

Skipton Jacky Jacky and his tribe at the opening of the Beaufort Railway.

Left Family of New South Wales natives engraved by
William Blake after a drawing by Captain King.
Above Engraving after a sketch made by John Hunter
after he found an Aboriginal woman and her child
hiding in the long grass.

Overleaf George Street, Sydney, in the 1850s, drawn
by F. Terry and engraved by J. Tingle.

145

Above General Post
Office, Sydney, in the
1850s; from a drawing by
F. G. Lewis.

Opposite The Illawarra
district, by Augustus
Earle, 1838.

hedges of clipped geraniums, the houses either stuccoed and whitewashed or
later in brick baked in beautiful soft colours. The interior woodwork was, more
often than not, cedar polished to a pleasing smoothness and heavily waxed.
It came from the great forests found along Hunter River Valley, from the north
coast, or later from the cedar brushes of the Illawarra district. These forests
are now practically non-existent having been worked out during the last century,
or destroyed, for the *Toona australis,* or native red cedar, is subject to attack from
a borer moth.

Cunningham writes that all you see are English faces, no other language is
spoken 'and yet you soon become aware you are in a country very different
from England'. Among the alien elements were the parrots which sold for
sixpence to a shilling each and which, not so many years ago, the settlers had
been shooting in the streets for their pies. Another unusual bird of 'strange
note' was the kookaburra or, to give it its correct name, the *Dacelo gigas,* the
laughing jackass or 'settler's clock' as the country-people call it. They still occur
in the residential parts of Sydney, and can be found roosting in any big tree,
sitting motionless, ruffled and rather portly and absurdly top-heavy with their
large domed heads and scissor-like beaks. Suddenly there will be a pulsing in
a white throat, a sound, half chuckle and half cluck which grows louder and

louder till, throwing its beak to the sky, a bird will break forth in ribald laughter. Again and again it peals off its cry to be caught up by others roosting in the neighbourhood.

The kookaburra by A. Alder.

The kookaburra is a species of giant kingfisher and lives on lizards, frogs, mice and fish. It is also a snake-killer and, although few people have witnessed the act, kills them in an unusual manner. Spying its prey, it will pounce on it, carry it up thirty or forty feet in the air, drop it and pounce again. This continues until the snake is too dazed to resist. Kookaburra or *gogobera*, is an Aboriginal name, that being their rendering of the noise it makes.

Tame kangaroos were great favourites among the settlers and one sees them in water-colours grazing on the lawns of their houses. Sir John Jamison, a Justice of the Peace, had one which became quite well known, following people into the house and 'gravely taking his station behind your chair at meal-times, like a lackey, would give you an admonitory kick every now and then, if you failed to help him as well as yourself'.[44]

As to the meals, they seem to have been fairly simple, rhubarb or pumpkin pie and wholemeal bread baked in dripping were considered luxuries, and appeared on Sundays. Fruit certainly was plentiful and in great variety and sold at very modest prices. The cutlery was mostly of iron, tin or wood, though there were the exceptions, and the decoration of the houses themselves was equally simple; the walls of the rooms were generally whitewashed and Indian cane matting was used instead of carpets, a sensible concession to the summer heat. The furniture, more often than not, was of local make, much of it being of cedar, polished to look like mahogany; rushes were used for caning chairs.

Dressing seems to have been as sensible as the decoration, white cottons during the hot months, blue jackets being exchanged for white ones in cooler weather. The better kind of straw hats were imported from Manila, the cabbage palm supplying the fronds from which the other kind were plaited.

On the whole there appear to have been few complaints, only one thing the settlers all regretted – the lack of any proper change of season. The most ordinary meadow flowers, taken for granted in England, were as carefully nurtured in Australia as the rarest exotics would have been in a colder climate. George French Angas writes that he remembers having seen 'an individual in tears at the unexpected sight of a primrose', and Cunningham waxes quite lyrical on the subject. He regrets the autumn leaves and the beauty of the buds in the spring and writes of the 'dull green uniformity of foliage from year's end to year's end'. 'Parrots chattering' must supply the place of nightingales singing and the pert, frisky robin, he tells us, is replaced by the lively superb warbler with his blue shiny plumage and his long tapering tail; but Cunningham can hardly have regretted the superb warbler, one of the most magnificent of the antipodean birds.

So much then for the exterior aspect of things. Every year, now, was to bring its improvements in the mechanics of living; in 1825 the famous Australian Club was founded, and a year later a subscription library had opened, and that same year the first street lamp shed its yellow light on the central square;

twelve months later a hundred of them had spread through the city. Stage-coaches were already running, and by 1830 there were hackney cabs plying for hire. A boarding school for young gentlemen had opened in Pitt Street and a similar organisation existing for young ladies, which, for the moderate sum of twenty pounds a year, instructed them in the different social graces. Mozart and Rossini could be heard being performed by an amateur musical society, an art school was founded, and by the 1840s Sydney had a choice of as many as eleven daily and weekly papers. Regattas were held in the harbour, there were also picnics and steeplechases. Cricket must have been played quite early on, for by 1832 one reads of a team of Aboriginal youths playing in a test match.

The year 1836 brings a fresh eye to the scene, that of the young naturalist Charles Darwin. Only twenty-six, not yet the great scientist and author of the most controversial book of the century, he sailed through the Heads aboard HMS *Beagle* on its way back to England after a five year survey voyage round the world. Impatient to get home, glutted with what he had already seen, the young naturalist was not over-enthusiastic about Australia. But neither is he entirely damning. He still refers to Sydney as Port Jackson, most people in England did and some were even still calling it Botany Bay. Describing the entrance to the harbour he tells us that the straight yellowish cliffs remind him of Patagonia. 'A solitary light house, built of white stone, alone told us that we were near a great and populous city.' Once past the Heads he comments on the nature of the sandstone, and he passes judgment on the 'beautiful villas and nice cottages'. He is surprised that some of the houses are two storeyed, and like everyone else, comments on the windmills. He is impressed with the amount accomplished, especially considering the poor quality of the land, 'scores of years have done many times more than a number of centuries have effected in South America'. He is good on eucalyptus. 'The extreme uniformity of the vegetation is the most remarkable feature of the landscape ... the trees nearly all belong to one family, and mostly have their leaves in a vertical, instead of, as in Europe, a nearly horizontal position: the foliage is scanty, and of a peculiar pale green tint, without any gloss.' He remarks on the lack of shadows in the bush, and riding over the Blue Mountains to Bathurst he just misses an engagement between two of the Aboriginal tribes and is amazed that they 'chose the centre of the village for the field of battle. This was of service to the defeated side, for the runaway warriors took refuge in the barracks'. In Tasmania he witnessed a *corroboree* performed in the light of blazing fires. The natives' 'heavy footsteps were accompanied by a kind of grunt', and the very ground 'trembled with the heaviness of their step'. The next day the party left for the Keeling Islands in the Indian Ocean. 'Farewell Australia!' Darwin wrote in his Journal. 'You are a rising child and doubtless some day will reign a great Princess in the South; but you are too great and ambitious for affection, yet not great enough for respect. I leave your shores without sorrow or regret.' He modifies these sentiments somewhat in a letter to his sister and admits that 'this is really a wonderful Colony; ancient Rome, in her imperial grandeur, would not have been ashamed of such an offspring'.

12 The explorers

We must now turn our backs on the sea, on the masts and rigging and the salty tang in the air; to the newness of white paint, of freshly quarried stone; to young, lovingly tended trees confined behind picket fences.

These trees – for only the botanists loved the eucalyptus – would certainly have been the dark formal spires of Norfolk Island's famous pine, the stiff *Araucaria*. They were, and still are, a great favourite with the public. Our generation seems to have relegated them to the beaches but the early settlers were in the habit of planting them as sentinels each side of their doorways with the result that, today, when driving out to the country, their gaunt silhouettes, rising above the flatness of roofs, nearly always proclaim an old building. But this is a detail and what concerns us in this chapter is on a much vaster scale, the opening up of the whole country.

As we have seen already the passing of the Great Divide had the effect of momentarily deflecting people's attention, and they turned from the coast to the interior, but what they saw when contemplating the huge unknown must have frightened them. No man really knew what those mountains hid; an immensity of land and possibly a kind of Australian Mediterranean, or more accurately a Dead Sea! It must almost have come as a relief when Oxley announced that all was not quite as lush as he had expected. It gave them a respite but it was only temporary. Human nature being what it is, it was impossible not to explore further. Man had got his foot into the door of an unknown continent and it would have been unnatural not to push on further.

It is a strange thing that all the capitals, with the exception of the federal capital of Canberra, are coastline cities, and yet one would hardly call the modern Australian sea-minded. They have no great Fleet nor has the country ever produced any particularly outstanding sailor. Even Sydney herself has turned her back on the sea and as Mrs Barnard writes in her charming book,[45] 'The average Sydneysider, like the average Australian anywhere when he thinks of himself in his national context, is haunted by the image of the bush behind him

Opposite Bivouac of travellers in a cabbage-tree forest, by Augustus Earle.

153

Norfolk Island's famous pine, the stiff *Araucaria*.

Opposite A native *corroboree*. Water-colour by Samuel Thomas Gill.

and not by the sea on his doorstep. His outlook is continental. Inland space and distance are printed on the back of his eyelids, even though he owns no more earth than will conveniently fit under his fingernails.'

An extraordinarily vivid picture emerges on reading the journals of the different explorers who have left their trails webbing the hinterland. Much of what they have written is hauntingly beautiful, and a great deal starkly frightening. How, one asks, were humans able to endure the ordeals they set themselves? Of course it is the harrowing accounts of weeks spent dragging through blistering deserts that linger on in the memory, while the opening up of thousands upon thousands of square miles of natural grazing are somehow taken for granted; these are not, anyway, the passages on which the explorers themselves dwell in any great length.

The different expeditions are far too numerous to be noted in chronological order and I hope that by concentrating on the leading explorers and the most important of their geographical discoveries a general picture of the whole may emerge. As to the question of dates, one is forced to ignore any methodical grouping of periods.

To begin I must return for a moment to Governor Phillip, for little mention has been made of his attempts at opening up the country. He was too busy to

154

move very far from the rocky precincts of Port Jackson; he did, however, visit Broken Bay, a branch of which he named Pitt Water after the Prime Minister. He also settled the Parramatta, Hawkesbury and Nepean River districts, naming the latter two rivers after men he was responsible to in the Government. The crossing of the Blue Mountains we know occurred in 1814. And, in 1802, Lieutenant John Murray in command of HMS *Lady Nelson* discovered Port Phillip, to be known as the Port Phillip District until 1851 when, breaking away from the parent state, it became Victoria, named after the Queen; its capital, Melbourne, was named after her Prime Minister. In 1823 Governor Brisbane sent Oxley north of Sydney to found a new convict colony. Sailing nearly seven hundred miles up the coast he entered Captain Cook's Moreton Bay, where he discovered a large river which he tactfully named after his Governor. Later the meeting of river and bay became the site of northern Australia's capital, the city of Brisbane in the future State of Queensland.

Allan Cunningham, the naturalist, another of Sir Joseph Banks's protégés, followed Oxley up north, but travelling further inland discovered the fertile Liverpool Plains, and Darling Downs districts, both of which were to produce some of the finest wheat in Australia. Cunningham had been employed as assistant to Aiton, the Manager of Kew Gardens and it was Aiton who had recommended him to Banks as a collector. He came to Australia for the specific purpose of collecting plants and during his forays discovered a considerable tract of new ground.

Cunningham's descriptions are more vivid than those of his contemporaries, at least he gives one a feel of the country and one sympathises with him when he writes of his tedious botanising 'through the gloomy woods, with scarcely trace of either Indians or kangaros'. He journeyed, day after day, mile upon mile, through forests of gum, that interminable bush of Australia. In Europe beech gives place to elm, to oak, and the oak in turn to birch and pine. But the eucalyptus of the Antipodes keep it in the family as species succeed species – some six hundred different varieties ranging in size from low scrub to the tallest hardwoods on earth.

The Darling Downs represent the limits of Cunningham's trek northwards. Had he persevered a few miles further, he would have noticed a sudden change, for it is after the Downs that the tropical north begins. The road today rises suddenly to a plateau of large gums that have been burnt, tumbled and charred by some long-extinguished fire, then, dipping suddenly, it twists through tropical jungle, a dark wall of verdurous gloom, looped overhead with vines, twisting from tree to tree. Enormous staghorn ferns attach themselves like green baskets to the trunks of giant hardwoods, their splayed and many-pointed leaves spread in great semicircular fans. Tree ferns and one of the *cycadaceae*, the most primitive of all flowering plants, make up the undergrowth, and it is amongst these dank surroundings that one will find the lyre-tail menura or superb lyre-bird, the king of all bird-mimics. The male of the species builds himself a dancing or display mound on which to perform, having a considerable repertoire of other bird calls including, even, sounds produced through human agencies. One bird, for instance, produces the whirring of an electric saw.

Opposite Rundle Street, Adelaide, 1845. Water-colour by Samuel Thomas Gill.

157

The hazards of exploration. Lithograph from *Tracks of McKinley and Party across Australia,* by John Davis.

Another peculiarity of these parts which adds a slightly sinister note is the *Urtica gigas,* or giant stinging-nettle tree. Fine specimens can grow up to forty feet and have large, heart-shaped leaves, armed with a formidable array of spiculae or shiny needles. Brush your arm against one of its leaves and it is a caress that electrifies, a shock as acute as a cut from a knife. Down by the shore on the mud flat you are likely to come across another somewhat disturbing manifestation – the gurglings of the *Megascolides australis,* south-eastern Queensland's mammoth earth-worm that, fully extended, can measure anything up to four feet. Seen out of the ground these worms look something like a length of iridescent garden hose, and it is the contracting of these faintly pink bulks as they slither through their lubricated tunnels that produces the weird noises.

I would like to include the extraordinary sea world of the Great Barrier Reef, the beauty of its colours and the strange life with which it teems but it is not within the scope of this book, and we must return to the sequence of events leading to the opening up of the interior. No longer confined, the pastoralists were able to pioneer for themselves as the need for more land arose. The incentive to probe any further was now one of a purely geographical nature – the call of the unknown, this, and certain political considerations. To hold a country one must be familiar with its coastline and establish strategic points along its shores. By and large these were the dictums that inspired the various expeditions mounted over the next half a century, and by the close of Queen Victoria's reign little remained to be explored – a few isolated parts of desert that had not been mapped, and these were eventually reconnoitred from the air.

While Cunningham was busy in southern Queensland, others were plotting the country west of the Great Divide, and it fell to Charles Sturt to unveil the Murray, the continent's only great river system; the fourth largest river in the world, snow-fed in the Australian Alps. Oxley, as we have seen, had traced the

Lachlan and the Macquarie Rivers into some swamps, and Hamilton Hume, with William Hovell the master of a merchantman trading with New Zealand, had crossed the Murrumbidgee and even actually discovered the Murray in its upper reaches, Hume naming their discovery after himself. They did not persist, however, and followed neither of the rivers in their course towards the sea, and thus were entirely ignorant of what they had discovered. Instead of turning south-west as the rivers flow, they continued on their course more or less due south in the direction of Port Phillip. As it turned out, both the Lachlan and the Macquarie, despite Oxley's swamps, were also tributaries of the Murray, as indeed are all the rivers of the western plains; a fact that remained for Sturt to unravel. In 1828 he got as far as the Darling River and the following year, travelling down the Murrumbidgee in a whaleboat, he suddenly shot into the Murray.

Sturt, born in India in 1795, was the son of a judge in the East India Company. Educated at Harrow he decided on an army career, and under the patronage of the Prince Regent, attained the rank of Captain. He saw service in Spain and against the French in Canada, and after Waterloo spent three years in the Army of Occupation in France. Garrison duty in Ireland followed and in 1826, at the age of 31, he sailed for New South Wales. Certain misgivings attended this last decision of his, but they were quickly dispelled and he seems to have taken an instant liking to the country. Popular, 'both monstrous handsome and lovable', he made friends easily. The Governor, Sir Ralph Darling, appointed him his Military Secretary and within a year he was despatched on different forays into the country, the end of 1829 seeing him on his great Murrumbidgee-Murray Expedition.

Sturt wrote well, charted accurately and made careful notes of everything he saw. He was even-tempered and knew how to extract the best from his men, the Aborigines, the military, and the convicts. He was, in short, the perfect traveller. Quickly he captures our attention. Leaving Sydney, the expedition struck out west over the plains. 'Neither beast nor bird inhabited these lonely and inhospitable regions, over which the silence of the grave seemed to reign. We had not, for days past, seen a blade of grass.'[46] From afar they spied the Murrumbidgee and Sturt describes the landscape, painting it almost in the manner of a young Corot. 'Occasionally groups of cypresses', he writes, 'showed themselves on the narrow sandy ridges.' But this resemblance to the lion-coloured plains of northern Italy is a pure invention of mine. In reality 'the wheels of the drays sank up to their axles' in mud and the horses floundered 'above their fetlocks at every step'. The river had grown deep enough for them to start assembling the twenty-seven foot whaleboat which they had brought with them, and the party must have been remarkably well organised, for within a week it was finished and with it another boat half its size which they had hewn from a giant forest tree. Both boats painted, they were moved alongside a temporary wharf ready for the loading.

'Reeds lined the banks of the river on both sides without any break, and waved like gloomy streamers over turbid waters; while the trees stood leafless and sapless in the midst of them.' Sturt feared that the river would peter out 'in one of those fatal marshes in which the Macquarie and the Lachlan exhaust themselves'. But, no, in some places huge trees almost blocked the way, 'under whose arched branches we were obliged to pass'. Their main worry was the roots 'which presented so many points to receive us'. Had they struck one of these boles at the rate which they were going they would certainly have been dashed to pieces. 'At about noon we stopped to repair, or rather to take down the remains of our awning, which had been torn away.' Grilled by the sun they swept on faster and faster. 'On a sudden, the river took a general southern direction, narrowed and started an ominous twisting.' At three in the afternoon, one of the men called out 'that we were approaching a junction, and in less than a minute we were hurried into a broad and noble river'. They were amazed at its size and in silent astonishment gazed about them as they floated over its slow-moving, glassy water. 'It is impossible for me to describe the effect of so instantaneous a change of circumstances.' Thus began the remarkable voyage down the Murray, a journey full of incidents especially when they met the Aborigines. Before this meeting, Sturt, not realising that this was the same river which Hume had named after himself, christened his discovery, 'laid it down' as he words it 'in compliment to the distinguished officer, Sir George Murray', the Secretary of State for the Colonies.

The Aborigines, when they made their appearance, were gathered in 'a vast concourse' under a long line of magnificent trees. They were painted and armed and shouting raucous war-songs. Sturt kept remarkably calm; 'we approached so near', he writes, 'that they held their spears quivering in their grasp ready to hurl.' He even makes notes of the various ways in which they were painted, some with their ribs and thighs picked out in white, making them look like skeletons, 'others were daubed over with red and yellow ochre and their bodies

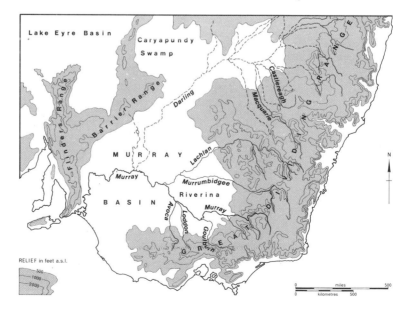

Map of the Murray River system.

160

Above River exploration in Australia in 1836. From a drawing by Major Mitchell printed in his *Journal of our Expedition to the Rivers Darling and Murray*. *Right* The slow-moving, glassy waters of the River Murray.

shone with the grease with which they had besmeared themselves. A dead silence prevailed among the front ranks, but those in the background, as well as the women, who carried supplies of darts, and who appeared to have had a bucket of whitewash capsized over their heads, were extremely clamorous'. The tension must have been extreme on both sides and fortunately for the whites the current came to their rescue, carrying the boat quickly downstream in mid channel. Disappointed, 'the natives ran along the bank of the river, endeavouring to secure an aim at us; but, unable to throw with certainty ... they flung themselves into a state of frenzy by loud and vehement shouting'. A moment's respite and then the current swept them again to within easy reach of the natives. So near that Sturt was about to take aim in the hopes 'that the fall of one man might save the lives of many'. Then a miracle happened; another tribe had made their appearance on the opposite bank of the river and one of them, hurling himself into the water, shot across and clambered up on to the bank where all the natives were gathered and immediately grabbing hold of the man whom Sturt was about to shoot, started haranguing him 'stamping with passion on the sand'. Sturt and the crew were so amazed that they just sat there watching this extraordinary display. They never quite understood, and it was only afterwards that anthropologists were able to explain. It was a question of tribal superstition, the Aborigines who had come to the explorers' rescue believed that one of their number was a reincarnation of a myth-hero who had traditionally led the tribe down the Darling River to the mouth of the Murray.

Along the way Sturt gives a depressing report on the state of health among the river tribes. They were riddled with syphilis, 'nor were the youngest infants exempt from it. Indeed, so young were some, whose conditions were truly disgusting, that I cannot but suppose that they must have been born in a state of disease'. But mostly Sturt and his party concentrate on the beauty of the scenery. Towards the end of their journey 'the cliffs under which we passed towered above us, like maritime cliffs, and the water dashed against their base like the waves of the sea. They became brighter and brighter in colour, looking like dead gold in the sun's rays.' Along the top of this unbroken wall the natives 'showed as small as crows and the cockatoos, the eagles, and other birds were as specks above us'. The whole valley reverberated to the 'harsh and discordant cries' of the cockatoo. Approaching the estuary Sturt writes: 'It is now near sunset; and one of the most lovely evenings I have ever seen. The sun's radiance was yet upon the mountains, but all lower objects were in shade. The banks of the channel, with the trees and the rocks, were reflected in the tranquil waters, whose surface was unruffled save for the thousands of wild fowl that rose before us, and made a noise as of a multitude of clapping hands, in their clumsy efforts to rise from the water.' Later on 'the full moon rose as we were forming the camp, and, notwithstanding our vicinity to so noisy a host, the silence of death was around us. The stillness of the night was only broken by the roar of the ocean now too near to be mistaken for wind, or by the silvery and melancholy notes of the black swans as they passed over us to seek food, no doubt, among the slimy weeds at the head of the lake.' The estuary in fact was a series of beautiful lakes blocked by sand bars at the entrance of the sea. The largest of these Sturt named Alexandrina after the first but little used name of the Princess who was to become his Queen.

Sturt had half expected a ship to meet him at Gulf St Vincent, where the Murray eventually seeps out into the sea. He had hoped to row there, and an attempt was made to drag the whaleboat over the sand bars, but it proved hopeless. Not certain of the ship Sturt dared not waste any time in a country almost completely destitute of supplies, and so the only alternative left was to return by the route they had come. After carefully checking the rations it was calculated that the return would have to be made – against the current – in about the same time it had taken to travel downstream. The voyage down had taken six weeks and in the end the return took three days less; a remarkable achievement given the conditions. But this was not the worst of it; Sturt had been banking on getting help from the depot on the Murrumbidgee, where the whaleboat had been assembled. On reaching it, they found it deserted. For nearly three weeks more the weary and half-starved men had to pull against a flooded river. They would fall asleep at the oars, and one of them became delirious. Sturt himself had his eyesight affected and for a time went quite blind and had to be led about by a servant. No one, however, actually died.

The next move must be counted as one of a political nature and should be seen as an act of pioneering rather than actual exploration. The effects, however, were the same; it meant occupying more of the country.

When Lieutenant-General Ralph (later Sir Ralph) Darling was appointed Governor of New South Wales in 1825, his commission extended over the eastern half of Australia, the part annexed by Cook and Phillip. Hardly one twentieth of it was actually occupied, the region was merely claimed as British territory. The remainder of Australia, comprising about two-thirds of the country, did not, as yet, belong definitely to any European nation. Clearly this was not a situation that could be allowed to go on for any length of time, and both the Governor and the Foreign Office were alarmed at the prospect of what might happen if no action were taken. The return in 1826 of Dumont d'Urville in *L'Astrolabe* decided matters. Ostensibly the Frenchman was on an expedition connected with the exploration of the principal Pacific islands, but it was feared he might also attempt to form a settlement on the western coast of Australia. To forestall him Darling gave orders for a garrison to be established at King George Sound situated at the extreme end of the Great Australian Bight, that part of Australia which had been entirely neglected on account of Dampier's unfavourable report. It had taken a threat of French occupation to shake the Government out of their lethargy.

James Stirling (a Captain in the Navy who had been given orders to evacuate the scurvy-stricken settlers at Fort Dundas, on Melville Island) happened to be in Sydney at the time of d'Urville's visit. Melville Island, some miles off the coast, due north of Darwin, in Australia's tropical waters, had been established on the insistence of the East India Company. They had hoped to use it as a treaty port in their dealings with the Malays. It had been an unfortunate siting and Stirling was responsible for evacuating the garrison to Sydney. He arrived during the period of the monsoons in the north and was obliged to delay the task. To occupy himself while he waited, he asked Darling for permission to explore the Swan River district on the west coast, his motives being a distrust of the French and the hopes of discovering some new place of settlement. Darling, delighted to have someone to prospect for him, packed Stirling off in HMS *Success,* sending with him the New South Wales Government botanist, Charles Frazer. They were gone three months and returned convinced that they had found a luxuriant Eden, rich valleys capable of producing any crop and a vast number of springs. 'Of all that I have seen', writes Stirling, 'in various parts of the world, it possesses the greatest natural attraction.'

Fulfilling his mission on Melville Island and back again in London, Stirling pressed for the settlement of Western Australia and suggested that the Colonial Office appoint him their Administrator. Both Darling and Frazer approved his plan, but Stirling tells us that London 'trembled at the thought of the expenditure involved'. Stirling, however, was an insistent man and further rumours of French intentions finally persuaded him. A chart of the Swan River was drawn up and a frigate under the command of Captain Fremantle hurriedly despatched from Cape Town to take possession of 'the western side of New Holland'. The official boat, with Stirling as Governor, was to follow later. It was to be a free enterprise, no convicts were to be transported, and to encourage settlement emigrants were offered special terms; a bonus of twenty acres for every three pounds' worth of goods imported. We are told that 'none of the country had been explored or surveyed and the coastal waters were virtually unchartered. It was left to the ingenuity of the settlers and the untried administrative capacity of Stirling to surmount all difficulties'.[47] The Colony of Swan River, in fact, 'was to be founded on a picnic episode lasting less than two weeks'.[48] There is no question, though, as to Sterling's integrity. In fact, so great was his belief in the enterprise, that he took his salary in the form of a grant of so many thousand acres.

Fremantle took possession in May 1829 and in June Stirling arrived with his family and civil officials in the *Parmelia,* followed closely by the *Sulphur,* a troop-carrier. The approach to the Swan River settlement was difficult and needed careful navigation. In trying to find a passage into the sound the *Parmelia* went aground off the mainland. The *Sulphur* narrowly escaped the same fate. It was winter and stormy, so the emigrants landed on Garden Island and camped there. The Governor and his lady received in their tent, and so did the others. One reads of thirty people sitting down to dinner 'and afterwards dancing, listening to music and playing cards till 2 a.m.'. Six weeks later the Colony acquired a capital a few miles up the river; Sir George Murray, the Secretary of State for the Colonies, had asked that it be named Perth after his native town. Land had been allotted to the first settlers by sectioning plots on a map studied in London, and it had been decided that priority of choice would be given to those who arrived before the end of 1830. Already, the advance guard, those who had carefully picked their acreages, were disappointed since the land adjoining the Swan River turned out to be very poor and further afield it was thickly forested and, until properly surveyed, quite useless. To further aggravate matters, more kept arriving, lured on by the glowing reports circulating in London. Impossible to satisfy them as far as land was concerned, they joined the encampment pitched in the dunes. And here again was a further problem: Fremantle (named after its founder), the port of the new capital, lay twelve miles distant, at the mouth of the river, and owing to the shortage of labour no roads had been built. The settlers were mostly well-to-do people and had brought with them a considerable volume of goods which now lay exposed to the sun and rain, rotting on the beach; carriages and pianos and veneered furniture, and mixed in with it, a collection of rusting ploughs. Thoroughbred horses and splendid cattle wandered, useless, in the bush. It presents a harrowing picture and one feels that it was fortunate for Frazer, the Government botanist, that he was safely beyond reach in Sydney. Stirling somehow seems to have escaped the public censure. His will to please and his unshakable faith in the venture kept him inviolate. As a business proposition the expedition was, of course, a failure, and it was only due to Stirling, rash and over-optimistic as he may have been, that the settlement was not abandoned then and there. People, however, did begin to leave, some going home and some to other colonies. The population sank from four thousand in 1830 to half that number two years later, and those who remained were obliged to swallow their pride and petition the Home Government for a shipment of convicts. The first batch arrived in 1849 and the last shipment in 1868 when the transportation of criminals from Great Britain ceased altogether. The intervening years saw the Colony gradually grow – to become what Stirling had always hoped it would be. The recent metal strikes in the north promise an even more brilliant future and economically speaking, it might well end up the most important state in the Commonwealth.

From the west we now turn to Victoria and South Australia. Again, as with the district round Perth, it was a question of pioneering, of opening up the country to grazers. The Henty family, a father and seven sons, were responsible in 1834 for the first permanent settlement at Portland Bay, while enterprising squatters from Tasmania established themselves at Port Phillip and Melbourne. It proved ideal country for the grazers, the sheep population increasing from twenty-six thousand in 1836 to well over half a million six years later, these figures swelling considerably by 1850. The value of the wool exported that same year, in fact, was just over a million pounds.

Sturt's discovery of the Murray, opening up nearly two thousand miles of navigable waterway, gave a major importance to the St Vincent Gulf district, the future South Australia, with its capital Adelaide named after the Queen Dowager. The first settlers arrived in 1836, Colonel Light, the surveyor-general, establishing the site for the capital the same year. Light had trouble with his superiors about his choice of position; a difference perpetuated on a tablet affixed to the Colonel's statue standing on an eminence above the city.

Right Self-portrait by Colonel William Light. *Far right* Edward John Eyre in 1845.

Extracts have been copied from his journal and he takes all the responsibility on himself and leaves it to posterity to decide 'whether I am entitled to praise or to blame'. Praise, of course, is the general consensus of opinion for he placed the town on either side of the River Torrens, giving it a belt of parkland, a feature of town-planning well ahead of his times.

The statue shows Light, all his weight on one leg, leaning a little forward, his feet encased in tasselled boots, his lithe figure shown to advantage by the skin-tight clothes of the period. There is also a self-portrait of Light in the Adelaide Gallery, and in this one can clearly trace his mother's exotic blood, for she was a Portuguese Eurasian; his father was a Suffolk man, who had become a trader in Penang. Light's contemporaries judged him 'a person of extraordinary accomplishments, a soldier, seaman, musician, artist and good in all'. He had been a Staff Officer at Wellington's Headquarters before he was thirty and the husband of the natural daughter of the third Duke of Richmond. The young couple had their own yacht in which they cruised the Mediterranean and then for some reason of which nothing is known they decided to separate. What a difference lies between the two worlds; a dilettante sketching the recent excavations at Pompeii and surveyor-general of South Australia, where he died of tuberculosis shortly after plotting out his handsome city.

Take the map of Australia and shade in all to the east of a straight line drawn from Brisbane to Adelaide, and this represents the part of the country that had been fully surveyed, including, of course, the small pocket to the west settled by Stirling. There still remained about three-fifths of the continent to be explored, and from 1840 on an unbroken succession of adventurous travellers risked their lives trying to map out the vast central territories.

Amongst the first must be counted Edward John Eyre, a young man of twenty-five, the son of a Yorkshire clergyman who had been encouraged to emigrate by his father in order to dissuade him from an army career. From managing a sheep station he graduated to 'overlanding', becoming one of the pioneering cattle herdsmen. Intent on opening up overland routes to the west, he gradually drifted into actual exploration. His early experiences took him north of Adelaide to Lake Torrens and north again to the glinting, salty shore of the 'Ghost Lake' that was eventually to bear his name. It covers some three thousand square miles and is the drainage basin for about double this area. Rarely filled with water, it is normally a waste of saline mud, covered with a thick salt crust. Eyre had set himself the task of crossing it and it was not long before the crust broke and thick black mud oozed up. The party plunged onward for about six miles, the mud becoming always deeper and deeper, till at length it half covered the saddles of their horses. Eyre was forced to retrace his steps, and the nearby Mount Hopeless marks his decision to 'waste no more time or energy on so desolate and forbidding a region'.

His next venture sent him a thousand miles along the shores of the Great Australian Bight in an east-west crossing of the continent; an expedition financed by the South Australian pastoralists who had hopes of opening up an overland stock-route between the two colonies. Eyre started out with a party of five white men and three natives, nine horses and some sheep. Only Eyre and Wylie, his faithful Aboriginal servant, finished the journey.

From the present Port Lincoln, situated on the left arm of Spencer Gulf, the expedition headed northward hugging the sweeping empty coast-line of the Great Australian Bight. At Fowlers Bay, three hundred miles west of Port Lincoln, Eyre sent most of the party back, afraid that there would not be enough water to support all of them. With him stayed James Baxter, his steward, a handsome, soft-spoken man of about thirty, and the three Aboriginal boys. He kept them, he writes, 'as they would be better able to put up with the fatigues and privations we should have to go through, than Europeans'. Their quickness of sight and their skill in trapping were further considerations.

Following Eyre through his journals one can almost feel the hot winds and stinging sands blowing off the desolate Nullarbor Plain (so called from the absence of trees), a name that suggests the hopelessness of the scene. Indeed, the coast Eyre travelled across has hardly changed and remains as sun blasted and lonely as when he knew it. At Eucla about halfway across the Bight, drifting sand dunes have engulfed the old telegraph station buildings and Eyre, marked as a village on the map, has been abandoned.

For the first few weeks Eyre and Baxter plodded through endless sandhills and had to dig for their water. 'I had nothing but a shell to dig with, and, as a very large excavation was required to enable a bucket to be dipped, my occupation was neither a light nor a short one.' The sand 'floated on the surface of the water, penetrating into our clothes, hair, eyes, and ears, our provisions were smothered with it, and our blankets half buried when we lay down at nights – it was a perpetual and never-ceasing torment'. Large horse-flies added to their misery. They had set out at the end of February, and by the first week of March they had reached the precipitous cliffs that form the striking sea edge of the Great Australian Bight; 'many battlements of masonry, supported by huge buttresses, and glittering in the morning sun. Still we keep moving on-wards and still the cliffs continue. Hour after hour passed away, mile after mile was traversed and yet no change was observable.' They were caught up on a waterless plateau. 'We were now about a hundred and twenty-eight miles from the last water; we had been four whole days and nights without a drop for our horses.' On the fifth day the wall of cliffs shelved, carrying the party downwards, enabling them to dig for water again in the dunes. It was only a temporary respite, however, for the cliffs rose again forcing the party to travel ant-like along the stony rim of the merciless Nullarbor Plain.

The next march they were for even longer without water, and Eyre was reduced to collecting the early morning dew with a sponge 'which was hanging in spangles on the dry grasses'. In April they contemplated abandoning the horses 'but there was another inducement to continue with them ... and how-ever revolting the idea might be at first, it was a resource which, I foresaw, the desperate circumstances we were in must soon compel us to adopt'. Here Eyre notes that for some time past the two eldest natives 'had been far from obedient', the reduced ration had made them sulky and discontented. Eyre then describes how their camp was arranged every night. Windbreaks were put up to lie under and the hobbled horses were turned out to feed. The party took it in turns to watch over them to see that they did not stray too far. One of the native boys had watched over them the night of 28 April, and it was now Eyre and Baxter's turn. 'The first watch was from 6 o'clock to eleven, the second from eleven until four a.m.'. Eyre gives us the details 'because of the fearful consequences that followed'. Eyre took the first watch. 'The night was cold and the wind blowing hard', clouds skudded rapidly across the moon and the horses rambled a good deal. Suddenly there was a flash, followed by the report of a gun from the direction of the camp. Eyre retraced his steps and presently was met by a frightened Wylie calling out for help. The other two native boys had robbed the camp, absconding with a quantity of food and the only good rifle. The shot Eyre had heard had been fired at Baxter who lay dying, wounded in the chest. Woken by the boys he had jumped up to stop them and they had killed him. Bleeding profusely, Baxter breathed his last in Eyre's arms. 'The frightful, the appalling truth now burst upon me, that I was alone in the desert.' Eyre spent a terrible night tortured with doubts 'in the wildest and most inhospitable wastes of Australia'. A fierce wind raged. He even suspected Wylie's loyalty 'who, for ought I knew, might be in league with the other two, who perhaps were even now lurking about with a view to taking my life. At last...daylight dawned' and poor Baxter 'with eyes open, but cold and glazed and dead' had to be buried. It was impossible for 'one vast unbroken surface of sheet rock extended for miles in every direction, and rendered it impossible to make a grave. We were some miles from the sea-shore, and even had we been nearer, could not have got down the cliffs to bury the corpse in the sand.' Eyre was obliged to wrap Baxter in his blanket, leaving his body 'enshrouded where he fell', and himself 'escaping from the melancholy scene'.

Three days after Baxter's death the cliffs subsided, and coming upon more fertile country, Wylie, his rifle in hand, was sent out hunting and returned with a kangaroo. Eyre notes with amusement that 'for once Wylie admitted that his belly was full'. In fact, judging by the quantity he ate, one might have supposed a serious, or even fatal, indisposition. 'He commenced by eating a pound and a half of horse flesh and a little bread, then ate the entrails, paunch, liver, lights, heart and two hind legs of the young kangaroo. Next followed a penguin found dead upon the beach, upon this he forced down the whole of the hide of the kangaroo after singeing the hair off and wound up his meal by swallowing the tough skin of the penguin.' Far from having any ill-effects 'it gave the young man a peaceful night of rest, curled up like a puppy near the glowing cinders of a brush fire'.

For over a month Eyre and Wylie struggled on, until on 2 June, at Thirstle Cove, near Esperance, they sighted the French whaler *Mississippi* which picked them up. After a rest Eyre insisted on completing his overland journey, and replete with fresh stores they struggled off through heavy rains and cold weather towards Albany, a further three hundred miles. They reached King George Sound, their objective, on the evening of 7 July, and stood looking down on Albany. Members of Wylie's tribe came running up the hill to greet them, while Eyre stood as lost in a dream gazing at the town he had 'so laboriously toiled to attain'.

It had been an incredible journey. Eyre had trudged over a thousand miles on foot and not once had he struck running water. Of course, the expedition had been a failure so far as concerned the pastoralists since stock could clearly never cross the Nullarbor Plain. Today a steel pipeline runs along the track of the Transcontinental Railway, taking water to the different halts, and when the weather is really hot one reads of kangaroos hopping around the pipeline, licking the moisture from seepages where the steel expands. But Eyre's courage and perseverance had been remarkable, and as a reward, he was made Resident Magistrate and Protector of the Aborigines on the Murray River, a new post created for the occasion, and three years later he was presented with the Gold Medal of the Royal Geographical Society.

The east to west crossing had been accomplished, and it now remained to cross the continent from south to north. Different attempts had been made to explore the interior, notably Charles Sturt's in 1844. With him, amongst others, went John McDouall Stuart as draughtsman, and it was Stuart who eventually discovered a practicable route from south to north. In the meantime others had paved the way for this little Scotsman to make the first break-through.

The vast arid zone of the interior represents about forty per cent of the total land surface of Australia, and most of it is entirely without water. All exploring is difficult and dangerous but, as Ernest Giles, who twice traversed the continent in 1874–6, once wrote, 'exploration of a thousand miles in Australia is equal to ten thousand miles in any other part of the earth's surface, always excepting arctic and antarctic travel'.[49] Sturt was unfortunate in that 1844 and 1845 proved to be drought years, amongst the most intense on record and 'even areas which in normal years nowadays are considered excellent pastoral lands were blazing deserts'.[50] He was the first white man to enter the terrible district now known as the Simpson Desert, and for six months he was trapped alongside the receding waters of a fast evaporating creek. At times the thermometer read 119°F in the shade and the earth became like plates of metal. Sturt writes that the bolts and screws in the wagons and boxes fell out, their combs, and the horn handles of their instruments split. Even their hair stopped growing 'and our nails had become as brittle as glass'. Supplies shrivelled in the heat and 'we found it difficult to write or draw, so rapidly did the fluid dry in our pens and brushes'. In their extremity they dug an underground room, deep enough to be beyond the dreadful furnace-glow above; to save themselves, in fact, from sunstroke. 'The stillness of death reigned around us, no living creature was to be heard; nothing visible inhabited that dreary desert but the ant, even the fly shunned it.' At one point kites swooped down on them out of the sky and came so close 'that they threw themselves back to avoid contact, opening their beaks and spreading out their talons'. The birds were so numerous that had they really attacked, it would have been fatal to the travellers. Suffering already the tortures of the damned from the heat, they had to sit by and watch the waters of their creek gradually diminish. 'From its original depth of nine feet, it scarcely measured two, and instead of extending from bank to bank it occupied only a narrow line in the centre of the channel.' In the end Sturt was obliged to strike tents 'which had stood for six months less eleven days'. Many of the men were suffering from scurvy which meant violent headaches, pains in the joints, spongy gums and a coppery taste in the mouth. Two of them died and the journey cost Sturt his health. When he arrived back from the expedition, his wife scarcely recognised him and his appearance gave her such a shock that her hair turned grey overnight.

Sturt had shown extraordinary perseverance and had made many scouting expeditions, but had never managed to pass the Tropic of Capricorn which cuts through the heart of the Colony. A sick and frustrated man, he returned to England in 1853 and died there in 1869.

More than ever, now, people were curious to know exactly what lay in the centre of the country they inhabited. Thomas Belt, an English geologist, came forward with an ingenious idea of attacking the continent from the north. He proposed that he and his brother should proceed by ship to the Gulf of Carpentaria and from there ride south to Cooper's Creek, where they would be met by another party coming from the south. It was a sensible plan but for some reason the Victorian Government turned it down. In 1859 McDouall Stuart, in love with the wide open spaces, pushed out again on his own beyond Lake Eyre, and the following year made his first attempt to traverse the continent, getting as far north as Attack Creek nearly two hundred miles beyond the present Alice Springs.

Who can blame Stuart for losing his heart to this beautiful country with its purple and orange mountains, its distances fading to a cerulean blue. The colours are quite extra-ordinary; towards evening the sky turns to turquoise and saffron, while the void above bruises to a deep violet. Beautiful also are its

The lovely *Eucalyptus papuana*, known as the 'ghost gum'.

creeks, or what in these parts pass as such. They are, in fact, just broad tracts of sand, a delicate coral in colour generally netted over with green, marbled paddy melons. For a few weeks in the year in which the creeks run, it can be seen how swiftly the water flows, the imprint of fast currents being clearly defined in the sand. Round these would-be water courses gather the Centre's different gums, principally the river red gum and the lovely *Eucalyptus papuana* with its snow-white bark. The river gums, as their name suggests, grow only near water, and like the willow they wear about them an aura of fluidity; lovely clean lines with a sparsity of dripping leaves. Indeed, from a distance they give an illusion of nearby water; their pale, upcurving branches of smooth, mottled bark, imitating the play of light and shade that they must reflect during the rains, when the creeks flow. The beautiful *Eucalyptus papuana*, or ghost gums as they are locally called, should be seen at night. They stand out like spectres becoming whiter and whiter as the moon climbs the sky, gleaming like satin in their nudity, their leaves falling about them like a shroud of grey mist. The country has not changed much since Stuart's days. In a strange way he still dominates the scene and scattered around are the places he named: the Finke River so christened after William Finke of Adelaide, a friend of his and a supporter of the expedition – and the hills: 'I name the Macdonnell Ranges after His Excellency the Governor-in-Chief of South Australia.'

A narrow-gauge railway now runs up from Adelaide to Alice Springs, and

171

beyond Alice a bitumen road follows Stuart's eventual trail to the Timor Sea. It all seems very easy now, but this was not the impression Stuart had when he was struggling northward, feeling his way. With no familiar landmark to guide him, he found it worse than a vessel at sea; 'the compass', he tells us, 'requires to be constantly in hand'. Near the Finke River he saw some black cockatoos with a flash of orange or red in their tails. It must be presumed that the dusty, pink and grey galahs were too ordinary for him to mention; they exist, however, in their hundreds and not a day passes without sight of these unwieldy, squawking creatures. They alight on a tree, a mass of palest grey, then taking flight again, and seen from underneath, they are miraculously transformed to a symphony of corals and pinks. Stuart does, however, mention the flies, and those familiar with the Centre will know that it is impossible to ignore them. It is not so much their numbers as their brutish persistence and their total disregard for life. A wave of the hand is quite useless with these desert leeches, for once settled on any part of one person, they stay there until mashed to death. It is impossible to eat without swallowing them along with one's food. Ants were another plague. Peter Warburton, who also explored these regions, writes of them with feeling. It was a drought year and in the end his party were reduced to travelling by moonlight on account of the heat. But before taking this decision the ants were unbearable; 'we cannot get a moment's rest . . . they will not allow us to have any shade.' Unable to shelter under the bushes he was 'compelled in sheer despair to throw myself on the burning sand. . . . This makes it too hot for the ants', and it nearly killed Warburton.

It certainly needed enormous will-power and courage to be an explorer in those early days and one can imagine Stuart's bitter disappointment when, having got to Attack Creek he was forced to make another retreat. He had nevertheless reached the Centre and climbing a hill planted a flag naming it Central Mount Sturt – later altered by others to Stuart. Undaunted, and subsidised by the Government, he made yet another attempt later on the same year and this time managed to penetrate the scrubland for a hundred miles beyond his 1860 terminus. While he was struggling back, a third expedition, unbeknown to Stuart, had set out from Melbourne to cross the continent, but aiming further east, hoped to reach the Gulf of Carpentaria by the Darling River and Cooper's Creek.

This expedition was the best-equipped and most expensive undertaking of its kind in the history of Australian exploration, and although successful, in that it reached its objective, it ended in disaster. Promoted by the Royal Society of Victoria the expedition counted eighteen men with camels, horses, and wagons. Twenty-five camels had been especially imported from India accompanied by three Pakistani drivers. Camels were better adapted to the country than horses. They did not need to wear shoes and could walk interminably over stony ground without bruising their feet, and, more important still, could travel for days without water. A Sergeant of Police named Robert O'Hara Burke had been put in charge, but he was a poor choice as a leader. He was good-looking, fiery, and romantic, but hopelessly unmethodical and impatient and worst of all,

Opposite The Waterhole, by Arthur Boyd, 1954.

Overleaf A mining camp at Bathurst. Oil painting by E. Tullock.

Far left Robert O'Hara
Burke.
Left William John Wills.

had no practical knowledge of the bush. Wills, the second in command, would probably have been better as a leader. The son of a Ballarat surgeon, he had been trained as a surveyor, had some experience of the outback and was more intelligent than Burke. But being young – he was in his twenties at the time – he had not the force of character to assert himself.

The expedition left Melbourne on 20 August 1860, led by Burke on a little grey horse. A crowd of cheering enthusiasts saw them off and it is through Wills's field books that we can follow the explorers. Reaching Menindee, some four hundred miles from Melbourne, on the Darling River, Burke formed a depot, left behind the greater part of his staff and equipment and set out for Cooper's Creek. Reaching his objective a member of the group was sent back to bring up the remainder of the party. Burke waited for them, but after six weeks became impatient and decided to make a dash for it, taking Wills, King, Gray, six camels, a horse and twelve weeks' provisions with him. He left five men behind at the Creek. On 28 March 1861 they reached the Gulf. Burke did not actually see the ocean, owing to swamps, but came close enough to make certain that it was there. Now followed the harrowing return journey. Ill already from the damp oppressive atmosphere of the tropics, the party struggled southward. For days it had been pouring with rain, with great leaden clouds that split open, shooting out livid forks of lightning. Crossing a creek by moonlight they rode over what they took for a log. It turned out to be a large snake 'larger than any I had ever seen, measuring eight feet in length, and seven inches in girth round the belly'. Killing it they ate it and the next day Burke had a violent attack of dysentery with giddy spells.[51]

More rain; every day it poured, the creeks were all flooded and they could make little headway through the squelching mud. Gray was caught stealing some flour. 'He explained that he was suffering from dysentery.' Wills made him report to Burke who gave him a thrashing. Two weeks later, Gray was dead.

Opposite The black
cockatoo. Plate from John
Gould's *Birds of Australia*.

John King.

Wills remarks that he had hardly spoken a word since they left the coast. 'Poor Gray must have suffered very much ... when we thought him shamming.' The party was now living on Billy their horse. He had been cut up into strips and smoked. All were suffering from a complete state of exhaustion and complained of a partial paralysis of the legs. The exertion required to get up a slight rise, even without any load, 'induces an indescribable sensation of pain'.

Making their way south they left the tropics and found themselves again in desert country. Landa, one of the camels, got caught in some quicksands beside a water hole. Attempts were made to extract him but to no avail. The next day they shot the animal 'and after breakfast commenced cutting off what flesh we could get at, for jerking'. Gradually, one by one the camels started dying and when finally they reached the depot at Cooper's Creek, which they had been counting on for help, they found it deserted. The party had left for Menindee that very day, taking most of the food and all the animals and the reserve stocks of clothing with them. A note explained that the men had waited four months, no one had come up with supplies, and the natives were becoming troublesome. Burke, instead of following the party, which would have been the sensible thing to do, struck out south-west for Mount Hopeless which represented the nearest point to civilisation. Dragging on, the three men became weaker and weaker and spent their time collecting, and pounding *nardoo*, a grass seed used by the Aborigines for food. 'I cannot understand this nardoo at all', wrote Wills, 'it certainly will not agree with me in any form.' They managed to get from four to five pounds per day between them and Wills got so weak he could no longer crawl out of his lean-to. Burke and King did the seed hunting, and then, leaving Wills with a supply and some water, went in search of the Aborigines. It was their only chance. For a while longer Wills wrote in his journal: 'I may live four or five days if the weather continues warm ... my legs and arms are nearly skin and bones.' His writing then trails off into an illegible scrawl and stops altogether. Burke died two days later. Only King had the energy and the sense to make himself useful to the natives who found him, and they supported him until a search party from Victoria came to the rescue.

Three months after the death of Burke and Wills, the indomitable little Stuart made another attempt to reach the north coast, and this time he succeeded. Leaving Adelaide in October, he was wading knee-deep in the blue tidal mud of Arnhem Land nine months later. A press conference gives us some of the details. The tide was right out and the beach very treacherous. 'There were hundreds of crab holes, and it was in one of these that Stuart bathed his feet and washed his face, as he had promised the Governor he would do.' 'I had an open space cleared,' Stuart writes, 'selected one of the tallest trees, stripped it of its lower branches, and on its highest branch fixed my flag, the Union Jack, with my name sewed in the centre ....' Almost immediately he started the return through the great empty landscape. He suffered from night blindness and scurvy, living on 'a little boiled flour', all he could manage to swallow; he started having haemorrhages and his men rigged up an improvised litter, slung between

Right The indomitable John McDouall Stuart.

Below Stuart and his party having planted the Union Jack on the shores of the Indian Ocean.

two horses. Three months later ten gaunt and ragged men, 'leading a string of limping, emaciated horses, came riding slowly, wearily, triumphantly, out of the mirage that filled the empty north. The Commander of the South Australian Great Northern Exploring Expedition, along with his faithful companions, had returned'.

Within nine years the overland telegraph stretched from Adelaide to Darwin, precisely along the route Stuart had travelled. At Darwin the line was connected with a cable that went under the sea to Java, Asia and Europe. Australia had become a whole.

179

13 Gold

For the first thirty years of her existence as a Colony, Australia had been strongly linked to Asia and the Pacific. It was a question of supplies since she was almost entirely dependent on importations from overseas. Then came a change as the settlers learnt to adapt themselves to the country and to understand her capabilities. Wool had not only opened much of the interior, but had also tied Australia to Europe. Wool and the whaling fleets produced two valuable exports for which England always had a ready market. There were no problems regarding the transportation of sperm oil since it never left the hold of the ships that would sail it back to the home country, while the wool, selling at anything from two to three hundred pounds a ton, was valuable enough to defray the expenses involved in carting it to the coast. In the ten years between 1832 and 1841 New South Wales exported whale products worth nearly two million pounds, while wool commanded still more important sums. Yet, despite the improved conditions, emigration to Australia remained slow. Parliament did what it could to encourage people, offering free passages, paying for them out of the Australian Land Revenue which was being collected from the sale of Crown Lands valued at five shillings an acre. But, as Professor Blainey writes, 'a working family in Britain who thought of starting a new life in a new land was not easily attracted to Australia. If a mill worker in Manchester or a farmer on a rented farm in Norfolk discussed the prospect of emigrating, the plans they made around kitchen tables were usually fixed on North America. They probably knew people who had emigrated there. The sea voyage was much shorter and decisively cheaper to New York than to Sydney, and if they eventually disliked living in North America, they had some hope of returning to England but if they eventually disliked their life in Australia they had only faint prospects of being able to afford the passage back to England. The ocean and all the disadvantages of isolation eliminated Australia as a goal for most emigrants who had to pay their own fare.'[52]

Opposite Detail of a ghost town.

Then, suddenly, in 1851, came the news that gold had been discovered.

Paul Edmund de Strzelecki from a miniature in possession of the Hon. P. G. King.

California's gold rush was to be duplicated on the other side of the world. A few months before the finds were published, Australia could number somewhere in the region of half a million inhabitants. Within ten years, this count had more than trebled.

It had been known that gold existed several years before the fact was made public. Already as far back as 1823 a convict working near Bathurst was found with a lump of gold in his possession. However, the officer in charge refused to believe that the man had picked the nugget out of the rocks and had him flogged for melting down stolen goods. The incident seems to have had no repercussions and the first official notification of a gold discovery comes from Paul Edmund de Strzelecki, a Polish explorer and scientist. Travelling round the world, Strzelecki arrived in Sydney in April 1839. We can follow him seven thousand feet up the highest mountain of Australia, named by him after the romantic Polish patriot General Tadeusz Kosciusko. The explorer apologises for associating the mountain with a country that had nothing to do with Australia and excuses himself for 'although … on foreign ground', he felt himself to be 'amongst a free people, who appreciated freedom and its votaries'. From the Alps he journeyed through Gippsland and crossed over to Tasmania where he was made much of by the Governor, Sir John Franklin, himself a well-known Arctic explorer.

Strzelecki was not a rich man and to help defray the expenses of his voyages he collected specimens which he sold in Europe. Among the specimens were 'specs of gold in silicate' found near Bathurst. He showed these to Sir George Gipps, Governor of New South Wales, who begged him to suppress all mention of his discovery, since an announcement of this nature would unsettle the Colony and probably give rise to mutiny among the convicts. Strzelecki compromised, and when his Journal was published in the *Sydney Herald,* he mentioned the gold but wrote that it did not exist in sufficient quantity to 'repay its extraction'. He believed quite the contrary.

There were others, however, who were not quite so easily silenced, amongst them William Clarke, a geologist clergyman who had been advised to emigrate to New South Wales on account of his health. Clarke also produced specimens for Sir George who, when shown them, turned and asked Clarke to 'put them away', intimating that they would all have their throats slit if he failed to obey him. Ignoring the Governor's injunctions, Clarke shipped his specimens to England where they came to the attention of the great scientist Sir Roderick Murchison. Sir Roderick read a paper on the subject before the Royal Geographical Society and in his address he drew attention to the geological similarity between the rocks of the Blue Mountains and those of the Urals in Russia. 'There was every probability that the one would be found to be as rich as the other was known to be in precious metals.'

So far as theory went, the matter had been fairly exhaustively explored but no one, strangely enough, had ventured, as yet, to make a serious practical effort. This is where Edward Hargraves come into the picture. An Englishman born in 1816, Hargraves had joined the Merchant Marines and reached Australia at the age of sixteen. Leaving the sea he worked for a while on a station and then joined a French ship heading for the Torres Strait on a tortoise-shell hunting expedition. Tiring of this, he sailed for the Californian gold diggings, stayed there for two years and in his early thirties returned to Australia. His venture on the banks of the Sacramento had brought him only moderate success but at least it had taught him the method of recovering gold – how to wash with a pan and cradle for alluvial deposits, something the other Colonists knew nothing about. In his book *Australia and its Gold Fields,* published in 1855, Hargraves tells us how immediately on reaching Sacramento he was struck with the similarity of the country to that which he remembered round Bathurst. Gold accompanies rocks of a certain class and Hargraves took note of the similarity of the Californian and Australian strata. He remembered one particular valley known to him in his youth and the idea of it haunted him. Perhaps in that silent spot he would unearth as much treasure as the more fortunate of his companions seemed to be gathering from the rocks and soil around them in California. Day after day the image of that winding creek recurred. The more fortunate his neighbours became the more vivid were his day-dreams, until, eventually, it compelled him back to Australia. His friends laughed at his expectations 'and treated my views and opinions as those of a madman'. Undaunted, he set out alone on horseback to cross the Blue Mountains. Within five days he was lodged in a little inn kept by a Mrs Lister. After dinner Hargraves told her of his project 'and begged her to procure a black fellow as a guide'. Although he knew the country well it had been some time since he was there and 'it is a matter of no small danger to attempt to penetrate alone the dense forest that covers the whole surrounding country'. Mrs Lister offered Hargraves her son who she assured him was familiar with the district. It was a question of hours only before they were bivouacked on the borders of the Summer Hill Creek, a tributary of the Macquarie – the valley of Hargraves' dreams. 'I felt myself surrounded by gold', Hargraves wrote excitedly. After a hasty meal he started immediately to pan for gold. The first trial produced a few grains. 'Here it is!' he exclaimed and four panfulls in succession produced gleaming particles of the precious metal. Hargraves was beside himself with excitement; a baronetcy would be his recompense and he saw the young Lister being knighted. 'My old horse will be stuffed,' he cried, 'put into a glass-case, and sent to the British Museum.' Given to flights of fancy he had allowed his imagination to get the best of him. Never raised to the peerage, he was, however, appointed Commissioner of Crown Land and granted the handsome sum of ten thousand pounds by the New South Wales legislature.

Edward Hargraves.

When first returning to Sydney, Hargraves tried to bargain with the authorities; for five hundred pounds he would show them the gold-bearing localities he had discovered. The Colonial Secretary replied that he must trust the Government and sent Hargraves back to Ophir – the biblical name given by Hargraves to his valley – in the company of Mr Samuel Stutchbury, the newly appointed colonial geologist. The Government had had its doubts and secretly believed that Hargraves' grains had been planted and were in reality

Californian gold. Stutchbury put them at their ease adding that the precious metal 'seems to be as regular as wheat in a sown field'. Within a week some four hundred people were stooping over Summer Hill Creek each with a dish in his hand, lost to the world as they washed and sifted the sandy, brown earth. Lumps valued at two hundred pounds were quite a common occurrence. The number of gold seekers increased; there was no holding them back. The lovely little gulley that so recently had been shaded by wattles and tea-trees was reduced to a muddy nakedness while the creek itself almost ceased to flow, choked by heaps of gravel that had previously formed part of its banks.

The news spread like wildfire and very soon the whole Colony was involved; shepherds deserted their flocks, shop-keepers closed their stores, sailors even left their ships. The price of labour soared. Men had to be tempted by four or five times the ordinary wage to stay in their jobs. Bathurst, the nearest town to the diggings, was quite literally paralysed. One reads that the Governor himself, reduced by the flight of his servants, took to grooming his own horses. Whether true or not, the very fact that such a report circulated, was a proof of the state things were in. One man, a successful tailor, was deserted by ten of his employees and, incapable of carrying on business without them, he followed them to the diggings where he eventually accepted the post of cook to the men he had formerly employed. Gold was a great leveller of classes, labourers often got a lift and the well-born a fall, 'gentlemen lost their gentility'. Shaw tells us that the amounts gathered by diggers were almost unbelievable, 'whilst their personal appearance is in no wise bettered'. He tells a story about the captain of a vessel who, wanting hands, explored the 'Rocks' in Sydney, a district where they were generally met with. 'In the course of his perambulations, he stumbled over a drunkard, apparently a tar, and asked him to join his vessel. "Where's your ship?" he asked. "That barque in the harbour," said the skipper, pointing one out to him. Pulling a wad of money out of his pocket, the drunk offered to buy her "And I will ship you with her"'.[53]

Another case relates to the wife of a Sydney Government official; who looking over a new shipment of dresses admired one in particular, but thought the price too high. 'Expensive is it?' said a digger who was standing close by. 'Allow me to make you a present of it, Ma'am; and Mr Shopman put a similar one out for my wife.'

Trollope, who can be considered a contemporary traveller, writes that it is difficult not to fall victim to the lure of the known presence of gold beneath the earth. 'It begets a fury in the minds of men compelling them to search for it – that a thing in itself so rich should lie buried in the dirt beneath their feet, loose among the worthless pebbles of the river, mixed at haphazard with lumbering rock – takes possession of his heart and brain – he makes no estimate as to the cost of his labour, does not weigh his chance of success – this gold may be got by the handful, if only the lucky sod of earth be turned.'[54]

There were absolutely no doubts as to the richness of the soil, children would often pick up particles of gold out of the gravel; a shrub pulled up from the ground would have nuggets hanging to its roots like clusters of golden grapes.

Then six months after Hargraves had made his discovery, a monster mass known as the Kerr Hundredweight was found on a sheep run by three young Aboriginal shepherds. The gold was beautifully encased in quartz, but Doctor Kerr, on whose land the mass had been found, was obliged to break the formation into several pieces in order to fit it into his saddlebags. A reporter writing for the *Bathurst Free Press* saw the hoard's arrival in town the next day. It had been stowed away in the back of a tandem drawn by two greys and the townspeople were gathering around gazing open-mouthed at the precious metal 'glittering in virgin purity'. Later the load was taken to the bank and heaped together on a table in the Board Room where 'they presented a splendid appearance, and shone with an effulgence calculated to dazzle the brain of any man'. Lieutenant-Colonel Munday, the Deputy-Adjutant General, was also at the bank and looking at the 'monster lump in a speculative light regrets that it was not hacked out of the earth intact. He would have had it tour in a circus – Mr Barnum would have realized £50,000 in a couple of years by exhibiting it around Europe and America with the black fellows who found it ... and would have sold it afterwards for at least twice as much as Dr Kerr got for it ....' – the round sum of £4,000, this being the market value at the time for 106 pounds of pure gold. One is pleased to hear that the three shepherds were well taken care of and among other things were given sheep, a dray and a team of bullocks.

In the meantime the rush to the New South Wales gold-fields caused serious worry to the founders of the newly established Colony of Victoria. In alarm at the prospect of being entirely depopulated, a number of leading citizens of Melbourne formed what was called the Gold Discovery Committee. They offered £200 to the first person who could lead them to a payable gold-field within two hundred miles of the town. Several people came forward but the first useful discovery seems to have been made at Clunes by a man named James Esmonds. Like Hargraves, Esmonds had practical knowledge of the work, learned also in the Californian diggings. He had, in fact, returned to Australia on the same ship as Hargraves. Esmonds made his discovery in July 1851, five months after Hargraves had first washed gold on Summer Hill Creek. A month later followed another Victorian find at Ballarat, which turned out to be the richest alluvial gold-field the world has ever known. In rapid succession followed further discoveries at Bendigo and at Mount Alexander near the present site of Castlemaine. By November there were about 25,000 diggers at work, acre after acre was dug up, pock-marked with irregular heaps of ochre-coloured sand, each with its shaft in the middle. Guards stood over three tons of gold heaped up in the Commissioner's tent, waiting to be carried to Melbourne. By the end of 1851 gold worth nearly nine million pounds had been taken from the Victorian fields and the next ten years were to swell this figure to a hundred millions. The States yield of gold far surpassed that of New South Wales, Bendigo and Ballarat alone almost equalling California's total output.

By the end of 1851 news had reached London and the outside world of the great new discoveries. By the middle of 1852, ships began to arrive freighted with thousands of men, who no sooner landed in Melbourne than they started for the diggings. During 1852, nearly 100,000 persons arrived in the country. By 1855 Victoria's population alone was greater than that of the whole of Australia before Hargraves' discovery.

These packed shiploads of gold seekers spelt considerable trouble; among the new arrivals were thousands of Chinese. In 1854 thirty-seven shiploads of them disembarked. The following year the Victorian Government imposed a poll tax of ten pounds a head upon all Orientals who landed in her ports. But the New South Wales Government did not follow their lead until 1861 which meant that the Chinese would just land at a port over the State border and make their way on foot to the different fields. On the diggings the Chinese lived in their own community and were for the most part diligent labourers content to occupy abandoned sites too quickly worked over by Europeans. 'Europeans', Preshaw, a Bank employee writes, 'take up certain localities, work for a short time, are dissatisfied, run off to a new place, and the abandoned ground is forthwith occupied by the Chinese. Perhaps within a few weeks the same Europeans are again disappointed and return to their old quarters, but find that they have really abandoned a good claim .... It seldom happens that Chinese take up new ground' and 'the consequence of all this was an appeal to the Gold Commissioners with the usual list of complaints against the Chinese; that they spoiled the water; are dirty and filthy in their habits; take up more ground than they are entitled to, etc. etc.'[55] The native-born Australians were particularly discriminating against the Chinese and on several occasions mass attacks were made upon them. They also played brutal pranks on them, like tossing sticks of dynamite in among the crackers with which they celebrate the New Year.

The 'Celestials' as they were called did not come to settle in Australia, but to make quick fortunes and return to their own country, which accounts for the almost complete absence of women among them, a lack, which no doubt, contributed to their bad reputation. Trollope, who was shown the Chinese quarters at Ballarat by the Sergeant of Police had no good word to say for them, found them dens of iniquity. 'A more degraded life is hardly possible to imagine. Gambling, opium smoking, and horrid dissipation ... boys and girls are enticed among them ... and become foul, abominable and inhuman.'[56]

By the late 1850s the Chinese working in the gold fields formed about four per cent of the country's entire population – an alarmingly high proportion. They were, however, a very temporary importation and at their departure appear to have left few traces behind them – two faded Joss Houses in Bendigo and Melbourne.

The early rushes occurred, for the most part, in wild, unsettled country, far from any established town and life in the camps was fairly rugged. A good road led from Sydney to Bathurst, but beyond that there were only bush trails. The same applied to the Victorian diggings. Hurriedly equipping themselves, the newcomers would set out, a few in carts, some on horseback, but for the

Detail of Joss House in Melbourne.

most part on foot, pushing wheelbarrows. There were no inns once they left the high road and the best they could hope for were roughly improvised 'coffee tents'. Life on the gold-fields called for a strong constitution and a robust nature. There was no hope of success unless the person involved was ready to accept all kinds of privations. James Bonwick, a prolific Australian writer, describes the diggings as having great attraction in spite of all the discomfort; the weather, the dust, the flies and the general filth. 'It was', he writes, 'the flow of animal enjoyment peculiar to bush life.' He adds that the diggings 'would be more tolerable if there could be cleanliness. But with water sometimes a shilling a bucket and that not easily obtained, the incrustations had to remain longer than agreeable.'[57] Conditions improved, of course, during the rainy season. Bonwick then gives his reader some practical advice, about shirts, for instance; coloured ones lasted longer without showing the dirt. When really so filthy that they could not decently be worn any more it was better to throw them away and buy a new one. This was cheaper than having them laundered.

As to diggers' fashions they seemed to have been set by the men from California; red or blue flannel shirts without coat or vest, moleskin trousers, leather belt and heavy lace-up boots. Australia's cabbage tree hat could replace America's felt one, and under it one would find a sunburnt countenance with a profusion of beard and moustache. More often than not, the digger's head would be swathed in veiling against the sandflies giving a somewhat comical aspect to these banditti-looking figures.

Once arrived at the diggings the newcomer, or 'new chum', as he was called, if just out from England, would find the place almost treeless and honeycombed with shafts and sinkings, some of them dangerously deep and close to the tents. When it rained these shafts filled with water making it dangerous to go out at night without a lantern. On an average most diggings could count about three deaths a week from people falling into these holes and drowning. The soft earth would fall in on them and choke them as they tried to claw their way out. Nearly everyone lived in tents which generally had built-in fireplaces made out of logs stuck onto one end. Sometimes log huts would be added to the tent and round them would run a picket fence closing off a small area in which the women of the family carried out their daily chores. One report I came across describes the women chopping wood with great axes, 'which they do not seem to swing but which rather swings them as they cut splinters from the stumps which ornament their digger landscape'. Later in the day one meets these same women surprisingly neatly dressed, for 'there is no lack of handsome mantillas, neat-fitting jackets, smart bonnets and parasols ... '[58]. Our same informant makes one of the diggeresses sound very glamorous in a large white hat with floating ribbons and a great flaring skirt.

The tents inside were desolate enough; bedding was usually laid on the ground and also served as chairs while boxes were used as tables. Mrs Clacy, one of the inmates, seems to have taken it all in good part and writes that 'Diagonese [*sic*] in his tub would not have looked more comfortless'. She admits, however, that 'in some of the tents the soft influence of our sex is pleasingly apparent; the tins are as bright as silver, there are sheets as well as blankets on the bed'. A dry sack acts as a carpet 'whilst a pet cockatoo chained to a perch screeches away in the corner'. Mrs Clacy makes no mention of the diggers' language which by all reports was 'something incredible in its violence'.[59]

In most of the diggings a gun would be fired from the Commissioner's Tent when it was time to down tools. Fires were then lighted and wreaths of blue smoke would curl up against the evening sky as the men prepared their meals consisting of the eternal lamb chop, or salt beef eaten with dampers (unleavened bread, something like a coarse pancake) and washed down with pannikins of scalding green tea. Johnny cakes, made from flour and water, with the addition of dripping, sometimes replaced the damper. Bread was far too expensive, costing six shillings a loaf. Potatoes were also luxuries, so were cheese, butter, pickles, ham, bacon and sardines. Fish was a great rarity, most of the brook trout having been choked to death by the washings. Plum pudding, or 'duff' as it was called, seems to have been the only extravagance commonly indulged in, being considered the regular Sunday dish. As for Sunday it was generally respected as a day of rest and parties would be met with strolling in the bush 'orderly and well dressed'. The naval officer who describes this scene, on a hurried visit to the Ophir diggings, also remarks on 'two very decent-looking women who had retired to a quiet spot, and were occupied with their book, apparently in devotion'.[60]

Above Photograph (from the Bernard Holtermann Collection) of a shanty hotel near the gold-fields dating from the early 1870s.

Right Another Holtermann photograph of a slab hut roofed in stringy bark.

'The one-storied sheds strung out along the main street would have had rickety wooden façades added for the sake of importance.' Photograph from the Holtermann Collection.

For amusement there was gambling and the dance halls where, for lack of women, hirsute performers paired off together in a rollicking mazurka, clumped out to the scraping of a fiddle. George Preshaw describes such a scene at Kiandra in the Snowy Mountains. 'There were only three dance girls, and those who were fortunate enough to secure one as a partner must have found it hard work dancing on a floor fully an inch thick in mud. Just fancy fifty diggers coming into a room with their muddy boots on, and walking about; what a nice state the floor would be in for dancing.'[61]

In the recently discovered fields people were housed as has been described already, in temporary, make-shift lodgings. The shops and amusement halls were also canvas and calico structures with wood frames. The local hotel would in all probability be just a large tent with stringy bark couches ranged down each side of a central gangway. Were the diggings at all successful wooden buildings would succeed the canvas, and these would be slab huts roofed in stringy bark. The one-storeyed sheds strung out along the main street would have had rickety wooden façades added for the sake of importance – stores, banks, public houses, a church or two and a few eating houses, sometimes even a theatre. Brilliantly lighted at night its fragile walls would tremble with the rough and hearty roars that greeted the performers; men like the well-known gold-field entertainer, Charles Thatcher, who sang popular songs, mostly traditional British and American airs. Handsome towns like Bendigo and Ballarat, which had been conjured up by the power of gold had more substantial buildings, of course, and it is in their theatres that the great Lola Montez danced, probably the most notorious of all the gold-field entertainers. Arriving from San Francisco in 1855 she was the first solo dancer to visit Australia, the best-known of her somewhat limited repertoire being *El Olle* and the Spider Dance, depicting the death agonies of someone bitten by a tarantula, a performance which astonished Paris. By the time she reached Australia she was already past her prime and had never, anyhow, been a very good dancer. However her reputation must have assured her of a good audience, for she had been, after all, Franz Liszt's mistress and had been raised to the peerage, with the title of Countess of Landsfeld, by King Ludwig I of Bavaria. The editor of the *Morning Post* describes her in 1848 at the height of her career as 'a very charming person and a delightful companion'. He found her manners distinguished and her palace in Munich the height of elegance; airy balconies and tinted muslin curtains, drawn close, adding a 'shell-like lightness to the atmosphere'. But she was seven years older and somewhat battered by life by the time she reached Australia. Mortlock saw her in Sydney and writes in his *Experiences of a Convict* that 'her eyes were brilliant and expressive; still I felt rather disappointed with her countenance and figure'. William Craig, a young miner, had no criticism to make. 'There is no mistaking the leading "star"' he writes, 'when she makes her appearance.' He does, however, refer to 'the traces of her former beauty', but finds her form 'willowy' and quite understands how 'she was able to bewitch a king and cost him his throne'. Both the Sydney and Melbourne papers gave Lola Montez poor reviews, but the Governor, nevertheless, asked her to perform in Melbourne and no doubt the dance he saw had been carefully edited.

Lola Montez – somewhat battered by life by the time she reached Australia.

From Adelaide Lola Montez finally set out for Ballarat and Bendigo, the centre of the gold-fields, where she was noisily appreciated and in Bendigo the audience showed its enthusiasm in more concrete form by showering her with nuggets. On leaving Australia, Lola Montez returned to America, remarried and settled in New York, dying in 1861 at the age of forty-three. The last years of her life she spent in Brooklyn helping destitute women.

An attempt has been made in the preceding pages to give an idea of life as it was led in a mining camp, but what of the actual mechanics? Digging was a precarious pursuit and the uncertain distribution of the mineral made the seeking of it a complete lottery. Shaw tells a story of two men at Mount Alexander who commence tunnelling horizontally into the bank of a creek; after penetrating thirty feet without discovering a speck of gold they gave up the excavation. A few days later a stranger had a try at the luckless shaft and collected fifty ounces in two days. Another barren hole abandoned by others had yielded over £2,000 worth of gold in a few weeks and it is these isolated cases of success that kept up the feverish excitement, a fever that never quite died out of the digger's blood until the day of his death. And who could tell, there was always the off-chance that the seeker would be the lucky person to find one of the freak nuggets which occasionally turned up. The 'Sarah Sands' discovered in 1853 was worth about £6,500. In 1857 the 'Blanche Barklay' worth £7,000 was discovered; and the following year produced the 'Welcome' which sold for £10,500, and was the greatest on record until 1869 the 'Welcome Stranger' was dug up, proving to be slightly the larger. The famous Holtermann nugget, the largest amount of gold ever mined in one piece, was not, technically speaking, a nugget, but a mass lodged in a reef of slate, the gross weight of which was 7,560 ounces and the actual gold content about 3,000 ounces. The same applied to the Kerr Hundredweight which was embedded in quartz.

Digging was a precarious pursuit and a complete lottery.
Above The lucky digger; lithograph by S. T. Gill, 1852. *Right* The unlucky digger.

192

Not only was mining a precarious undertaking but also an arduous one. Hall, a store-keeper in Melbourne, writes that his hands blistered to such a degree 'that blood oozed from them down the handle of my spade'.[62] Others report enormous blisters covering the whole hand and there are endless cases of bad backs. At times those stricken were unable to stand up and had to move around on all fours. Bonwick tells us that in spite of the out of door life the miners as a class were not particularly healthy. 'Most of them look pale and haggard and the work underground, excessive toil, discomforts and neglect, too often bring on disease....' Cramps, colds, rheumatism, bad eyes, diarrhoea and dysentery were the prevalent complaints and most attacks of sickness resolved themselves in fevers. One pictures men shaking with ague in their tents and needless to say the medical attention was not of the best. Many who came to the diggings fell ill and died leaving absolutely no clue as to their identity, and had to be buried in nameless graves. Amongst the minor annoyances there were the mice. 'They are English mice and they swarm. We find it one of the most difficult things in the world to catch them.' The mosquitoes were even worse 'the very air seemed made of them'[63] and only with the coming of dawn did they disappear. The author of this account tells us of the only effectual way of getting rid of the fleas – just spread your possessions near an antheap.

Far more aggravating, and the cause, in the end, of serious disturbances among the miners was the question of licensing fees. The Crown, technically owning all the land, claimed the mines as the property of the Government. It did not claim the gold found on this land but threatened prosecution against all those digging without authority. Authority took the form of licences for which a fee of thirty shillings a month should be paid. The money thus raised was expected to cover the expense of extra police and other exigencies arising out of the gold-fields. It was a perfectly reasonable arrangement, and the trouble lay

A Commissioner collecting licences. Unsigned water-colour.

in the impecunious state of the diggers. Their average monthly earnings worked out at about eight pounds per man. To those who were fortunate the fee appeared but a trifle but for those who earned little, or nothing, there was no resource but to evade payment. Every conceivable trick was resorted to in order to dodge the Commissioners. Avoidance of payment became a feat and 'was elevated to a virtue' as one of the men put it. At least one man in every five systematically paid no fees and aware of this the police were in the habit of stopping every man they met and demanding to see his licence. If he had none, he was at once marched off to jail or a place that served as such. Here again was another problem and as William Howitt writes it was rather the mode of collecting the tax than the actual tax itself that made it increasingly unpopular. 'It has frequently happened that one individual has been called upon to produce his receipt half a dozen times in the course of one day. ... Men who were found without licences on their persons but who had them in their tents were dragged off to the Government Camp, and allowed no explanation but were fined from three to five pounds' and clapped into chains if they remonstrated. The trouble here lay in the kind of men being employed as police. With an acute shortage of labour those in command had to accept almost anyone who could be persuaded to wear a uniform. At best the recruits were young and inexperienced and at worst they were brutal and corrupt. Tax collecting amongst them became a sport and was referred to as 'man hunting' whilst the diggers in their turn began referring to the foot-police as 'blood-hounds'.

The Chief Commissioner was an important official at the diggings and paraded on horseback in a kind of undress military uniform with an orderly riding at a respectful distance behind. Such a person was the famous bully, Mr Armstrong, known in Bendigo as 'the flying demon'. Lord Robert Cecil, the future Lord Salisbury, describes him in his diary as a very striking man, 'well-made, tall, muscular, with keen "flashing" eyes, a splendidly clever countenance, perfect temper, and a quiet, fearless energy'.[64] Intelligent he might have been but according to Howitt he was also quite mercilessly cruel. He tells this story of him and quite understandably changes his name to Hermsprong.

'A poor Irishwoman was left a widow with several children, the youngest of which was only a few days old.' It was discovered that she was selling grog. Hermsprong 'appeared before her tent with his myrmidons, and, ill as she was, summoned her out'. She did not deny the accusation, 'but said that her husband being killed by an accident, her countrymen had advised her, as her only means of support for herself and little children, to sell grog, promising to give her their custom; and the poor woman said piteously, "what, your honour, was I to do."

'Without replying to her remark, Hermsprong turned to the police with him, and said, "Fire that tent!"'

The children were still inside, the baby asleep and the police, 'to a man refused to execute this diabolical order'. Hermsprong swearing at them and threatening their dismissal 'leapt from his horse, stalked up to a fire burning before the tent and seized a flaming brand' did the job himself.

'The poor woman, uttering a frantic cry' rushed in to save the baby, 'and, followed by her other children, came out and stood shrieking and tearing her hair like a maniac, while her tent, and all that she had in the world, consumed before her eyes...'.[65]

For two years this monster was allowed to stay in office, till eventually public opinion could no longer be ignored. When dismissed he showed complete indifference and replied that he did not mind being turned out, 'for in these two years I have cleared fifteen thousand pounds'. His salary had been four hundred a year!

Small wonder that the diggers nursed a growing feeling of resentment against the police. A riot at Ballarat, an unfortunate incident at Bentley's Hotel where a digger got his skull sliced open with a spade, brought the matter to a head in an armed clash known as the Eureka Stockade. Five hundred miners had taken an oath to fight for their rights and liberties. A man named Peter Lalor, about twenty-five years old, of a 'handsome presence' was elected leader, and under a blue flag adorned with the stars of the Southern Cross they took their stand on a hill behind a hurriedly constructed enclosure. The next morning, 3 December 1854, a Sunday, some infantry and cavalrymen and a hundred police proceeded quietly to the stockade from the Government Camp. Immediately fire was opened on them by the insurgents, and the issue was joined. In about fifteen minutes all was over, the untrained miners being no match for the Government forces. Six men on the Government side were killed and thirty-four miners fell. Lalor, badly wounded, managed to escape. The loss of the miners' lives, however, was not entirely in vain, a general amnesty was proclaimed and a Gold-Fields Commission appointed. Their report recommended the abolition of the licensing and instead suggested the issue of the miner's right, giving to the holder, on payment of a pound a year, permission to dig in any part of the Colony.

Conditions for miners had improved, but now the gold being so avidly sought for was becoming difficult to find. The alluvial deposits in river beds and gulches had been worked out and such simple methods as washing and panning, or cradling, were no longer of any use. Deep shafts had to be driven down into the earth and a considerable amount of expensive machinery became necessary. The great days of alluvial mining were over. Rushes did occur after the 1850s but in general it had become a matter of reefing and quartz crushing conducted by big companies. The prospector was replaced by the wage-earner, and, although production remained high, relatively fewer men were engaged in mining.

During the 1870s gold was found in Queensland and twenty years later in Western Australia. Coolgardie became Australia's foremost gold-field closely followed by Palmer field in Queensland. But Western Australia has been the main producer in recent years, being the source of approximately eighty per cent of all the gold produced in the country, an impressive figure totalling a little over a hundred million sterling; a tally that ranks Australia fifth among the gold-producing countries of the world, those of greater output being South Africa, USSR, Canada and the United States.

14 Clippers and coaches

By 1850 the average passage to Australia took about four months, some thirty days faster, that is, than ships making the same run earlier in the century. Conditions on board the emigrant ships were still fairly primitive, however, and the passengers were divided into three classes: cabin, intermediate and steerage, with the fares running from seventy pounds for a cabin to fifteen pounds, steerage. The first class accommodation was very cramped. It was like being shut up in a box, while the intermediate, or second class, had four or six berths to a cabin. As to the steerage passengers, they had to sleep in open berths in a huge dormitory where there was no question of any privacy, the berths being separated by low wooden partitions; and it was quite usual to have a second tier of berths only three feet above the lower. The food varied according to which class you were travelling and only the cabin class was supplied with necessities, the other passengers having to furnish their own supplies, including all their bedding and sheets. Pamphlets were handed out by the shipping agents and in them the passengers were given all kinds of useful advice; what they should wear and what they were most likely to need; tin plates and dishes, a vessel for holding the day's allowance of water, candles, a camp stool, a looking-glass. From another source one learns that 'a bottle of disinfectant fluid and perfumed pastilles to burn occasionally will be found useful'. The same person tells us that 'on the day the ship sails there is often so much confusion and the cook is so drunk, that there are no meals to be had. It would be well, therefore, to have a sort of picnic provision in a basket for the first dinner and supper'. Enough linen should be taken to last the four months as there would be no opportunity for laundry work, 'the only water ever available for such purposes being the rain collected from the sails'. More advice follows for the ladies, they 'should be cautious not to wear thin-soled shoes while the decks are damp after washing or rain; diarrhoea is a frequent result of this practice'.[66]

The sailing time to Australia, already much faster than it used to be, was to be cut still further after the discovery of gold. The great majority of gold-

Coming South, by Tom Roberts, 1886.

seekers were well off enough to pay handsomely for their ticket to El Dorado, and the shipping lines were not slow to take advantage of the situation. The Californian rushes had been responsible for encouraging New England ship builders to design faster ships and, by cutting off superfluous parts and stream-lining the hull, America's naval architects produced the 'clipper', a magnificent looking vessel with clean, sweeping line; a kind of greyhound of the sea. Professor Blainey describes them beautifully in his excellent book *The Tyranny of Distance* and calls them 'graceful temples of science'. He writes that 'the age of steam-ships had arrived but no steam-ship in the world could equal the speeds of the American clippers in the lonely latitudes of the Southern Ocean. The American clipper was the consummation of centuries of ship-building, the most glamorous ship that ever went with the wind. She had her swift glory on the eve of the dethronement of sailing ships as the sea's speedsters, and perhaps her finest achievements were on the Australian run.'[67]

To match the cleaving prows of these sea greyhounds a new and quicker route to Australia was inaugurated, known as the Great Circle. It had been thought out by John Towson, an English watchmaker who made the chronometers with which navigators reckoned their longitude at sea. His theory was a simple one: the shortest distance between two points was the arc of a great circle. Between the Cape of Good Hope and Melbourne a ship that forsook the traditional route along a latitude of about forty degrees and instead cruised far to the south could save over a thousand miles. Using this route a ship saw no land all the way from the Irish Sea to the coastline near Melbourne. Furthermore, between the tip of South Africa, on the way out, and the tip of South America, on the return, they sometimes covered more than four hundred sea miles a day. The winds, never dependable, prevented them, of course, from maintaining such a pace, but had they been able to do so, they would have gone from Liverpool to Melbourne in something like thirty days. From sixty to sixty-three days seems to have been the fastest sailing time recorded. Reading down the list of ships, one is taken by some of their manes: the *Mermaid* and the *Shalimar*, *White Star*, *Lightning* and the *Flying Scud*, one of R. W. Cameron's celebrated Pioneer Line of Australian Packets, the ship belonging to my grandfather which made a record run from New York to Melbourne with 140 passengers on board in 1892.

Duncan Dunbar was among the first of the shipping magnates in the British Isles to adopt the clipper. He named his after the family, beginning with the *Phoebe Dunbar*, followed by the *Dunbar* of tragic fame. She was a favourite passenger packet and was commanded by James Green, a popular captain. Due in from England, Sydney was waiting impatiently for her to arrive. Her crowded passenger list counted a high percentage of mothers and daughters – daughters who had been years abroad at school. The *Dunbar* by rights should have berthed on the evening of 20 August 1857. She was off Botany Bay soon after 7 p.m. but the weather was stormy with a strong wind from the southeast and with very poor visibility. But let Mark Twain tell the story, for he does it well. With him we board the *Dunbar* flying towards Sydney Heads and as he writes 'the happy home-comers were busily doffing their sea clothes and putting on their finery – these poor brides of the sea', as he calls them. Before the Heads were sighted, darkness came on and there was a miscalculation. They were nearer to the entrance than had been imagined. Mark Twain in Australia towards the end of the century would have met people connected with the tragedy so he writes almost from experience. 'It was said that ordinarily the Captain would have made a safe offing and waited for the morning; but this was no ordinary case; all about him were appealing faces, faces pathetic with disappointment. So his sympathy moved him to try the dangerous passage in the dark. He had entered the Heads seventeen times and believed he knew the ground. So he steered straight for the opening.' The miscalculation in miles was to cost them their lives. Instead of the opening, breakers appeared right ahead.

Entering Sydney Heads on a rough day. Water-colour by Conrad Martens, 1854.

The Master tried desperately to clear the rocks but there was not enough room to alter the ship's course and shortly afterwards she was hurled broadside against the cliffs. 'There was no saving the ship. The great sea swept her in and crushed her to splinters ... not one of all that fair and gracious company was ever seen alive again.' Of the persons on board only one survived – a young able-seaman named James Johnson. The sea had 'flung him up the face of a precipice and stretched him on a narrow shelf of rock mid-way between the top and the bottom, and there he lay all night'. By chance he was discovered the next morning and handed to safety with ropes. Johnson must have had a very practical turn of mind for Twain tells us that he hired a hall in Sydney and exhibited himself at sixpence a head.

During the peak period of Australia's gold rushes as many as two ships a day arrived from Liverpool and Boston. But the clippers' reign was to be brief as steam communication gradually drove canvas from the sea. It took steamers some time, nevertheless, to beat the records set by these elegant ships. The steamer *Great Britain* entered the Australian run in 1852. Six-masted, built of iron, with a screw propeller she was one of the biggest ships afloat and carried 137 in her crew. Sailing from Liverpool with 630 passengers she reached Melbourne in just over eighty days, three weeks longer than the records established by the clippers. But with the years came experience and advanced techniques, with the result that the latest steamer SS *Canberra* can now make the run from Southampton to Melbourne in twenty-five days.

Gold was not only to streamline travel by sea but also on land, and again it was to America that Australia turned. Her needs were similar and circumstances had put Americans in the lead, her gold rushes having occurred earlier than those of Australia. The geographical considerations also played their part; the great distances and the wild reaches of the west were similar in almost every respect to the unopened spaces of the Antipodes. America needing a tough, reliable coach for travel across rough country where there were few roads had developed the Concord, and Australia copied her. The Concord differed from other coaches mainly in its springs; the body instead of being mounted on iron springs, was suspended on flexible leather straps known as through-braces. When encountering rough ground the body tended to produce a rolling motion instead of bouncing up and down. This put less strain on both the vehicle and the horses, and was certainly more comfortable for the passengers, although the motion did sometimes cause sea-sickness. Wheels and under-carriage were stoutly made and American hickory, a very light wood, was largely used in the body work. Square, unadorned, their sides curtained with canvas, these coaches looked what they were, thoroughly utilitarian – a counterpart in carriages to the model T Ford in the world of motor cars.

As mentioned already a number of Americans emigrated to Victoria in the early gold-rush days, among them Freeman Cobb, John Peck and James Swanton, men who had worked, or at any rate were familiar with, the great coaching organisation of Wells Fargo and the Adams Express Company in the United States. When Cobb first arrived the only reliable transport to the gold-fields were the bullock-drays and quick to size up the situation Cobb decided to form a partnership with Peck and Swanton and together import some American coaches, complete with first-class horses and drivers, 'Yankee whips' who had learned their trade with Wells Fargo. The company had an immediate success and regular services were started from Melbourne to Bendigo, Ballarat and Castlemaine. They advertised four departures a day with a load of some sixteen passengers. There were frequent changes of horses and being lightly constructed the coaches could keep up an average speed of nine to ten miles an hour. Bendigo to Melbourne, almost exactly a hundred miles, could be done in less than a day. Cobb made a fortune and sold out to a syndicate headed by another compatriot, James Rutherford. The company extended the Victorian services, established coach-building works, obtained a mail subsidy and re-placed the American drivers with Australians. When eventually the railways drove these horse-drawn vehicles from the busiest roads, Cobb and Company moved to the back country of Eastern Australia and by 1870 were harnessing 6,000 horses a day, their coaches travelling some 28,000 miles a week, and not until 1934 did the company go out of business, ousted in the end by the bus rather than the railway.

Cobb and Company's apotheosis would appear to have been the Leviathan, the largest coach ever built in Australia. It carried eighty-five passengers and was drawn by twenty-two horses, while a driver and two postilions were needed to manage the reins. Like all Cobb's coaches it was painted yellow and the horses had pale blue rosettes over their ears. It must have been a splendid sight, but not very practical with the general condition of the roads.

The particular construction of Cobb coaches was important, of course, in the success of the company but its real fame lay in the reliability and resourcefulness of its men. Some of their drivers were real heroes, as well known in their day to the youngsters as Ned Kelly had been. 'Knights of the Ribbon' they were called, and the most remarkable amongst them was a young man from Tasmania, Ted Devine, or 'Cabbage-tree Ned'. It must have been an exciting experience sitting up on the box watching him handle the leader without once using the whip. Silent and in complete control, hands light and steady, he kept the horses well bunched, with heads together, all trotting in perfect rhythm. Even the coach seemed to keep time, swaying along on its leather straps in unison with the rest. Yet despite Ted Devine and the soft springs some of the trips must have been pretty rough. 'Every two or three minutes', writes a traveller in 1846, 'the wheel goes into a hole or over a stump with such force as would almost throw you out of your seat.' It can be argued, of course, that Ted Devine would have avoided the stumps, but he could do nothing about the roads.

Emily Soldene, a successful singer in *opéra bouffe* touring Australia in Offenbach's light opera, *Geneviève de Brabant,* describes such a ride for us. Not only gifted with a fine mezzo-soprano voice, Miss Soldene was also quite a dab with her pen. She rides to Melbourne in a Cobb coach drawn by six young horses and reading her memoirs is almost to experience the ride for oneself. 'I liked to sit on the box', she writes, 'though it made one sick, not with fright exactly, but with excitement and the anticipation for some possible calamity.' Miss Soldene describes the road, a soft, sandy track cut into deep ruts, winding in and out among huge trees, 'sharp corners, unexpected fallen trunks, monster upturned roots, every kind of obstacle, six horses always galloping, the coach banging, creaking, swaying from side to side. Then suddenly we go, down over a mountain as steep as the side of a house, down into and through a rushing, roaring, tumbling, bumping, yellow river! Splash! Then with a "houps!" "hi!" and a big lurch, out again and up the opposite side, galloping, always galloping, breathless, the driver shouting, cracking his whip, and the horses shaking the water from their sides, tossing their heads, and jingling their harness; then out onto the land, soft and springy, covered with mossy turf and beautiful trees like an English park; away over more sand, leaving the mossy turf, and ploughing through sharp cutting, tough, rusty-looking tall grass, growing in huge tufts far apart. At last we come to a hut, full gallop, and the driver, without any preparation, pulls the horses up on their haunches.'

The reader is left almost breathless and Miss Soldene climbs down, her hands blistered with holding on. 'It was all lovely', she writes, 'except for the jolting.' It is certain she did not have the young Tasmanian for her driver for he would most certainly have given her a smoother ride.

Not only were the roads very rough but also dangerous. One of the results of the gold-rush was a revival of bushranging. Robbers roamed the scrub around the diggings and made frequent forays, attacking not only isolated travellers but even gold escorts when it was known that they were carrying bullion.

202

15 The bushrangers

The gold-fields naturally attracted all kinds, especially the 'old lags' the class of convict who, having served part of his time, had been liberated on condition of good behaviour. Hundreds crossed over from Tasmania and once arrived in Victoria found 'only too great an opportunity for the display of their criminal propensities and perverted behaviour'.[68] Quickly tiring of the hard work involved in mining, they took to bushranging and forming into bands swept the country, robbing in all directions. One particular band went so far as to board a ship whilst it lay at anchor in Hobson's Bay (a part of Melbourne harbour), overpower the crew and remove gold to the value of £25,000 – remarking, as they handed the boxes over the side of the vessel, that this was the best gold-field they had ever seen.

Victoria was only recently established as a separate colony and further encumbered with a monstrous influx of emigrants, her state of affairs was understandably somewhat disorganised, and this applied in particular to her police force; the roads were patrolled but only by a skeleton staff. To try and stem the flow of undesirable emigrants the legislature passed what was called the Convict Prevention Act. No person who had been convicted, and had not received an absolute free pardon, should be allowed to enter the colony. It further stipulated that all persons who came from Tasmania should be required to prove that they were free, before being allowed to land and any ship's captain who brought a convict into the colony was to receive a heavy fine. These restrictions helped but did little to relieve the problem regarding the bushrangers. These became so brazen that two ex-Tasmanians dared to 'bail up' passers-by on the St Kilda Road near the very centre of Melbourne and heading them into the shrubs robbed them there. The gold escort from the McIvor diggings was also plundered, its guards shot-up and over two thousand ounces of gold made off with.

New South Wales, not having the spectacular finds attributed to her neighbouring state, fared better in the beginning than Victoria and was relatively free

Opposite Ned Kelly. A portrait photograph he requested for his family and friends when he was told that there was no hope of a reprieve.

A gold escort; arrival at the Treasury, Sydney.

of bushrangers, but this state of affairs was of short duration for over the next decade a new school of bushranging came into being. The bands were no longer made up of ex-convicts but of native-born youths drawn largely from the sons of poor settlers who chose to take to the road partly out of a misguidedly romantic sense of adventure. They became known as the 'wild colonial boys'; men such as Frank Gardiner, Ben Hall and John Gilbert, and later the Kelly gang. They became, one might almost say, national heroes. 'In England', Professor Ward writes, 'the fame of Robin Hood or Dick Turpin pales before that of Drake and Nelson, and in America Sam Bass and Billy the Kid are almost entirely eclipsed by Washington and Lincoln. In Australia, however, whilst every child knows something of Ned Kelly, Macquarie, even to a great many adults, is just the name of a Sydney street favoured by men in the medical profession.'[69]

Few of these bushrangers committed brutal or cold-blooded crimes and generally speaking took pains to avoid unnecessary violence. The country people had a sneaking regard for their pluck and bearing and admired their dashing appearance, superbly mounted on stolen thoroughbreds. One of the newspapers reporting on their local gang, details (with affection, one feels) their attire, their 'broad-brimmed Manila hats turned up in front with an abundance of broad pink ribbon, satin neck-cloths and splendid brooches. The bridles of their horses were profusely decorated with rings and watches'. Many country people were in league with these 'wild colonial boys' or were afraid to report their movements to the police. The youthful law-breakers, in fact, took some pride in their reputations and were careful to behave accordingly. It would seem that even the law itself looked upon their activities with a certain lenience. David Collins, the Judge Advocate, tired, one presumes, of passing judgement

204

Left Bailed-Up, by Tom Roberts, a reconstruction of the Eugowra Rocks robbery. *Below* Ben Hall.

on petty thieves is said to have considered highway robbery 'one step towards refinement and at least a manly method of taking property'. Hardly a statement warranted to curb the miscreants.

And what about the 'wild colonials' themselves: Frank Gardiner, the illegitimate son of a Scottish free settler, and an Irish-Aboriginal servant-girl was born near Goulburn in 1830, and was already a talented horse-thief when still in his teens. His chief exploit appears to have been the holding up of the gold escort at Eugowra Rocks where he stole gold dust and notes to the value of £14,000; Eugowra was a daring feat which later was to inspire the painter Tom Roberts to do his well-known *Bailed-up* which he took the trouble to paint near the actual site of the robbery. Ben Hall, another of the 'colonial boys', is supposed to have been among those attacking at Eugowra Rocks and reading about him it is difficult not to be attracted to the man. Born in 1837, the son of an emancipist stock-man he had trained under his father and when twenty-five had leased a small farm near Wheogo in the Grenfell district and married the pretty daughter of a local squatter. In due course they had a son and Ben Hall, a hard-working man, was doing well with his farm. But from this time on, Hall appears to have been the victim of circumstances, more sinned against than sinning. Early in 1862 he was arrested on a charge of highway robbery but there seems to have been little or no evidence against him, indeed it looks very much as if the charges had been trumped up by an incompetent police inspector. Despite the lack of evidence he was sentenced to a month in gaol. When released he returned home to find that his wife had deserted him and absconded with a former policeman, taking their son with her. Some weeks later Hall was again arrested and this time on returning home he found that the house had been

205

burned – by the local police, so the neighbours told him. Small wonder, after this treatment, that the unfortunate Hall took to the high road. He and his gang, anyhow, are credited with a healthy number of hold-ups in different small New South Wales towns. At Canowindra he occupied the place for three days, issuing written passes to inhabitants wishing to leave the town temporarily. He showed a certain verve and for three years completely baffled the police. In the end Hall met his death betrayed by an informer. He was found sleeping near a creek by a party of seven policemen. Surrounding him they shot him, so the story goes, in cold blood as he awoke.

Hall lies buried in Forbes Cemetery and in the 1920s, the tomb, much neglected, had a new headstone placed over it, paid for, one reads, by an ageing man named Harry. Could Harry have been Ben Hall's son? One hopes so.

There were other bushrangers; Frederick Ward, alias Captain Thunderbolt who held the roads between Newcastle and the Queensland border. Another was Andrew George Scott who called himself Captain Moonlight. Moonlight and his gang raided a large property near Wagga-Wagga, detained all the guests and spent the week-end at the station, inviting others up from a neighbouring inn. One of the fifty-two 'guests' managing to escape warned the police and in the scuffle that ensued, a member of the gang got a bullet through his chest: 'Oh, God,' he cried, 'I am shot and I am only fifteen!'

There were also the Clarkes of Araluen who operated near Braidwood. Three brothers, they were more desperate than most and had several deaths to their name, and a reward of £5,000 on their heads. In the end one of their gang turned informer and betrayed them. James, the second brother, was already in prison, so only Thomas and John were brought to Sydney for trial. The crowds turned out to watch the notorious Clarkes, expecting to see 'burly, bearded desperadoes' and they were amazed when two 'beardless, sheepish country youths' appeared on the scene. Their age, however, did not excuse them and they were dutifully hanged after warning their brother James to pay heed to their end.

William Brown, a youthful bushranger, one of the Brady gang, was hanged at Hobart Town in 1826.

There were other minor bushrangers, but by and large, they had practically disappeared when, in 1878, the Kelly gang, a band of four, flashed onto the scene. Two were brothers, Ned the eldest and Dan the youngest of the three Kelly boys, Jim, the middle one, never being able to join the gang since he was already under arrest for horse stealing. With Ned and Dan were two young friends of theirs; Steve Hart and the tall and handsome Joe Byrne, just twenty-one. Their background was similar to that of the majority of bushrangers – the native-born offspring of Irish emancipists, brought up in the tradition of English tyranny and stories of British injustice, interpreted for them at close quarters in the brutality of the Australian prison camp.

The Kelly story is too well known to go into again in as much detail as it deserves. It is nevertheless gripping enough to be retold in a very condensed form. John, the Kellys' father, died when Ned was eleven years old, leaving their mother with eight children to feed. Poverty-stricken she moved to a slab hut near Glenrowan in north-eastern Victoria, a district now known as the

Kelly country. A lone widow, unable to make a living from farming, she turned the hut into a shanty house to provide meals and accommodation for the drifting streams of men travelling up and down the country roads; a motley collection of stockmen, cattle-duffers and horse thieves. The police had their eye on Mrs Kelly's bush hotel and it was not long before Ned was arrested for minor offences, two of them never proven. Jim as already mentioned, was given a five year sentence for horse stealing while Dan, only sixteen in 1877, was sent to jail on a trumped up case sworn to by false witnesses. No sooner was he released than they were after him again and a newly-enlisted constable named Fitzpatrick, attempting to arrest him, stormed into the Kelly's house. Fitzpatrick had been drinking and in any event was no match for young Dan who, resisting arrest, disarmed the policeman and, using a wrestling hold, forced him to the floor. In falling Fitzpatrick slashed his wrist against the door, an incident which he later elaborated on at headquarters, the cut becoming a bullet wound and the wrestling match a deliberate attempt at murder. The next day a whole posse of the law returned to arrest Dan, who in the meantime had taken to the bush. Not finding the boy the police arrested Mrs Kelly, charging her as an accessory. Ned was away in New South Wales at the time and when he heard

The remains of the Kelly homestead near Glenrowan.

about his mother's arrest he swore vengeance, declaring, quite rightly, that his family were being persecuted. The local Superintendent of Police had, in fact, openly stated that he considered them troublemakers and there was no question that he was deliberately harassing them in the hopes of driving them out of the territory. Mrs Kelly was sentenced to three years in Melbourne's Pentridge Jail, and her arrest, entirely unwarranted, was the direct cause of the drama to follow.

At this point the Kelly brothers took to the hills, the Warby Ranges behind Glenrowan to be joined by Steve Hart and Joe Byrne and through an intermediary they all four made an offer to surrender if Mrs Kelly was released. There was no response to their offer and throughout the latter part of 1878 police patrols were out looking for the boys, openly boasting that if they found them they would 'blow them to pieces'. On 25 October the Kellys came across four men heavily armed but not in uniform, camping by Stringybark Creek. They were, of course, the police for when actually tracking the gang they usually posed as horse dealers, or surveyors. Ned and Dan, aware that they would probably shoot to kill, decided not to give them a chance. Ned shot three of them dead, and a fourth escaped. After the Stringybark shooting, there was no turning back, the gang were exiled for ever if they wished to stay free. It was war now to the finish – months of hiding amongst barren ridges and stealing stealthily through the lengthening shadows of night. Young and high spirited they might even have enjoyed the first few months. Better mounted than the police, and justly proud of their horses, the four had little trouble in eluding the law moving freely between the homes of their relatives, and camps in the ranges close behind. So ably, in fact, did they conceal their movements that rumour supposed they shod their horses backwards. They made complete fools of the police and Ned wrote that he was 'not a bit afraid of them and know if they alone hunted me I would never be taken'. They showed their contempt for the law when robbing the bank of New South Wales at Jerilderie where they raided the police station, shut the police in their own cells and donned their uniform. The Government responded nervously by augmenting the police force and increasing the reward for the renegades' capture, putting a price of £2,000 on each of their heads, or the equivalent, in present-day currency, to about £30,000 for the four.

Ned now came out with a series of statements to the press, surreptitiously posting them to the editor. One ridiculed the police wearing civilian clothes. He had no wish, he said, to take innocent life but since 'the justice are afraid, or ashamed to wear their uniform' it was going to be difficult to differentiate. In another statement he stresses the fact that 'I have never molested workmen or farmers, except when they came between me and the police. I have never taken from a poor man when I could help it ... but I'll rob the banks, and if I get my hands on any mortgages, I'll burn them'. After this, notices announcing rewards for the Kellys' arrest were posted up in every village and town, 'and in many cases no sooner posted up than silently, by night, torn down.'[70] Children began playing games 'police and the Kellys' and the Kellys emerged alive and victorious from dozens of breathless encounters. The gang had become heroes to the people of the streets. Their deeds made exciting reading and became material for popular bush ballads.

High above the mountains,
So beautiful and grand,
Four young Australian heroes
In bold defiance stand.
In bold defiance stand, my boys,
The heroes of today.
So let us join together, boys,
And shout again horray!

Even the people who should have been most against them could not help but admire them, especially the women. Ned with his hazel, almond shaped eyes and curly dark hair became the object of feminine hero-worship and Joe Byrne, with the reputation for having a girl in every town of the Kelly country, also came in for his share of adulation.

The police, becoming desperate, called in some Queensland Aboriginal trackers to help them in their search. 'Black devils' Ned called them, writing that 'they could track him over bare stones'. One by one the Aborigines discovered the gang's hideouts, putting whole districts out of bounds. Life was becoming more difficult and a little after this, early in 1880, reports started coming in of thefts amongst the farms in the neighbourhood of Greta. Mould-boards had been wrenched off the ploughs. The black trackers pointed to the marks of high-heeled riding boots known to be worn by the gang, but this did not help much for what would they be wanting with mouldboards? It was only afterwards, at Glenrowan, that the police found out. Heating the metal over fire the gang had been hammering out a sort of primitive armour, shaping it over logs. 'Two round metal shields, laced together and supported by straps, protected the back, the chest, and stomach; and to these was riveted an apron covering the thighs. Only Ned Kelly wore a helmet – a cylinder, falling over the nape of the neck behind and, in front, two hinged pieces with a slit between them for the eyes'.[71] The total weight was nearly a hundred pounds and the young outlaws tested them by firing bullets at one another from ranges decreasing to within ten feet. Mrs Skillion, Ned's favourite sister, is said to have spent her evenings quilting the headpiece to protect her brother's head from the iron. The armour was Ned's idea since he was convinced that the black trackers would eventually lead the police to their last hideout and the armour, he hoped, would enable them to shoot it out.

For sixteen months, from February 1879 until June 1880, the outlaws remained in hiding. The police paying secret agents got hold of a young man named Arron Sherritt, a friend of Joe Byrne's, to inform on them and the gang hearing of this decided to take revenge; appearing one evening at Sherritt's hut, they shot him dead. Ned was becoming careless, money and supplies were running out and the black trackers were making it increasingly difficult to move around. Ned decided on a grand gesture; they would wreck the special train they knew would be sent with more police and trackers when Sherritt's death was reported at Melbourne. Did he hope to convince the authorities of their invincibility, or perhaps force their hand in obtaining Mrs Kelly's release by using hostages? Whatever the reason it was a desperate move. The train left Melbourne at 10.15 p.m. one Sunday and approached Glenrowan about 3 a.m. the next day.

In 1880 Glenrowan was a quiet little hamlet, consisting of a few houses, a general store and two bush hotels. The gang descending on it had no difficulty in taking possession: herding everyone into the Glenrowan Hotel they moved in to await the train, having first taken the precaution of forcing some men to tear up the rails north of the town. The train was late but eventually it was heard steaming into the station – and then it stopped. Somebody had managed to sneak out and flash a lantern on the line to warn the driver. It was still not too late, the outlaws could have got away. But Ned decided to stay and shoot it out. 'A man gets tired', he explained later, 'of being hunted like a dog in his native land. I wanted to see the thing end.' Donning their armour in the moonlight they lurched onto the verandah in front of the hotel. On beginning to fire they found that the weight of the metal impeded their movements and so retired back into the hotel, all except for Ned, who worked his way round the back hoping to take the police by surprise. In the heat of the fray he probably hadn't realised the extent of his wounds for he had been shot in the foot and the arm and lost so much blood that he fainted and lay unconscious for some hours, hidden in a wood, while the police fired continually at the hotel, sending a constant rain of bullets whistling through its flimsy walls. Just before dawn, Byrne, standing in the bar, was felled by a bullet.

During the shooting further reinforcements had arrived, making a total of fifty in the investing force. At 7 a.m. Ned Kelly regaining consciousness returned to the fray – but let Mr Brown tell the story, he is a specialist on the subject. Constable Arthur, behind a log, eighty yards from the hotel 'was lighting a match when he heard someone behind him. He turned, and the sight so surprised him he let drop the pipe from his mouth. Advancing through the light timber ... was a huge figure dressed in a grey cotton coat reaching past his knees. Most extraordinary of all was the head. Arthur goggled for some seconds before he concluded it was some madman who had conceived the notion of storming the hotel with a nailcan on his head. "Go back, you damn fool," he shouted, "you'll get shot".'

Further conversation followed and eventually Arthur 'fired at the helmet thinking to knock it off. The figure no more than staggered, and continued to advance, slowly putting one foot forward after the other with a macabre lurching motion. An opening in the helmet looked like a huge mouth. At this Arthur fired a second shot. The figure staggered again and still came on. Arthur fired at the body. He heard the bullets hum off. He was completely astonished.' Another policeman shouted that it was a ghost. The scene must certainly have presented a spectral quality with the ground mist of dawn swirling up and

around the staggering figure whose deep voice echoed loud from behind his visor. Laughing derisively and 'rapping his steel breast-plate with the butt of his revolver', Ned called his mates.

'Come out, boys, and we'll whip the lot of them', he cried. Dan and Steve came to the rear and commenced firing but were soon forced back again by a rain of bullets. Ned had twelve policemen shooting at him, firing at his legs and arms with double-barrel shot-guns. 'The outlaw tottered. His voice boomed under the helmet. "I am done. I am done." He could sustain the great weight no longer.'[72] He sank to his knees and fell back against a log.

The shooting at the hotel went on; the police had been firing at the house incessantly since five in the morning. It was now three in the afternoon and they appeared to be in a state bordering on hysteria. Someone had gone as far as tele-graphing Melbourne for arc lights and a small cannon. Finally they decided to

'Advancing through the light timber...was a huge figure...' Engraving from the *Illustrated Australian News*

211

Joe Byrne's body was taken to the Benalla police station and two days after his death was strung up outside to be photographed.

set fire to the hotel with kerosene. A Roman Catholic priest, Father Matthew Gibney, who had been standing among the crowd of onlookers, came forward at this point and volunteered to go into the building. There was some hesitation but Gibney just went ahead shouting back that it was his duty. Inside he found Byrne lying in the corridor dead, and the other two outlaws 'stretched full length, side by side on the floor with bags rolled up under their heads'[73] and their armour of plough shears laid to one side. A dog lay beside them shot through the heart. There was time to lift Byrne's body from where it lay in the corridor before the flames took over. Nothing could be done about Dan and Steve and only later were their remains dragged from the smouldering embers. It was supposed that they had committed suicide by poisoning.

Ned, shaken but dignified, was carried to the train where a doctor dressed his wounds while they steamed off towards Melbourne. In jail Ned proved a model prisoner and pale and self-controlled carried himself with great dignity while in Court when he was being charged with the murder of the three policemen at Stringybark Creek.

When asked if he had anything to say why sentence should not be passed on him, 'Kelly for so long silent rose and addressed the Court in a quiet, conversational tone as if quite at home, yet clearly and in excellent English so as to be heard distinctly throughout the Court room'[74]. He remarked that it was rather late to speak now but wished he had insisted on examining the witnesses himself. It would have shown matters in a very different light. It was impossible not to be moved by his speech. 'I do not pretend', he said, 'that I have led a blame-

212

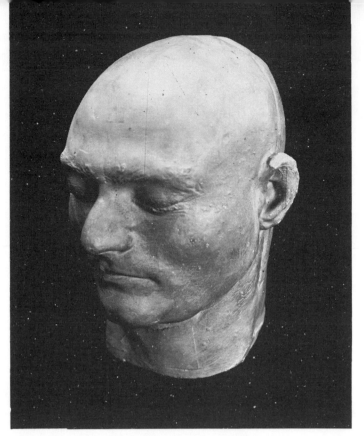

Ned Kelly's death mask. After his execution his head was cut off, shaved and oiled and a clay impression was made of it.

less life or that one fault justifies another; but the public, judging a case like mine, should remember that the darkest life may have a light side, and after the worst has been said against a man, he may, if he is heard, tell a story in his own rough way, that will lead them to soften the harshness of their thoughts against him, and find as many excuses for him as he would plead for himself.' 'For my own part', he told them later, 'I do not care a straw about my life...' he had no qualms about dying. 'I fear it as little as to drink a cup of tea.'

To while away the last hours in his cell, Kelly sat on his bunk singing bush ballads. His sang-froid seems to have upset his warder who reprimanded him. It was not seemly for a condemned man to appear so cheerful. Kelly's final visit was from his mother, detained in the same prison as himself and her last words to him were: 'Mind you die like a Kelly, Ned.'

On the eventful day Ned rose at 5 a.m., prayed for twenty minutes, and then lay down again. At 8.45 they removed his irons and the litany of the dying was administered. Some thirty people, officials, police and the press were present standing in the basement above which passed a gallery in which the gallows were placed. He appeared and his arms were tied and a white cap put on his head. They then walked him to the trap where the hangman stood with an oiled noose. A few seconds and the bolt was drawn.

There is some confusion about his last words. He did, in fact, make a remark: 'Ah well, I suppose it had to come to this', or was it 'Such is life'? Both were reported but no one could be quite certain. Perhaps the shorter of the two phrases is the most likely.

213

16 Melbourne, Queen of the Gold-fields

As we have seen already Melbourne and the Port Phillip district was surprisingly long in being established. Hobart, Brisbane, Perth and Adelaide, all antedated them. Nor did Melbourne, like other state capitals, originate under official auspices. It was given birth by an association of enterprising settlers from Tasmania. Needing new land on which to graze their stock, they had delegated John Batman, one of their number, to prospect for them. Crossing Bass Strait from Launceston, Batman entered Port Phillip and making his way up the Yarra, fell in with native inhabitants of the region. Batman was enthusiastic about the land and felt that in order to occupy it, he should make some form of exchange with its original owners; an unusual way of thinking for a man of the nineteenth century. Admittedly the exchange can hardly be considered a fair one but nevertheless it was better than nothing. For so many blankets and axes and a certain quantity of flour, Batman became the owner of 600,000 acres, a good slice of Victoria, a small pocket of which was to become the fair city of Melbourne.

In duty bound, Sir Richard Bourke, the Governor of New South Wales, repudiated Batman's purchase. Having neither licence nor authority he and his associates were considered to be trespassers on Crown Land. However, having made a formal protest, Bourke then took a more practical view in a despatch to London. 'It would be more desirable', he wrote, 'to impose reasonable conditions on Mr Batman and his associates than to insist upon their abandoning their undertaking.' The Home Government agreed with their representative and in May 1836 Bourke sent a police magistrate to inspect the new settlement, two years later appointing Charles Joseph La Trobe as Superintendent and eventually as Lieutenant Governor.

Robert Hoddle, a surveyor working for Bourke, planned the future city and with remarkable foresight provided for wide boulevards sweeping out to its eventual suburbs. However grandiose the plans they did not immediately constitute a city and the early settlers described Melbourne as a scattering of

Opposite The delicate tracery of cast-iron balconies is a distinctive feature of Melbourne.

215

John Batman, the founder of Melbourne.

weatherboard cottages and tents, with a few brick structures in between. Bullock drays bumped over the wheel ruts sending up clouds of dust and on dark nights it was difficult to keep to the streets. There were still wide intervals between the houses on either side, and if the vacant lots were not fenced off one found oneself riding off into the bush.

Then suddenly came the gold discovery of 1851 and almost overnight Melbourne swelled to Hoddle's plans and became a city, its harbour crowding with ships flying flags of every nation. By 1852 the streets of the city are still unpaved 'yet the shops which line them display the choicest articles and although the people live in tents, yet inside there may be perceived rosewood furniture and Turkey carpets'.[75] By the end of the year Melbourne was averaging about two hundred buildings a month. They grew, not in stately rows, but rose at intervals prominently amidst the surrounding desolation. For some reason difficult to explain the windings of the Yarra were completely ignored and, as Trollope remarks, it seems to have little to do with the city which spreads across two hills and across the valley which separates them. The founders, apparently indifferent to the scenic effects, did, however, take trouble over the layout and the general scale of its public buildings. The Town Hall was begun as early as 1856 and in the ensuing forty years were planned a whole plethora of similarly grandiose Victorian fantasies.

But before getting lost in these exuberant flourishes of builders' art there was the strange phenomena of the prefabricated buildings which appeared by the hundreds in numbered packing cases. A vast iron church made to the order of the Bishop of Melbourne arrived from Bristol in 1853. It measured seventy feet in length and fifty feet in breadth and could comfortably accommodate a congregation of seven hundred. The exterior was of galvanised iron, the interior being lined with thick planking covered with canvas and papered. Felt was stretched across the ceiling as an insulator from the heat. Topping it off came a forty foot tower and the completed assemblage cost only £1,000, a very reasonable price when one takes the transport into consideration. Two-roomed houses were also being sold at a cost, crate included, of £150 each, and in 1855 Melbourne ordered an enormous theatre designed on the lines of Paxton's Crystal Palace. Until very recently some of these prefabricated houses were still standing but a hunt for them proved abortive. Should any traces remain they can only be lengths of galvanized iron incorporated in somebody's garden wall. Two very fine examples of prefabrication do, however, remain: one is Governor La Trobe's cottage where he lived throughout his term of office from 1839 to 1854, and the other, Corio Villa out at Geelong, forty-five miles from Melbourne.

Corio Villa, or the 'wedding-cake-house' as it is called, has a curious story.

Opposite Bedroom in La Trobe Cottage, recently restored by the National Trust of Australia.

Overleaf A Cobb & Co. coach. Water-colour showing a corduroy road made of saplings.

Opposite A room in La Trobe Cottage, with a portrait of Lt. Governor Charles La Trobe by Sir Francis Grant.

Right Collins Street, Melbourne, in 1839. Water-colour attributed to William Knight.
Below The same street in 1853, two years after the first gold strike. Tinted lithograph by Thomas Edmund.

A street of prefabricated houses and the church ordered by the Bishop of Melbourne.

Late in 1855 an unusual shipment arrived from Glasgow and was unloaded at the pier; a motley assortment of cast-iron sections, classically moulded urns and heavy, wide-gauged roofing irons. To complicate matters further, there were no particulars of sender or receiver and for six months these cast-iron shapes lay cluttering up the wharf. When eventually the port authorities began to make enquiries they found that the foundry responsible for the shipping had been burnt out shortly after it opened and that the plans for the house had perished in the fire. It would appear that the 'pieces' had been shipped by some settler who intended to collect them on his arrival. In any event no one appeared to claim them and to rid themselves of this cumbersome jigsaw puzzle, the port authorities decided to put them up for auction. The attendance was small and Mr Alfred Douglas, the Geelong Harbour Master, acquired the lot for some few pounds and hauling the sections up the hill managed somehow to assemble them in proper order, thus finding himself the proud owner of what amounted to a small mansion, fretted around by an arched verandah.

The two things that never failed to impress people visiting Melbourne were firstly the rate at which it was growing and secondly its size. In no time it had outstripped its parent city, Sydney. Mark Twain refers to it as 'that juvenile city of sixty years', and estimates its population at half a million, some 200,000 more than Sydney. Almost overnight the 'Queen of the Gold-fields' had become the largest city of Australasia and Trollope, writing in 1871, judges it 'the greatest congregation of British human beings outside the British Isles'.

Melbourne was founded on gold and, when the output of gold began to diminish, industrial enterprises, financed by the accumulation of wealth from the mines, came to the rescue. There appeared to be no limit to the amounts at the architects' disposal and given unlimited credit they saw no reason to stint themselves and consequently indulged to the full. Parliament House, planned in the first high flush of the gold boom, rises in great fluted columns above

Corio Villa.

impressive flights of stairs; a handsome Treasury followed in 1862, and the Mint in 1869. The whole gamut of epochs and styles is run; engaged columns, rustications, pediments and pointed arches; from the Gothic north to the honeycombs of Islam, and from Palladio through to Wren and Hawksmoore. Every fashion and every known architect was drawn on. The builders had no compunction in borrowing from the past. Indeed, they conceived it to be their duty, and as Robin Boyd, the architectural historian, writes, 'they thought that nothing but the best from all past ages was good enough for this rich young country which they were helping to build at the bottom of the globe'.[76]

Foremost amongst the borrowers was Joseph Reed who arrived in Melbourne during the gold rush of 1852. As Boyd points out, he used a different historical style for almost every building he designed; Gothic for the churches, a successful Italian Renaissance pastiche for the State Library, and a much less successful one for the Town Hall. His smaller buildings often had a Romanesque flavour, while the Exposition Building, his most ambitious undertaking, where the ceremonial opening of the first Commonwealth Parliament was held in 1901, is hard to tabulate. It has, possibly, an American flavour and reminds one of buildings in Chicago of the same period. An interesting point is its connection with Dame Nellie Melba; her father, David Mitchell, was its contractor, and his daughter was already singing her way to world fame while it was being built. Handsome also is the great domed library of the Supreme Court and Government House by William Wardell who adapted the design of Queen Victoria's Osborne House on the Isle of Wight. Setting apart a special wing, he gave the Governor an enormous ballroom. It flattered the Governor but drew a sniff of displeasure from his Queen who failed to appreciate the competition. The grandeur of the building contrasts strangely to La Trobe's modest little prefabricated cottage which has been removed from Jolimont by the National Trust and re-erected in the Domain.

223

Wardell, with Reed, must be counted amongst Melbourne's most prolific architects and by far the most successful of Wardell's ventures is his St Patrick's Cathedral. As luck would have it, it escaped being endowed with bad copies of medieval glass and the bright Australian sun flows in, filtered by amber-tinted windows, playing in soft, golden motes over what Robin Boyd considers to be the best Gothic interior to have been built in the last four hundred years. High praise indeed.

Melbourne University holds another surprise. One approaches it up a double avenue of palms, a variety of palm that is indigenous to the Middle East and which was brought back in the form of seedlings, by Anzac[77] troops serving in the First World War. The surprise, however, is not the avenue but the quadrangle beyond the main entrance which is pure Tudor, built in 1854.

What one might call the 'Gold Style' when applied to purely domestic architecture was not as successful there as with public buildings. Possibly the owners were responsible and were too high-spirited to hear of restraint. One generally

A good example of the 'Gold Style'.

finds an almost embarrassing profusion of detailing; classical mouldings too deeply cut, and the capitals on bastard columns ridiculously over-leafed. Richard Twopeny, a journalist writing at the turn of the century, describes the interior of such a house. With tongue in cheek he tells us that turrets and flag-staffs abound and that 'the owners' notion of furniture begins and ends with upholstery. The frowsy carpets and heavy solid chairs of England's cold and foggy climate reign supreme beneath the Austral sun'. In the same essay Twopeny takes us on a tour of a millionaire's house. 'On entering the drawing room the first thing that strikes the eye is the carpet, with a stiff set pattern large enough to knock you down, and of a rich gaudy colour.' You raise your eyes and there opposite you is 'the regulation white marble mantel-piece, more or less carved, and a gilt mirror which we hope is not protected from the flies by green netting'. Pictures and knick-knacks rarely extend beyond the company's precincts. It would be considered a waste of good money to put pretty things in the bedroom. However, Twopeny admits that the Melbourne houses 'are certainly more expensively and perhaps better furnished than in any of the other towns. The Victorians have a much greater love of show than any of their fellows'.[78]

Twopeny is not the only writer to intimate that the average Australian of the last century made few, if any, concessions to the climate. Trollope complains bitterly that he saw 'a great pudding come into the room all afire when it has been so hot that one could hardly bear a shirt on one's shoulder'. The *Illustrated Australian News*, throughout the period of its publication, always made much of Christmas, and the subject was a great favourite with the engravers on its staff. For Christmas of 1865 we see crowds picnicking on a beach with their

Christmas in Australia.
Engraving from the
Illustrated Sydney News.

puddings, while a subsequent number of the same magazine sets the scene on a station verandah with ladies voluminously swathed and hatted plying their fans with the thermometer reading 120°F in the shade. It might be mentioned in passing that the summer months in Melbourne are much easier to bear than in Sydney. In Sydney 90°F is impossibly humid while 112° in Melbourne, though uncomfortably hot, is at least very dry.

Not all the houses were as Twopeny described them and among the exceptions must be counted 'Como' recently acquired by the National Trust. Built early in the 1850s it was bought by the Armitages in 1864 and has remained in the family until taken over by the Trust in 1959. One reads of the cherry-picking parties in the garden during the month of November, they became a regular feature in the round of entertainments and Mrs Charles Armitage appears to have been quite a character. She always slept with a loaded revolver under her pillow and her children remember being woken and taken out onto the verandah to watch their mother firing into the air to frighten trespassers. Left a widow in 1877, she took her children to Europe to complete their education and fresh milk being unobtainable during the long sea voyage, two cows were added to the entourage. A souvenir of this tour is a Swiss music box which still tinkles away in the drawing room.

Belonging also to this period is Mark Twain's spirited description of the Melbourne Race Meeting at Flemington. The big race is the Melbourne Cup and it has been run annually since 1861. It is Australia's National Day and as Twain writes 'it overshadows all other holidays ... overwhelms them I might almost say blots them out'. The women's clothes have been ordered months ago 'at unlimited cost, and without bounds as to beauty and magnificence. And so the grandstand makes a brilliant and wonderful spectacle, a delirium of colour, a vision of beauty. Champagne flows, everybody is vivacious, excited, happy, everybody bets. ... Day after day the races go on, and the fun and the excitement are kept at white heat; and when each day is done, the people dance all night so as to be fresh for the race in the morning. And at the end of the great weeks the swarms secure lodgings and transportation for next year, then flock away to their remote homes and count their gains and losses, and order next year's Cup Clothes, and then lie down and sleep for two weeks, and get up sorry to reflect that a whole year must be put in somehow or other before they can be wholly happy again.'[79]

Another established Melbourne custom are the weekends at the seaside on Mornington Peninsula, the eastern arm of Port Phillip Bay, due south of the city. Sorrento and Portsea are the two fashionable resorts and the peninsula at this point is only a mile across and has a sheltered beach on the bay shore, and an ocean beach on the other. In the 1860s Sir Frank Gavan Duffy, Chief Justice of Australia, bought land in the vicinity and built a house, calling it Sorrento because the surroundings reminded him of Italy. Others followed suit and a resort grew up named after the house. Portsea developed simultaneously and very soon a paddle steamer service was operating between the two places relaying them to the city. Wagonettes would meet the passengers at the Sorrento

The 'Husbands' boat'.

pier. A February number of the *Illustrated Australian News* of 1874 carried an article on what it jocularly refers to as 'The Husbands' boat'. The women, it explained, were lodged in rented cottages and had been sent ahead so that they escaped the unpleasant heat in summer 'when the suburbs became but portions of one vast Sahara'. There they waited for their husbands who would join them over the week-end. 'A steamer', as the *News* puts it 'started from Melbourne with its freight of lords of creation on Saturday afternoon' returning them to their desks on Monday morning. Portsea and Sorrento are still fashionable and there is a well-bred understatement about people's houses. Honey-coloured limestone and bleached wood are the building materials while fragile paper nautiluses decorate the mantelpieces. Sandy slopes fall away from the rough lawns of their seashore gardens, anchored with tufts of pale saltbush and twisted ti-trees, tugged into weird shapes, protect them from the prevailing wind.

For anyone visiting Melbourne the magic hour today is between five and six of a still, summer evening. Walk through its residential districts, starting in south Yarra, skirt the handsome Botanical Garden, then cross over the river to East Melbourne to Carlton, Fitzroy and Parkville. The traffic in these areas is not yet wearisome and it is here, in the mottled light of its tree-lined streets, that one gets the full flavour of the city, a remarkable tribute to the full-flood of Victorianism. Nearly every street, every house, whole terraces are laced over with an elegant tracery of cast-iron balconies. Façade after façade composed of iron columns, frieze, brackets, and balustrades throw delicate shadows on the recessed walls behind. Cast-iron gates and fences often close off a small garden thus completing the composition. It is the custom to paint these terraces all in

Left The Melbourne Botanical Gardens.
Below House at the corner of Powlett and
Gipps Street, unusual because of its openwork
cast-iron columns framed in wood. The
pendentive friezes are also in wood.

one colour and more often than not the whole house, the whole terrace is coated in white. The effect is enchanting. Not even the famous Garden District of New Orleans can do any better.

The first iron castings arrived from Great Britain in the 1830s and were, of course, destined for Sydney. But smelting of native ores took over very quickly and before the end of the century over a hundred Australian foundries could be counted, forty-two foundries producing castings in Victoria alone. At first local craftsmen copied imported designs and then by degrees local flora and fauna were incorporated; tree ferns, emus and kookaburras swallowing snakes, Aboriginal masks and trophies with native weapons. But the tree fern was the great favourite, its graceful fronds lending themselves admirably to a delicate, stylised design. Later, as the demand for ornamentation increased the builders turned to cement. Elaborate façades of brick were thrown up to hide the roof line and onto these were slapped parapets decorated with every known conceit; swags, urns, faces, shells – all cast in cement. Iron balconies joined the pedimented ends.

An example of cast cement building.

One of the interior courtyards of Melbourne's new Art Centre, built by Sir Roy Grounds.

As a contrast one must also stop and look at Melbourne's latest pride. This is its National Gallery, referred to as the Art Centre and reputed to have cost the city sixteen million dollars. The Centre, apart from its galleries, incorporates an art school, a theatre, and a concert hall capable of seating 2,500. Sir Roy Grounds, its architect, has chosen a severe style with somewhat chunky proportions, a contemporary version, if you wish, of a Roman palace of the Renaissance. Beautifully set stone walls unbroken by window openings, rise to a glazed clerestory. A great arch, reached across a bridge spanning a moat, marks the entrance; the doors, slightly recessed, being set in a glass screen curtained with sheets of falling water. This prodigal use of water in a country notorious for its aridity, gives a certain air of luxury; not unlike the great shallow bowls which used to continually overflow, splashing in the sunshine, from the corners of Sir Edwin Lutyens' Viceroy House in New Delhi. Once past the screen of water the interior sustains our first impressions of solid prosperity. It is immediately welcoming and soft under foot with thick yellow wool carpeting running from wall to wall, even rising up some of the vertical faces, deadening all sound. Stainless-steel escalators carry one up to the galleries faced through-out with large panels of pale smoky wood cut from the giant mountain ash, one of the many eucalyptus, the tallest hardwood in the world. The Museum's showcases are cleverly lit with black metal fittings that disappear into the frames. Particularly successful is the room housing the Oriental porcelains. The colours are warm and soft and beyond the cases zig-zags a wall of smoked glass giving onto an interior courtyard floored with grey pebbles and planted with bamboo, animated by great jets of water that spurt up spasmodically and splash down noisily through circular grills.

There are three internal courts and a great empty hall roofed over by panels of stained glass designed by Leonard French, described as 'a translucent Persian carpet in the sky'. There is no space here to elaborate on the Museum's fine collection of Australian and European paintings – Australian painting, or a certain aspect of it comes in another chapter – but suffice it to say that, as a whole, the Gallery gives a very pleasing sense of quiet and luxury rarely attained by the great galleries of Europe.

It would be impossible to leave Melbourne without reference to Adam Lindsay Gordon, the first poet to sing the praises of Australia's great outback. A life-sized bronze statue of him stands to his memory near Parliament House, and it shows him tall and lean, seated on a chair, dressed in a Crimean shirt, well-fitting cord breeches and top boots. His friends described him as being always very neat. They also talk a lot about the far-away look in his grey-blue eyes and the statue succeeds in making you feel that he gazes out, not on Melbourne traffic, but on some distant point that we cannot see.

Gordon arrived in Australia when he was twenty and during the sixteen years he lived in Australia he became entirely absorbed and identified with the country. His *Bush Ballads and Galloping Rhymes,* the last collection of his poems to be published, are filled with sensitive, nostalgic evocations of the out-back. Few have caught better the atmosphere of the bush; the outback with its terrible solitude, its sun-filled days and glittering nights. Gordon was a wonder-ful horseman, had an iron nerve and a magic influence over horses and would compose, it seems, to the clopping rhythm of his horse's hooves. Indeed, if one reads some of his verses aloud, the wonderful ride for instance in *From the Wreck,* one can almost hear the galloping of his horse. He was serving in the Mounted Police when he wrote this particular ballad and it tells of the time he was detailed, with one other, to warn the nearest telegraph station of a ship-wreck, the *Admella* having been driven ashore off the rocky coast of South Australia near Cape Northumberland:

> And faster and faster across the wide heath
>   We rode till we raced. Then I gave her her head,
> And she – stretching out with the bit in her teeth –
>   She caught him, outpaced him, and passed him, and led.

The poem ends with the young mare's death. She died of strain, one presumes.

> A short, sidelong stagger, a long, forward lurch,
>> A slight choking sob, and the mare had gone down.
> I slipp'd off the bridle, I slackened the girth,
>> I ran on and left her and told them my news;
> I saw her soon afterward. What was she worth?
>> How much for her hide? She had never worn shoes.

A scribbly gum or *Eucalyptus racenosa.* 'When the gnarled, knotted trunks eucalyptian seemed carved, like weird columns Egyptian'. From Gordon's *Bush Ballads and Galloping Rhymes.*

One reads how Gordon would compose while riding, halting his horse under the shade of some tree and casting his leg over the pummel of his saddle for a desk. John Riddock, a friend of his, would often ride out with him, and writes that 'he would mumble away in the saddle with his thoughts far away, and it was absolutely impossible to get anything out of him'. He would scribble on any odd piece of paper; when he wanted to publish something it was quite a business collecting all the bits and pieces. *The Stockrider* he wrote lodged in the limb of a gnarled old gum tree that had taken his fancy.

Gordon was a lonely person and would shut himself off from those around him. When horse-breaking he would pitch his tent as far away as possible from the station buildings. Probably his upbringing had something to do with his reticence, he was, after all, far better educated than the majority of the people he came in contact with. Yet despite the difference of background, he was capable of making strong attachments. Billy Trainor, a clown in a travelling circus, became one of his closest friends. Because of Gordon, Trainor gave up his job and took up horse-breaking[80] and when the poet shot himself Trainor went and bought the adjoining lot in the Melbourne cemetery where he lies buried. Gordon was the bushman's ideal and certain of his lines became homespun proverbs. The following lines are a perfect example

> Life is mostly froth and bubble,
>> Two things stand like stone,
> Kindness in another's trouble,
>> Courage, in your own.

This kind of verse would be found hanging on the walls of many an outback homestead.

Gordon's father had been an army career man and, after years of service in the Bengal Cavalry, was invalided home. He first went to the Azores, renting a pretty house among vineyards on the Island of Fayal where Gordon was born. From there, the family moved to Cheltenham, popular amongst retired East India Company officials on account of its clement weather.

As to Gordon's mother, she was a spoilt East Indian heiress, tall and graceful with a very long neck and something of an eccentric. Bored with life in Cheltenham, she spent most of her time travelling abroad, swathed in long clinging muslins while everybody else was learning how to manage the cumbersome hoops bulging out their cinolines. Gordon's father to help defray her extrava-

gances, started working again. A gifted linguist, talking Hindustani like a
native, he became Professor of Oriental languages at Cheltenham College, a
post which he held until his death. Both parents incidentally were related to the
Duke of Richmond, and in fact were first cousins.

Young Gordon was eleven when they left the Azores and as might be expected attended his father's school, graduating in 1848, to the Royal Military
Academy at Woolwich, later keeping some terms at Merton College, Oxford.
Good at sports, but not studiously inclined, and totally undisciplined, he seems
to have been a constant worry to his masters and later, inheriting his father's
passion for horses, got involved in the rough and ready world of the training
stables, 'skylarking around' as he himself terms it, with jockeys and boxers,
even fighting with the great Tom Sayer. Gordon's 'skylarkings' must have
been of quite a serious nature for even his father, who adored his only son,
thought it advisable that he get away for a year or two from his associates. Many
sons of good families went to Australia lured by the rolling acres of empty land
and together the two decided that was the place young Gordon should go.
There was a sad parting on the gangway of the ship 'when neither father nor
son could speak–so utter was their misery'.[81] Later in memory of this voyage
he wrote *An Exile's Farewell* and how sad the third verse:

> How brightly gleams the orb of day
> Across the trackless sea!
> How lightly dance the waves that play
> Like dolphins in our lee!
> The restless waters seem to say,
> In smothered tones to me,
> How many thousand miles away
> My native land must be!

And then the last line:

> Some briny drops are on my cheek,
> 'Tis but the salt sea spray!

There is also a pathetic ode to his sister which appears in

Whisperings in Wattle-boughs:

> Oh, tell me, sister dear, parting word and parting tear
> Never pass'd between us; – let me bear the blame.
> Are you living, girl, or dead? bitter tears since then I've shed
> For the lips that lisp'd with mine a mother's name.

Gordon's ship berthed at Port Adelaide in November 1853. With him he had
brought a letter of introduction to the Governor of South Australia, Sir Henry
Young, but the young man scorned to use it and instead enlisted in the South
Australian Mounted Police as a trooper. Leaving the police he became a horse-
breaker and in 1862 married a Miss Park, the niece by marriage of the owner of
an inn where he had been recuperating from a bad fall. Maggie Park was barely

Adam Lindsay Gordon.

five foot high and Gordon addressed her always as 'girl'. 'She has more pluck', he wrote to a friend, 'in her little finger than ever I had in my whole body.' They were married at Mount Gambier a few miles from the coast, about midway between Melbourne and Adelaide.

The place is famous for its blue lake, a curious natural phenomenon that has never been satisfactorily explained. The lake is of volcanic origin and lies at the bottom of a crater and every year, usually late in November or early December, suddenly, almost overnight, turns to a vivid, indescribable blue. The blue then gradually fades as the weeks pass, becoming sombre and dark and almost forbidding in appearance. Carbonate waters are usually clear and chalky blue in colour when in sufficient depth, and since Lake Gambier has a high calcium carbonate content its surprising blue is to be expected. What is surprising, however, is the overnight change, late in the year, from dark to vivid electric blue.

This eerie place is the site of one of Gordon's most famous exploits. An obelisk marks the place where he jumped his horse, *Red Lancer,* over a post and rails running around the narrow rim of the lake. One day returning from a kangaroo hunt with a party of friends, they had dared Gordon. Very short sighted, never able to see beyond his horse's ears, the leap could have proved fatal. The rails were of normal height but the ledge, the further side, is exceedingly narrow and falls away abruptly to drop four hundred feet, sheer down to the lake, which is very deep. If Gordon had made the slightest slip both he and his horse would have gone hurtling down to their deaths.

234

Near Mount Gambier is to be found the pretty little cottage Gordon purchased in 1864, after his marriage. He lived there for two years and these were
probably the happiest times of his life. The couple would walk and ride over the
cliffs at Cape Northumberland. Gordon was a powerful swimmer and would
swim summer and winter, striking out two miles or more into the bay. He had a
total disregard for danger, taking no notice at all of the sharks or the powerful
rip tides. It was here he wrote his *Song of the Surf* and as always in his poems,
there is a touch of melancholy.

> White steeds of ocean, that leap with a hollow and
> wearisome roar
> On the bar of ironstone steep, not a fathom's length
> from the shore,

and then

> You break, with a rainbow of glory, through the spray
> of your glittering tears,
> Is your song a song of gladness? a paean of joyous
> might?
> Or a wail of discordant sadness for the wrongs you
> never can right?

The following verse describes the drowning of a swimmer:

> When against the rock he was hurl'd, and suck'd again
> to the sea,
> On the shores of another world, on the brink of eternity,

the swimmer could well have been himself.

In 1865 Gordon was elected to the South Australian House of Assembly as
a Member for the District of Victoria but he had no gift for public speaking and
taking the money he inherited at his parent's death, he opened a livery stable at
Ballarat and it was while at Ballarat that he won his first great race, the Melbourne
Hunt Cup. He won three steeplechase races at Flemington in one afternoon,
two of these on his own horse. It was a record that put him at the top of the list
as chief amateur steeplechase-rider in Australia.

Skilful and brave a rider as he was, his eyesight caused him a series of bad
falls. More than once he fractured his skull and in 1870 he had a particularly
bad fall from which he never really recovered. 'Since that heavy fall of mine',
he writes, 'I have taken to drink. I don't get drunk, but I drink a good deal
more than I ought to for I have a constant pain in my head.' A combination of
his health and money worries exaggerated his habitual state of melancholy and
taking his rifle one morning he rose at dawn and walking off into the scrub,
shot himself. 'Girl', his young wife, remembers a faint brushing of his lips as
he crept silently out of the room.

17 The first Australian painters and the Heidelberg School

The early drawings and water-colours of Australia were mostly the work of topographical or natural history draughtsmen. The men sketching were not really interested in landscape as such, they found the country monotonous, even hostile, and, if for some reason or other, they attempted a painting of this nature it was more likely to be a view of a distant town framed by a kind of vegetation they would like to have found there: the brown and sepia trees of eighteenth-century Europe. They appeared incapable, or stubbornly refused, to render the eucalyptus in its true colours, nor would they allow it its graceful but individual habit of growth, and, although it is invisible, one feels that ivy clings to the mottled, falsely lichenous trunks of the horticultural fantasies they limned in their stead. Tree ferns and the exotic *Xanthorrhoea*, or grass tree, were among the few concessions these painters were willing to make and these, judiciously placed, in conjunction with a kangaroo or two or a group of wandering natives were considered indulgence enough for a land the majority of the 'exiles' found disappointingly commonplace.

Amongst the early painters only two men seemed to have really interested themselves in trying to depict the real character of the country; one was John Glover, who had had a long and successful career as an artist in England, and the other an Austrian, Eugène von Guérard, whose father had been a Court painter to Francis I. Glover, a great admirer of Poussin and Claude Lorrain – he owned two Claudes of his own–had, like the masters he tried to emulate,[82] made a lifelong study of light and on emigrating with his family to Tasmania at the age of sixty-three it was the luminosity of this new land that struck him; the brightness of the Pacific sun and the haze of its dying as it burnished the

Opposite Spring Street, Melbourne, by Charles Conder, one of the nine by five paintings from the 1889 exhibition.

Overleaf Landscape by Eugène von Guérard.

slim trunks of a grove of river gums. 'There is a remarkable peculiarity', he writes in 1835, 'in the trees of this country; however numerous, they rarely prevent you tracing through them the whole distant country.' Several canvases of his bear witness to the truth of this observation.

Twenty-two years separate the two men whose paintings are so strikingly similar that they could, in fact, lead to some confusion for those not familiar

Grass trees at Yankalilla, with the red kangaroo. Drawing by George French Angas.

with their work. Von Guérard, trained in Vienna at the height of the Biedermeier period, was one of the romantic realists. It was the fashion, as with the Pre-Raphaelites a little later, to try and render what they saw in all its exactitude, down to the minutest details. Von Guérard, like Glover, was struck by the light and the way it caught the foliage of Australia's unique trees. He, perhaps better than any other, caught the particular way in which a stand of distant gums cushioned the distances of a hilly landscape, the young tender growth at the top of the trees reflecting a glitter that was almost like glass.

Glover and von Guérard were not the only painters attempting landscapes. Nicholas Chevalier, born in Russia of Swiss parents' and Louis Buvelot were also exhibiting large canvases, and with them a third, William Charles Piguenit, a native-born Tasmanian, of French extraction. Highly proficient in their art, they were not as successful as either Glover or von Guérard at capturing the elusive quality of the Australian countryside, and their views, if found in a London sale room, would not immediately proclaim their distant

Opposite Landscape by John Glover.

241

Tree ferns. Water-colour by Nicholas Chevalier.

Conrad Martens; a self-portrait.

origin and at the first hurried glance could easily be attributed to one of the painters of the Barbizon School.

Conrad Martens is yet another painter to be considered, and Martens can almost be classed as one of the founders of the Australian school. He was an English-born German whose father had been posted to London as Austrian Consul. Retiring from the diplomatic service, his father had moved to the country and Martens was brought up in Devonshire. With a talent for drawing he had been allowed to apprentice himself to the romantic water-colourist, Copley Fielding. In 1833, aged thirty-one, he left on a trip for India and on his way there met up with Captain Fitzroy and Darwin on the *Beagle* anchored at the time at Rio. Augustus Earle, the expedition's topographical draughtsman having fallen ill, Martens was offered the post and accepted. He stayed with them for two years and left the expedition at Valparaiso, and instead of going to India made his way across the Pacific to Sydney where he remained until his death in 1878.

Martens was a prolific painter, working mostly in washes and water-colours. Typical of his time, he concentrated largely on romantic views, working in and around Sydney. The sun sets over the harbour in a blaze of Turneresque light that picks out the prominent landmarks, whose crenellated walls are mirrored in a glassy sea shot with all the colours of a milky opal. His views are charming and much collected and yet they fail, except when dealing with the tropical north, to capture the essential spirit of the country. The trunks of his eucalyptus are correctly observed and sweep upwards, untidily peeling their bark, but when it comes to the foliage it becomes the burnt umber, lateral spreading growth of Europe not the downfalling of pointed leaves, the true character of the

242

Australian gum. It is the trees of a soft Devon that Martens has in mind's eye, they assert themselves in his supposedly foreign scene–willy-nilly he has transported them to Botany Bay! and as Marjorie Barnard so aptly puts it, 'the light and air eluded his brush. Its beauty haunted and escaped him'.[83]

It was to elude all the painters who plied their brush in this new colony, and it was not until well on in the nineteenth century that artists, encouraged by the revolutionary tendencies exhibited by the Impressionists abroad, were able to break away from the old influences and paint what they really saw.

Four men were responsible for what became known as the Heidelberg School; Frederick McCubbin, Thomas – better known as Tom – Roberts, Arthur Streeton and Charles Conder. McCubbin was the son of a Melbourne baker who had been apprenticed to a coach painter and Roberts was the son of an editor working on a small English newspaper. At the age of thirteen he emigrated to Australia with his widowed mother and having only the most rudimentary schooling started off working as a photographer's assistant. Arthur Streeton's father was a schoolmaster in the State of Victoria and Streeton himself was apprenticed for a time to a lithographer. As for Charles Conder he was sent to Australia to work for an uncle when he was sixteen and later got a job doing engravings for the *Illustrated Sydney News*. McCubbin and

A View of Sydney Harbour, by Conrad Martens.

Above Arthur Streeton at the age of 24, painted by Tom Roberts in 1891. *Above, right* Charles Conder, by Toulouse-Lautrec.

Roberts, born in 1855 and 1856 respectively, were the oldest in the group by about ten years. Streeton and Conder were practically the same age. Roberts, the acknowledged leader of the movement, studied painting under Eugène von Guérard, the Curator of the Melbourne National Gallery, and afterwards went to England for four years. Returning to Australia in 1885, he met Streeton who had also studied at the Melbourne National Gallery School. Roberts at that time was spending his week-ends painting in the country at Box Hill, camping out with Frederick McCubbin, who was shortly to become Master of the National Gallery Drawing School. Both men were impressed by the young Streeton's work and asked him to join them on their painting expeditions. Charles Conder joined the group after meeting Roberts, who was on a brief visit to Sydney in 1887.

While in Europe Roberts had had no direct contact with the controversial Impressionist painters in France, but he nevertheless felt the repercussion and felt it strongly enough to return home fired with a zeal for the great outdoors – with the intention of painting in the *plein air*, an unusual procedure in those days. The outdoors for young working men meant week-ends in the country camping, and Heidelberg was the name of the district near Melbourne that became their favourite haunt. Heidelberg is now a suburb, but in Roberts's youth it was still only a small township above the city overlooking the green Yarra Valley, a quiet place laced with willow-fringed backwaters. From tents the painters moved to á large weatherboard house at Eaglemont and later to the stables of an old stone house called Chaterisville, sitting in a neglected garden.

They were still camping but under more comfortable conditions. Their fare consisted of chops and tomatoes cooked on an open fire swilled down with billy-can tea. 'Give me one summer again', writes Conder to Roberts from London in later years, 'with yourself and Streeton – the same long evenings – songs – dirty plates – and the last pink sky. But these things don't happen, do they, and what is gone is over.'

Young, enthusiastic, the painters soon attracted others to them. Their work, strictly speaking, was not Impressionistic; no divided touches of broken colour, rather an ordered but free interpretation of what they saw. Whistler rather than Manet was their master and through him no doubt they were conscious of the newly fashionable Japanese prints. Conder's judicious placing of blacks and his treatment of greys in his delicious *Departure of SS Orient* hanging in the Melbourne Gallery is very reminiscent. Above all the group was passionately nationalistic, especially Roberts and Streeton. It was the mystique of Australia they wanted to capture; the blinding light of its beaches, and the startling whiteness of a woman's dress as she moved under the luminous shade of her parasol, across the sand; the heat-haze of noon that smudged the distances between the trees and the hot wind that sent the dust spiralling in clouds over burnt hill-sides. Their blacks are luminously black and their colours clear and limpid. They mastered the anatomy of the gum tree, and one can almost smell the pungent odour of the fires that flicker round the billy-cans. Their ground is dry underfoot and loud with the crackling of the eucalyptus' untidy litter. Streeton, in a letter he wrote to Roberts, expresses in parts what he felt about Australia. '.... and the great gold plains, and all the beautiful inland Australia, and I love the thought of walking into all this and trying to expand and express it in my way. I fancy large canvasses all glowing and moving in the happy light and others bright, decorative and chalky and expressive of the hot trying winds and the slow immense summer. It is *immense* and droughts and cracks in the earth, and creeks all baked mud ... I love Australia ....' Certainly, Streeton succeeded in showing us a beautiful side to this strange country, and he and Roberts, together, were the first painters to really discover its true character.

The Heidelberg School held their first exhibition in August 1889 at Buxton's Gallery, Melbourne and it was advertised as an *Exhibition of Nine by Five Impressions*. Nine by five represents the exact measurements of a cigar-box lid and the paintings were rapid sketches in oil. Streeton, just twenty-one, exhibited about forty paintings and Conder, a year younger, produced about the same number. They were reasonably priced, the most expensive painting being seven guineas, and, in spite of a sneering press, they sold very well.

Conder left Australia for Paris in 1890, never to return, and Roberts and Streeton, attracted probably by the beauty of the harbour, moved to Sydney, where they established another of their temporary camps at Sirius Cove, a picturesque spot on the harbour, below Mosman, the site of the present Taronga Park Zoo. Roberts had just started on his remarkable canvases depicting outback subjects typical of the Australian scene: *A Mountain Muster, Shearing the Rams* and his splendid *The Breakaway*. 'Paint what you like and

Spring, by James Jackson, a rapid oil sketch that shows the brilliance of light so typical of Australia. The painting is later in date than the majority of the Heidelberg School's work but never-theless shows a strong influence.

love what you paint', he writes, 'and on that I have worked; and so it came that being in the bush and feeling the delight and fascination of the great pastoral life and work I have tried to express it.' How fortunate for us that he felt like this. The result has been an unforgettable series of paintings.

McCubbin also planned a whole sequence of paintings depicting bush life but, as Bernard Smith writes in his *Australian Painting*, a note of melancholy creeps into his scenes 'in sharp contrast to the sun-drenched optimism and gaiety of spirit which animated the landscape impression of Roberts and Streeton'. *Down on his Luck*, depicted an unsuccessful gold digger and the *Lost Child*, inspired no doubt by Marcus Clarke's pathetic tale *Pretty Dick*, are two of his subjects. Children getting lost in the bush was a common occurrence in frontier life and McCubbin's painting is the study of a little girl, quietly crying amongst a tangle of undergrowth and trees. It is sad but not as traumatic as the story which McCubbin was half illustrating. The writer brings out the full horror of such an experience and Marcus Clarke's *Pretty Dick* is hard to forget: they called him Pretty Dick when he was yet a baby on board the *Star of Peace*, an emigrant ship. Pretty Dick's father was a shepherd and lived in a log hut on the edge of the plain and had five thousand sheep to look

The Lost Child, by McCubbin, painted at Box Hill in 1886.

after. Everyone on the station called him Pretty Dick, even the cockatoo. 'He was a slender little man with eyes like pools of still water.' His skin, 'where the sun had touched it, was a golden brown, and his hands were the colour of the ripe chestnuts his father used to gather in England years ago'. He had 'hair like a patch of sunshine, and a laugh like rippling water', and despite his name he was a manly little fellow.

The story is set in the middle of a blistering summer and 'Pretty Dick sat gazing between the trunks of the gum-trees into the blue distance'. He then turns towards the dark ranges and remembers the creek running deep in the bush. With Clarke we experience Pretty Dick's every emotion. Wandering further than he had intended, he gets lost. Towards the first evening he sees the overseer a long way away and shouts. But the distance is too great and the man, if he had heard him at all, took his cry 'for the scream of a parrot'. Terror grips the child, another hot day and then on the second night the poor little boy is delirious.

'They looked for him for five days, on the sixth, his father and another came upon something, lying, hidden, in the long grass at the bottom of a gully in the ranges. A little army of crows flew heavily away. The father sprang to earth ... Pretty Dick is lying on his face, with his head on his arm ....'

247

18 Horizons

Dying in 1943, Streeton was the longest lived of the four principal Heidelberg painters and a great deal happened to his country during the three-quarters of a century that represented his life-span. This young nation which he had learned to interpret so well had played an heroic role in two of the old world's major conflicts, and between the wars had forged its independence, founding a Federal capital in the A.C.T., Australia's Capital Territory, a division of land which represented a compromise between Sydney and Melbourne. Both cities coveted the prestige of the Federal Parliament but both agreed that neither should have it.

Melbourne with the help of her gold had progressed rapidly and for years had been a serious rival to Sydney. By 1911, however, Sydney had regained her old ascendancy, and as things stand she can now boast some 300,000 more inhabitants than Melbourne. Sydney now shines with skyscrapers sheated in glass, rearing upwards framing her harbour; and out in front, right at her heart, projecting into the sea, rides the most beautiful, certainly one of the most expensive, buildings ever erected – her Opera House. It sits like a great, pearly white nautilus borne up out of the deep – a twentieth-century Taj Mahal. As a building it has been much criticised and the pessimists have prognosticated the direst of futures as far as its acoustics are concerned. Even should they prove right, which is highly improbable, even should it turn out nothing but a magnificent shell, it will remain nevertheless a very remarkable achievement – the world's most monumental piece of sculpture.

But enthusiasm projects one too quickly for one must consider Sydney's splendid nineteenth-century buildings. Measured alongside those of Melbourne, they certainly hold their own; for instance, there is her splendid

Opposite Sydney Heads. Water-colour by Conrad Martens.

Overleaf Early Morning, Heidelberg, by Walter Withers.

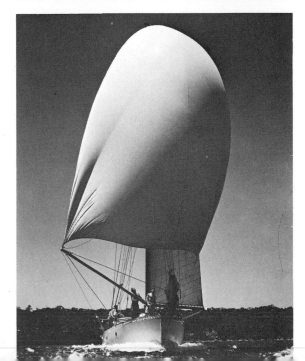

Top The sweeping roof of the Sydney Opera House, like a great, pearl-white nautilus, is strongly reminiscent of the billowing sails of yachts in Sydney harbour *(bottom)*. *Middle row* Model of the Sydney Opera House.

Opposite Glover's house and garden in Tasmania, by John Glover.

253

Above Sydney University.
Marble figure by A.
Simonetti of John Henry
Challis, one of the
University benefactors.
Above, right Marble
figure by P. Tenerani of
William Charles
Wentworth, the founder
of the University.

Post Office with its fine sculptured details, a portrait of her architect James
Barnet appearing over one of the arches carved by a stonemason who saw him
as a kind of bearded Moses, prophetically pointing a finger. There is also the
magnificent ugliness of the Town Hall, the tortured work of at least eight
different architects; and the Romanesque extravagances of the Queen Victoria
Markets which takes up a whole city block and now house, rather awkwardly it
must be admitted, a battery of offices and shops. There are numerous private
houses judiciously situated on the different points of the harbour, built in the
Tudor and romanticised Gothic revival styles with plastered brick-work and
gabled roofs edged with wooden bargeboards of fretted lace. It was the fashion
towards the end of the nineteenth century to use dark liver-coloured bricks
but daubed now, in whitewash and surrounded by lawns, frangipani, jacar-
andas and magnolias, these houses take on quite another air. Sydney also has
its cast-iron; streets of terraced houses faced with balconies line the steep
roads of Paddington, Paddington being a district the equivalent to Chelsea in

London. There are also some very fine examples of cast-iron work at Hunter's Hill, and further afield still, in the country at Bowral.

Vaucluse House and Lindsay are amongst the handsomest of the large private houses in the Tudor style, Vaucluse once the home of the renowned William Charles Wentworth, now a State Museum, and Lindsay serving as the headquarters of the New South Wales division of the National Trust.

Amongst the scores of architects practising in Sydney during the second half of the nineteenth century by far the most important was a romantic little figure, the son of a rich London merchant, called Edmund Thomas Blacket. He was twenty-five when he landed in 1842 and with him he brought his wife, a pretty woman he had married much against his family's wishes. It would seem that he had no formal architectural education behind him, although he must have had some sort of academic training, for he was already building the first of an incredibly long list of churches and secular buildings by the end of the following year. In all he designed fifty-eight churches and in middle age

Edmund Thomas Blacket, at the age of 25.

was referred to as 'the Christopher Wren of Australia'. St Mark's on Darling Point was one of the most successful of his Gothic interpretations, another being St Stephen's, Newtown, one of the suburbs. Both churches were topped with remarkably well-proportioned spires. As Mr Herman points out, he was, architecturally speaking, a copyist 'following plan forms settled by long tradition, but he was able to arrange parts with such a sure touch and harmony of material, scale, and proportion, that true architecture resulted'.[84] His placing of buildings was also remarkably happy, they seemed inevitable on their sites.

Appointed Colonial Architect in 1849, Blacket resigned the post five years later when promised the commission for the main building of Sydney University. Work was started in 1854 and completed in about 1860. Included in the buildings he was responsible for are the Quadrangle and the Great Hall with its fine cedar ceiling inspired by London's Westminster Hall. The carving throughout is remarkably firm and crisp and one's only regret is that Blacket did not draw from the country's unique collection of fauna when designing his gargoyles.

255

Sydney University:
central door, east front,
looking towards the Quad.

Opposite Australia Square,
Sydney.

Let us jump now to the present, to our own century, to the excitement of a shining new Sydney; the cylindrical tower in Australia Square sweeping in vertical lines rising six hundred feet above street level, its forty-seventh floor a revolving roof-top restaurant that turns at the rate of one mile every twenty-two hours, and completes a full circle while one is eating. There are other revolving restaurants in the world, but none have the stupendous view that Australia Square offers its visitors. Sitting at one's table, feeding off the sweetest oysters in the world, one overplanes the city – Phillip's Sydney Cove. How prophetic his words that echo across the years: '... anchor so close to the shore' he writes to Lord Sydney, that 'the greatest ships may unload'.

It is said of Sydney that she has the atmosphere of a city on everlasting holiday and from this vantage point, at the top of Australia Square, the reason is plainly apparent. Beyond the tongues of houses, each side of the Heads, runs a perimeter of golden beaches; to the south, Bondi, Coogee, Maroubra, Malabar, Cronulla, and to the north Manly, Collaroy and Narrabeen – the list is endless. A good proportion of the population of Sydney – just over

256

two and half millions, more than half the population of the entire State – spend much of their free time on these beaches.

The beaches I have named are surfing beaches and on most days of the year great green-blue waves crash in a roar of whirling foam obliging one, if one is anywhere near the water, to shout to be heard. Flags mark the area on the beach between which you are supposed to bathe, some two hundred yards which is patrolled by trained life-savers, mainly young men in the sixteen to twenty-three age-group who belong to the different clubs. They sit on the beach beside reeled life-lines and are on the alert for anyone in difficulty. During the last sixty years 130,000 lives have been saved, and one supposes a good many further rescues have gone unrecorded. Dangerous rip-tides are generally the cause of the trouble, the swimmer gets tired and a big wave breaks over him, he swallows water and then panics. It is surprising how even the strongest swimmer can be drowned in these circumstances. Mass rescues are quite common and one is recorded at Bondi towards the end of summer 1938. Forty people were pounded unconscious by a series of huge waves that hit the beach without any warning. The ordinary waves are usually called swells and they travel in sets of from three to seven and are generally the aftermath of heavy seas somewhere out in the wide ocean. Leaving the storm areas they fan out, much like ripples in a pond, and it is these huge giants that the Sydney surfers ride.

The Pacific Ocean produces the finest surfing in the world and the three shores upon which the experts consider the surf best are, in order of precedence, Hawaii, which has the largest waves, then Australia and thirdly California.

Surfing as a sport originated in the Pacific Islands, among the Polynesians. Sir Joseph Banks while on the *Endeavour* writes of watching the natives perform in Tahiti. 'It was in a place where the shore was not guarded by a reef as was usually the case. Consequently a huge surf fell upon the shore and a more dreadful one I have not often seen.' Banks tells us that the best European swimmer would most certainly have been drowned and yet 'in the midst of these breakers ten or twelve Indians were swimming'. One can imagine the scene; the glass-green waves turning over in the sun, breaking into a crashing, tumbling mass of foam that sweeps headlong onto the pebbly beach, lacing the shore-line. The sea edge is smoking with the fume from the waves, a mist that sweeps upwards obscuring the feathery heads of palms growing out from the nearby point. Into these huge, crashing monsters, rising twenty to thirty feet high on the skyline, plunge the young, cinnamon-coloured Tahitians, their black hair falling in shiny, black snakes on their square shoulders. Banks says that they were using boards ripped out from the stern of an old war canoe. In Hawaii certain sexual implications were involved with the pastime. Should a man and a woman ride in on the same wave together, it was the custom to consummate a still closer union on the beach. The missionaries, when they arrived, took a dim view of the promiscuity involved and, by dint of constant preaching, managed to curtail the procedure.

Swimming as a sport was not as yet a habit indulged in by Europeans and by degree the natives themselves lost interest in it. A sister I met stationed on the Isle of Kauai remembers surf boards being used as writing desks in the school room where she taught. An old sport among the islanders, it was not until the 1880s that Sydney saw its first real surf rider. He was a Hawaiian named Tommy Tanna, employed as a gardener's boy at Manly. Large crowds would gather to watch him speeding in on his board towards the shore. His admirers, had to be early risers for local by-laws forbade swimming in the surf between sunrise and sunset. Municipal authority frowned on total immersion in daylight, which was regarded as immodest and the glorious beaches were principally a playground for children. Women did not start to bathe in public until about 1910. A newspaper editor called William Gocher was the first to revolt against these stringent rules and one Sunday in September 1902 he strode boldly out at midday on Manly Beach and repeated the procedure on various occasions, openly challenging the police to arrest him. Finally public opinion forced the Manly Council to rescind its by-law.

In 1906 the first surf-club in the world was founded at Bondi and more followed. In 1922 the Surf Bathing Association of New South Wales changed its name to the Surf Life-Saving-Association of Australia and the movement by this time was a national one. Today there are well over two hundred clubs and active lifesavers can be counted in their thousands. Each club has its surf-boat crew and to be a member is a demanding pastime and means perfect physical fitness, constant exercise and often fairly strenuous dieting.

Surfing is an intoxicating sport and once mastered it becomes almost like a drug. At least some part of the long summer day must be concentrated to it. It is between you and the wave; the wave leads and it is for you to catch its rhythm. The slightest shift of body weight and the board responds. The light out there on the surf is blinding, like snow under the sun and the intense whiteness forces you to screw up your eyes. Not all the waves are to be ridden. You must learn to differentiate, to pick and choose. It is the great swelling wave that you must catch and these sometimes appear enormous. Heart in mouth you decide and suddenly you are borne aloft as if on the wings of foam – you ride the elements. For four, five hundred yards you lose the heaviness of your limbs. You have timed it right and remain poised on the crest the whole way, gathering speed as the wave breakers touch the shore. Surfing must be the nearest humans come to flying. Again and again you return. It is only sheer exhaustion that forces you ashore where, wrinkled with cold, you are compelled once more to struggle clumsily with your legs. It is hardly surprising that with such a sport within a quarter of an hour's drive from your office the city should exude so buoyant a spirit. But surfers or not the Sydneysiders have, most of them, an innate robustness about them, the sun-touched colour of an outdoor people. The sun is in the air and the tang of the sea is in the blood. One is immediately conscious of a certain optimism, of a kindness born of content. No pallid, harassed city dwellers these people and all of them in some way or other worship the sun and their wonderful beaches. If not beach lovers, then they find their recreation in flecking the rippled surface of their harbour with the sails of racing skiffs.

Sydney, more than any other, is a city of the sea and its streets, figuratively speaking, echo to the crash of Bondi's surf. The light is glorious. Walk of a morning up Macquarie Street, past the colonnaded portico of the Mitchell Library, skirt the Botanical Gardens and then turn and face downwards towards the city. On one corner stands the copper encased building of the State Office block with its black granite fountain tumbling its water in spiral snail-like form. Beyond runs Phillip Street with the great concave front of the Wentworth Hotel, and Chifley Square with the glass wall of the Qantas Building. From the roof of the P & O Offices flags flutter bravely against the Pacific sky, for there is always some degree of wind. Sydney's weather depends on its winds. Southerly busters generally start at the end of a hot day and the temperature can drop twenty degrees in as many minutes. Hot, humid weather sets in when the wind blows in from the tropic north, or north-west, bringing dry heat from the central deserts. This particular day we evoke a mild southerly buster is blowing that tugs at the flags. From the P & O Building the road dips straight down to Circular Quay and dipping further, but to the left, one comes to Australia Square with its great tower; its open air restaurants; its fountains and trees, and on a platform, out in the front, a giant, black iron Calder.

Sydney is an exciting city, optimistic, enthusiastic, and in the last few years even cosmopolitan. A sufficient number of Latins have emigrated to spice its food, giving rise to a string of amusing little restaurants. The people live in a manner appropriate for the climate. I remember lunching with a friend of mine, Marion Hall Best, I imagine Sydney's leading decorator. During the summer months she tents over her patio in circles of brilliant colour and it becomes a deliciously cool retreat, the pavilion of a Mogul Prince or a scene from Scheherazade as interpreted by Bakst. It is the most successful room I have seen for entertaining in hot weather.

A few architects, but not as many as one would wish, are designing exciting houses. Guildford Bell in Melbourne is one of this number. He is a man with an instinctive sense of quality, and a calm, measured feeling for proportion. Two buildings of his stand out well above the average; one, the painter Russell Drysdale's house, and the other a swimming pool and pavilion he designed for Mr James Fairfax; a beautifully restrained composition built of marble and stone matchlessly cut and joined. And then, inevitably, of course, comes the famous Opera House. Few buildings can equal it for creative originality.

In 1955 Sydney announced that it intended to build a National Opera House and the question of the design was to be decided by holding a world-wide competition. The entries were to be judged by four architects, two Australian, one English and one Finnish American, the late Eliel Saarinen. Over two hundred designs were received and after much deliberation design No 218 was finally selected, the work of a thirty-eight-year-old Dane called Joern Utzon. Utzon at the time had few buildings to his credit but had travelled fairly extensively. A scholarship had taken him to the USA and to Mexico. He had met Le Corbusier and Frank Lloyd Wright and knew Mies van der Rohe. He was not, however, at all well known, and his designs when submitted were little

View of Russell Drysdale's
house designed by
Guildford Bell.

more than elaborate sketches. Michael Baume, the Financial Editor of the
Bulletin, the author of a concise and unprejudiced account of the dramas
connected with the building of the Opera House, writes that Utzon's 'did not
even fit between the boundaries set to the site', and that 'before his winning
entry could be shown publicly, a university lecturer in architecture had to draw
up what he understood to be the side elevation. There was no indication that its
major hall would accommodate the 3,000 to 3,500 audience stipulated in the
competition' and 'there could be no coherent estimate of the cost because
Utzon did not know how to build it, let alone whether it would stand'. Furthermore 'Utzon's ignorance about how to build his winning design was shared by
all the experts involved in the project, including the international panel that
awarded him first prize and the structural engineer who promised to build it'.[85]

Considering these facts it showed great courage on the part of the judges to
have chosen Utzon's plans in the first place. Their report to the Government
also shows admirable foresight. 'We have been impressed by the beauty and
the exceptional possibilities of the site in relation to the Harbour and we are
convinced that the silhouette of any proposed building is of the greatest importance. We feel strongly that a large massive building, however practical,
would be entirely unsuitable on this particular site.' Again and again when
sifting through the other plans they returned to Utzon's drawings. They were
doubtful about them perhaps in the beginning, however, they were convinced
in the end 'that they present a concept of an Opera House which is capable of

becoming one of the great buildings of the world'. They were perfectly aware that there would be much criticism but 'we are, however, absolutely convinced about its merits'.

Utzon's own views on the subject also make interesting reading. As already explained the Opera House juts out on a point, the same point that Captain Phillip had originally reserved for Bennelong, the Aborigine he had practically adopted. Utzon in his plans was obviously very influenced by the siting of the proposed building. The peninsula is overlooked from all sides and stands at an acute angle dominated by the huge over-stretching, multiple parkway of Sydney Bridge.

'There can be no backsides to the building and nothing can be hidden from view, not even from the air – the building must form a free-standing sculpture in contrast to the square buildings surrounding it.

'The difference in character of the two components forming the building – the massive and imposing base, and the light and graceful shells on top of it – is emphasized by the choice of materials. The base is clad in granite-aggregate panels underlining its relationship to the ground, while the shells are covered with white glazed tiles. Separating the two are the glass walls, which will under-line the lightness of the shells and the feeling of open space on a platform on top of the base.'

Utzon took infinite pain over the tiles; five inches square, they are assembled in sets on chevron shaped tile-lids and shade from palest buff to white, the edge of the chevron being darker than its centre, a colour variation that one is not conscious of from a distance. Once in place they gleam softly taking the play of light from the sky, reflecting the cloud shadows, and are, in themselves, like great static cumuli. It would seem that Utzon discovered the particular glaze used in their manufacture while on his travels in the Far East and got a Swedish firm to experiment on the degrees of light absorbed. Once satisfied with the result it was decided to manufacture them on the spot – several millions of them.

Work began on the foundations in 1959 and its state opening was planned for 26 January, Australia Day, 1963. It is still not finished and has cost, so far, a good seven times its original estimate, somewhere in the region of fifty million dollars. There is certainly not the slightest doubt that had the eventual cost been known the Opera House would never have been built but how fortunate for us that things worked out as they did, and that Utzon's vision now dominates the harbour with its bold upsweeping forms.

So unorthodox a conception as Sydney's Opera House was bound to be attended by difficulties when it came to the actual building, they were endless and are a whole story unto themselves, far too long and complex to go into here. The real tragedy is that the man who conceived this extraordinary building is no longer in charge of its construction. Utzon resigned in February 1966, almost seven years after he had started the work. There had been a whole chapter of disagreements on structural matters, the culminating point being Utzon's insistence on having a plywood interior for the two great halls, his argument being that they would be like the 'inside of a string instrument'. But as Mr

Utzon took infinite pains
over the tiles of the
Sydney Opera House roof.

Baume points out 'what a violin sounds like from the inside, may have little relevance to its sounds outside'.[86] Not one of the great concert halls or opera houses have thin wooden linings. Their auditoriums are solidly lined with either plaster or heavy wood panelling and under the circumstances it is hardly surprising that those responsible for the final decision fought shy of approving Utzon's untried theories on acoustics, at best a highly unpredictable quality.

The firm of architects elected to take over the project estimate that the Opera House will be completed in 1972 at a further cost of some thirty-five million dollars. State lotteries finance the project and all one can do is to applaud a people courageous enough to give the world something so uniquely beautiful. Purists can argue that Utzon's designs are dishonest, well known architects have stated as much in print, declaring that his beautiful superstructure is nothing more than a superficial camouflage. They argue that in his plan form comes ahead of function. 'The inside of the building', they claim, 'had to be fitted into the limits set by the sculptural shapes.' Perhaps? Let us wait for the final judgement. Many might possibly regret having committed themselves.

From the Opera House we now jump to the ferries that skid around off Bennelong Point – they are typical of the Sydney scene. Double-ended, like trams they arrive at the wharf, the skipper moves to the other end and off they plough in the opposite direction without having to turn round. It is estimated that these Sydney ferries carry about fifteen million passengers a year, a pale shadow, we are told, of their former bustle. Before the Sydney Harbour Bridge was opened in 1932, they reached a peak of nearly a million passengers a week.[87]

Circular Quay is their terminal and to board them you drop a token into a slot and walk through a turnstile – they have no conductors. The Manly Ferry serving the northern-beaches is the largest in the service and several of them have sailed out from England under their own steam. The ships serving Manly have to be seaworthy to cope with the heavy seas that come sweeping in through the Heads, for their route takes them straight across the wide opening. During the last war a miniature Japanese submarine, sneaking into the harbour, blew up one of these ferries while she happened to be carrying a shipload of naval ratings.

Going to Manly by ferry used to be a regular Sunday outing towards the turn of the century and for some 120 years Sydney's inhabitants have been making the trip, first in a paddle-wheeler worked by horses on a tread-wheel and later by iron-screw steamers. It was and still is an invigorating experience – half an hour of sun, water and wind straight from the Pacific. Most of the ferries are still pleasantly old-fashioned with varnished wood-work and polished brass fittings, but lately two smart new hydrofoils, fitted with powerful Mercedes-Benz diesels, have appeared on the scene. Made in Italy they can travel at thirty-six knots thus cutting the crossing of eight miles to Manly down to a brief quarter of an hour. They have their own glassed-in landing stage and showing off slightly in front of the other ferries, they take wing, skimming over the top of the lapis blue water. It is an excellent way of seeing the harbour.

Australians like the Americans are air-minded people. They have the climate to be so and the distances to make it worth while. Most of the large station-owners have a landing strip and fly their own planes. It was in this manner that I spent a weekend at Yulgelbar on the Clarence River, 350 miles north of Sydney. The property had been bought recently by the Baillieu Myers of Melbourne and Guildford Bell the architect had been called in to attend to its shadow-haunted neglect. For forty years this crenellated house, the dream of a pioneer in stone, had been drowsing alone in the bush. Built round a central patio, flanked on its river-front by two towers and a colonnaded terrace, it had, and still has even without its towers, a distinctly exotic look. Rough lawns dip down to the river and up a slight rise over which marches a stand of grass trees, like strange Aboriginal sentinels from the past. On top of the rise sits a classicised gazebo where the original owners were in the habit of taking their afternoon tea. A carriage-way winds up to the top and they say that Aboriginal maids struggled up the hill with the silver at tea-time. At any rate the ritual, today, is somewhat simplified; towards evening a jeep bumps you up to the top and whiskies and sodas are substituted for the loaded tea-tray.

Yulgelbar is an Aboriginal word and means 'place of little fishes' and the story of its building is as romantic as the style of the house leads one to suspect. It had belonged to the Ogilvies; the original Captain Ogilvie had served under Nelson at the Battle of Trafalgar and after the wars with Napoleon had emigrated to Australia with his sons. His eldest son, Edward Ogilvie, became a pioneer grazer and in his wanderings discovered the upper reaches of the

Yulgelbar. *Left* Painted in
the days of its neglect by
Donald Friend.
Below View from the
house on to the Clarence
River.

Clarence. It was rich land and his sheep prospered and with the rise of prices in wool at the outbreak of the Crimean War he soon found himself a wealthy man. A tour of Europe followed and while in Ireland he met his future wife, a Miss de Burgh from County Kildare. It is told about him that he first saw Miss de Burgh in church and almost immediately fell in love with her. Anyhow they were married soon after the meeting – she a young bride of eighteen, he a man of forty. Returning to Australia in 1859, he shipped with him a quantity of bricks, a Scottish carpenter and a whole boat load of German masons. In his portmanteau he carried the plans of his dream house – Yulgelbar. The architect, possibly Ogilvie himself, appears to have been inspired by the building fashion of southern Spain, where the Moors had once ruled. There is something almost Mexican about the house, which, of course, is perfectly logical since architecturally they derived from the same influence. The foundation stone was laid in 1860 and the castle (for that is how it is locally known) took six years to build, the mortar for its bricks being made from crushed oyster shells brought by bullock cart from the mouth of the Clarence River, eighty miles away. When finished it was sumptuously appointed with great chandeliers and heavy teakwood furniture carved in India. Ogilvie was fond of entertaining and gave great receptions insisting that his guests dress for dinner. But since few of the local farmers would have possessed such a thing as a stiff shirt and a black tie let alone the clothes to go with it, Ogilvie is said to have kept a wardrobe full cut to different sizes and any guest without a dinner jacket was fitted out for the evening. The footmen were all Aboriginal and were dressed in silk knee breeches with powdered wigs and once dinner was over they would hang this finery on pegs in the pantry and stalk home to their wurlies in the park, stark naked.

The present housekeeper's mother was married at Yulgelbar and she has photographs of the garden as it used to be in 1905; a carriage drive winds down to the river between beds of roses and there is a beautifully tended croquet lawn. Among the views were some faded portraits of the Ogilvies' daughters, eight of them in all and when the family was sent on a visit to England during his later years, they made friends with the poet Robert Browning who called them his 'Australian octave'. Ogilvie died in 1896 after a fall from his horse and the family remained a further thirty-six years in the house before it was sold to its present owners.

Since distances are of hardly any consequence in Australia there were few parts of the country that I did not visit, Tasmania included. But the Island should be a subject all on its own and well deserves attention if for no other reason than the number of fine old houses that exist, scattered over different parts of the country. Somewhat isolated and the smallest of the states, Tasmania is also, economically speaking, the one that has the least to offer and has thus escaped the boom years that have done much to change the rest of the land. She is the poor country cousin, out of the swim of things and has remained unspoilt and old-fashioned. Her towns have an air of distinction and the beautiful countryside has remained almost completely inviolate.

Malahide. *Above* In 1845;
lithograph by Royston
and Brown.
Right The house as it
stands today, restored by
the present Lord Talbot
of Malahide.

Killymoon, built between 1842-8.

To mention only a few of the houses there is Malahide, an original grant made to the Talbot family in 1824 and now restored and lived in for part of the year by its present owner Lord Talbot of Malahide, a keen botanist who has lately published a comprehensive work on the native flowers of the island, and is a direct descendant of its original builder. Among my own personal favourites comes Killymoon, and the seignorial Panshanger, a house of calm classical design; the miniature Palladian Ballochmyle and the romantic, empty Bona Vista with its beautifully finished masonry. Ross Bridge, designed by John Lee Archer, Tasmania's leading architect, and built between 1830 and 1836, is

Opposite Skyline of Sydney harbour.

Overleaf, left Patio arranged by Marion Hall Best in her Sydney house.
Right Sydney Opera House as seen by William Dobell.

268

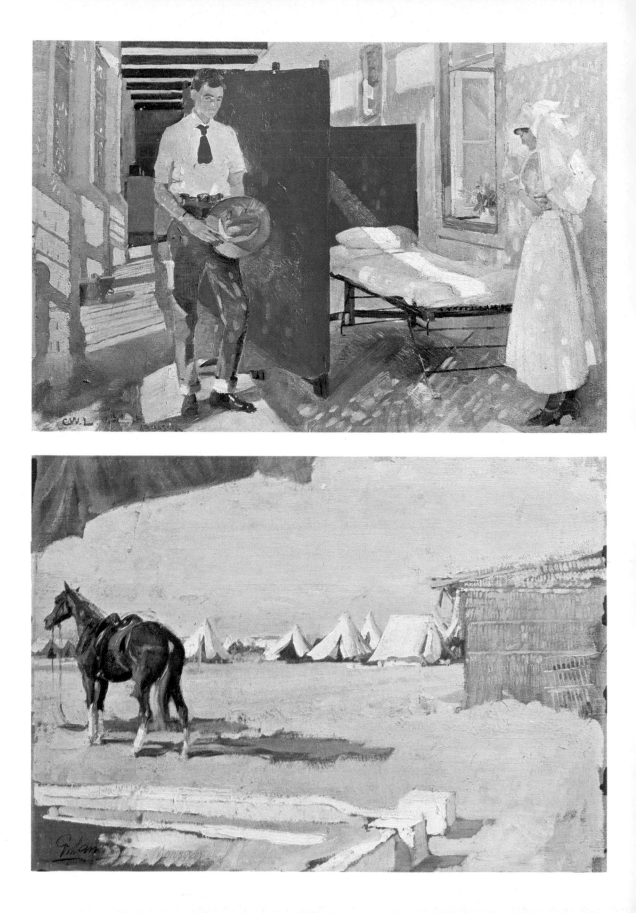

Panshanger. *Above* The house in
the mid-nineteenth century;
coloured lithograph by Day and
Haghe. *Right* The house as it stands
today.

Opposite, top Troops Ward, Abbasia,
by George Lambert.
*Bottom Moascar as Seen from Banjo
Paterson's Tent,* by George Lambert,
painted during the Middle East
Campaign.

Ballochmyle, built during the 1830s.

Portrait of the Rev. Dr Bedford, drawn by Wainewright while in Tasmania.

considered to be the finest bridge of the period still existent in Australia. Convict built of local sandstone it has the strangest voussoir stones facing its arches; a glutinous foliage-motif incorporating animals and humans which have more the appearance of having been squeezed out of a sugar icing mixer than actually carved.

However hurried and lacking in space one cannot leave Tasmania without mention of Thomas Griffith Wainewright, a fascinating personality and a highly accomplished painter; a literator, a friend of Fuseli and Blake. Transported for forgery but suspected of having poisoned three members of his family by measured doses of strychnine, he is better known for his misdeeds than for his talents, which were considerable. Bernard Smith judges him 'the most accomplished portrait draughtsman at work in Australia during the Colonial Period'.

While in London Wainewright is known to have made a portrait sketch of Byron which has since disappeared and both Dickens and Oscar Wilde have written about him. He is Julius Slinkton in Dickens's *Hunted Down*, a short story commissioned by America for a thousand dollars, a high price to pay in those days. Wainewright was forty-three when he was transported for life, and in his middle fifties when he died of disseminated sclerosis, a disease of the central nervous system. The *Melbourne Spectator*, writing about him after his death, describes him as having had deeply set eyes with long hair and a snake-like expression with a vaguely sinister air – a down-at-heels Mephistopheles. His conversation and manners, we are told, were winning in the extreme and grossly sensual. 'If commissioned to execute the portrait of a lady, he would always endeavour to give an erotic direction to the conversation.'[88]

Another interesting character is George Augustus Robinson, a little bricklayer who single-handed braved the wilds of Tasmania and made contact with the few remaining Aboriginal tribes there. They were hostile to the whites and were gradually dying out and his idea was to try to save them from extinction by isolating them on an island. It was a noble effort but an abortive one for they just pined away, being carried off eventually by a variety of chest complaints. Truganini was the last of her race and died at an advanced old age at Hobart in 1876.

Charles Darwin in the *Beagle,* and Thomas Huxley sailing the Pacific in HMS *Rattlesnake* in 1847, the world's first anthropologists, were amongst the earliest to notice the difference between the Tasmanian Aborigines and their northern brothers. Huxley discovered certain negroid traits and compared them to the inhabitants of New Caledonia, supposing that they had migrated from there on large rafts. Certainly in the paintings one sees of them they appear different from the mainland Aborigines; their strange hair styles making them look like Egyptians. They wore their hair in long rats-tails thickened with a mixture of animal fat and red ochre, a mixture that on hardening served as a natural helmet, looking exactly like an early predynastic wig.

Head of a Convict, very characteristic of low cunning & revenge!

Self-portrait by Thomas Griffith Wainewright, made while serving his sentence in Hobart. The mocking inscription is written in his own hand.

A sepia drawing by Wainewright. Many of his earlier drawings were 'tinged with voluptuousness which tumbled on the borders of the indelicate'.

Canberra is another impression again. When I first went there twenty-two years ago, it was in its infancy, as ephemeral as one of Ledoux's magnificent schemes – a capital in search of a city. Tattered curtains hung at the long windows of its concert hall, rotted by the sun, for they were always drawn and its doors were seldom opened. The only people to be met with in its streets were its gardeners, straw-hatted, shirtless and bronzed, clipping the hedges, or the grass, round the bole of a cypress. It was a baffling experience for diplomats. They found themselves *en poste* in the country, their social life confined to picnics and snowy trips to Mount Kosciusko. But Canberra has grown considerably since then, its population doubling between 1950 and 1959, and doubling again by 1966. Though still uncrowded it must now number some hundred thousand.

It is a pleasant garden-city lying two thousand feet above sea level, set in a gentle hollow surrounded by a rim of lion-coloured hills. The nights are almost cold and the mornings fresh, sparkling with dew, the skies pale, and shadows soft and dusty blue. Tests were made as to the type of trees best suited to the soil at this altitude with the result that the city has avenues of north American firs, birches, cottonwoods and Mediterranean cypresses. Elms and beech mingle with the kurrajongs and the wattles of Australia. Of course there are the eucalyptus, but it is a relief that for once they have not been allowed to dominate the scene. Intelligent controls have also prevented land developers from ruining the approaches to the city; there are no hoardings, no television aerials and no neon-light advertising.

The actual site was officially ratified in 1911 and the A.C.T. (Australian Capital Territory) itself covers an area of a little under a hundred square miles, approximately twelve thousand acres of which is covered by the city area. An international competition for the city plan was won by an American from Chicago, Walter Burley Griffin, who had practised in partnership with Frank Lloyd Wright. His runner-up was the distinguished Finnish architect Eliel Saarinen. Various names were considered by the Cabinet for their new capital, one an almost unpronounceable combination of the different State capitals. 'Myola' and 'Shakespeare' were among the other names suggested. Canberra, the eventual winner, is of Aboriginal origin one of its meanings being 'the meeting-place' – very appropriate. The chosen name was kept a close secret until the naming ceremony, which was performed by Lady Denman, the wife of the Governor-General, at Capitol Hill on 12 March 1913. In pronouncing the name she placed the emphasis on the first syllable – Can-b'ra – which is the accepted and correct pronunciation.

The task of translating a blue-print into a city came at an unfortunate moment. The war delayed development for many years and it was not until 1927 that the Federal Parliament could transfer from its temporary seat in Melbourne. Burley Griffin had centred his whole design round an extensive artificial lake and for years it was Canberra's stock joke and remained a miasmic swamp where cows grazed. Hardly the proper note for a State capital! It is only since 1964, by the damming of the Molonglo River at Yarralumla, that

Griffin's water has reflected the beautiful Australian clouds as he had intended.

There is no denying that Canberra has charm, but on my recent visit, I was disappointed in its scale. One cannot help making a comparison with the other world capitals of recent construction: Washington, New Delhi, Brasilia and Shandrigar. And Canberra in the comparison emerges very much the minor statement. The buildings appear flat, squashed almost, as if some giant hand had pressed them into the landscape; not at all suitable for the role Canberra plays and will increasingly play in the world affairs of today.

For me, as for most people, I think, Canberra's Australian War Memorial Museum is the most moving thing about the city. It stands away by itself up against a hill, a domed building flanked by two colonnades bordering a rectangular pool. Its lines are square and severe, its walls devoid of any ornament. It looks vaguely oriental, something Lutyens might have built in Palestine. It is not a particularly distinguished building but the collection it houses and the manner in which it is displayed are remarkable. Room after room of relics; paintings, sculptures, photographs, maps, uniforms, models and last but certainly not least, eerily realistic dioramas. Without windows and with only artificial lighting these rooms have managed, in some extraordinary way, to recapture the atmosphere of the different wars in which Australian soldiers have been involved, from the Sudan campaign onwards. Europe's first Great War lives here in these great halls, clear and vivid under the uncompromising glare of electricity, more poignantly alive than one would have believed possible. The walls are saturated with the suffering, the memories of those fast-receding years. The air is heavy, haunted by the countless dead. Though unspoken, one hears the whispered echo of the old familiar names, Passchendaele, Menin Gate, and Ypres, Cambrai and Vimy Ridge. How wonderfully Australia's War Museum evokes the past and the very feel of the landscape. From the Gallipoli Galleries you move to the Near East. The clear light and bright sands of its dioramas then give way to the sombre hues of a Flanders sky, leaden and grey; stretcher-bearers struggle through a morass of mud. The wounded lie slumped up against the side of a shell-hole. One sees the graveyards with their garish trophy of mauve and white beads, crosses are knocked awry among the sticks of trees, above which rises the ruins of a steeple. In a later room paintings depict the endless dog fights with the Japanese in the skies over New Guinea and then finally a canvas by Dennis Adam showing the Japanese surrender on board HMS *Glory*. It is all there. Lost to the outside world one forgets the hours and it is closing time before one realises it. The Last Post is played and a notice asks you to stand fast and then move quietly to the exit.

One emerges a stranger to Canberra's smiling hills, sad with a heavy sadness that will not pass for several hours. One's spirits revive, however, as one's plane touches down in vital, shining, welcoming Sydney. And then comes another break for as Trollope writes: 'Sydney is one of those places which when a man leaves it knowing that he will never return, he cannot leave without a prayer and a tear. Such is its loveliness.'

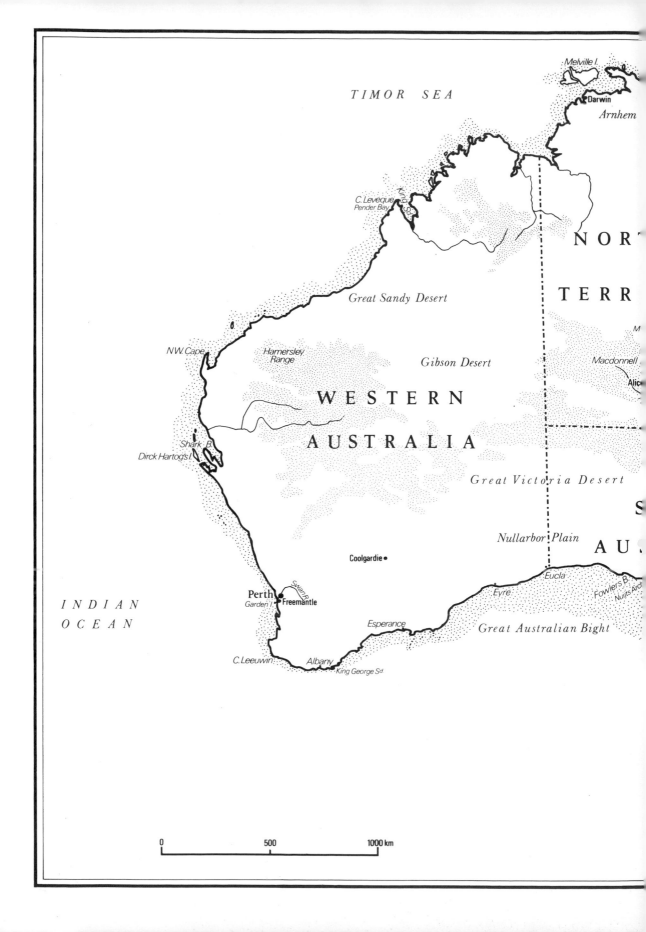

Notes

1 *Australia and New Zealand* by Anthony Trollope, London, 1873.

2 *The Land of Promise* by William Shaw, London, 1854.

3 *Following the Equator* by Mark Twain, Hartford, 1897.

4 *The Tyranny of Distance* by Geoffrey Blainey, Sydney, 1966.

5 After the publication of *A New Voyage Round the World*, Dampier had written *A Discourse of Winds* in which, it is still considered, there is a valuable pre-scientific essay on meteorological geography.

6 Cook in his Journals spells his name wrongly as Magra.

7 *The Tyranny of Distance* by Geoffrey Blainey, Sydney, 1966.

8 *A Narrative of the Expedition to Botany Bay*, London, 1789, and *A Complete Account of the Settlement of Port Jackson, in New South Wales*, published four years later.

9 *Admiral Arthur Phillip* by George Mackaness, Sydney, 1937.

10 *Experiences of a Convict* by J. F. Mortlock, Sydney, 1965.

11 *Australia and New Zealand* by Anthony Trollope, London, 1876.

12 As Stockdale points out in *Governor Phillip's Voyages*, it is perfectly understandable that 'Botany Bay should have appeared in a more advantageous light than to Governor Phillip...their objects were very different; the one required only shelter and refreshment for a small vessel, and during but a short time; the other had great numbers to provide for'.

13 The exact spot where the ceremony took place has never been established, but it is generally accepted to have been mid-way on the western shore of the cove on the present site of Sydney Cove Terminal.

14 *Voyage of Governor Phillip*.

15 *Two Years in New South Wales* by Peter Cunningham, London, 1827.

16 *The World of the First Australians* by R. M. and C. H. Brendt, Sydney,

17 *An Account of the English Colony in New South Wales* by D. Collins, London, 1798.

18 *Following the Equator* by Mark Twain, Hartford, 1897.

19 His *Illustrationes Florae Novae Hollandiae* begun in 1803 was abandoned after the issue of the plates.

20 *Australian Painting* by Bernard Smith, London, 1962.

21 *A Voyage to Terra Australis*,

22 *The Australians* by Arnold L. Haskell, London, 1943.

23 *The Tyranny of Distance* by Geoffrey Blainey, Sydney, 1966.

24 *The Convict Ships* 1787–1868 by Charles Bateson, Glasgow, 1959.

25 *Stories of Australia in the Early Days* by Marcus Clarke, London, 1897.

26 *The Land of Promise* by William Shaw, London, 1854.

27 *Australia. A Social and Political History* edited by Professor Gordon Greenwood, Sydney, 1955.

28 *The Life and Adventures of John Nicol, Mariner*, Edinburgh, 1822.

29 *Experience of a Convict* by J. F. Mortlock, London, 1964.

30 *Australia and New Zealand* by Anthony Trollope, London, 1873.

31 *Their Shining Eldorado* by Elspeth Huxley, London, 1967.

32 *Settlers and Convicts* by Alexander Harris, London, 1847.

33 'Reasons for the Entire Abolition of Flogging' by Alexander Harris, *The People's Journal*, April, 1846.

34 Charles Rowcroft writing in the *Sydney Gazette*.

35 *Our Antipodes* by Colonel Charles Mundy, London, 1852.

36 *Lachlan Macquarie, His Life, Adventures and Times* by M. H. Ellis, Sydney, 1947.

37 *The Early Australian Architects and their Works* by Morton Herman, Sydney, 1954.

38 *Lachlan Macquarie, His Life, Adventures and Times*.

39 *Lachlan Macquarie, His Life, Adventures and Times*.

40 The convict, James Hardy Vaux, compiled a glossary while undergoing a term of hard labour at Newcastle. In his foreword he writes that an acquaintance of his, a distinguished magistrate, had suggested he do so for use in court to help interpret the evidence given by prisoners.

41 *Two Years in New South Wales*.

42 *Savage Life and Scenes in Australia and New Zealand* by G. F. Angas, London, 1847.

[43] *Australian Painting* by Bernard Smith, London, 1962.

[44] *Two Years in New South Wales.*

[45] *The Sydney Book* by Marjorie Barnard, Sydney, 1948.

[46] *Two Expeditions into the Interior of Southern Australia, 1828–31*, London, 1833.

[47] *Australian Dictionary of Biography.*

[48] *The Hentys. An Australian Colonial Tapestry* by Marnie Bassett, 1954.

[49] *Australian Explorers* by Kathleen Fitzpatrick, London, 1958.

[50] *Ibid.*

[51] Of the meals made by the different explorers one in particular, described by Ernest Giles, sticks in my memory. Giles and his party were caught in the Gibson Desert and when nearly dead from thirst and starvation, they providentially come across a creek. Giles crawls to the water and just as he got the bank, he heard a faint squeak, and looking around he saw a small dying wallaby which had evidently been thrown from its mother's pouch. It only weighed about two ounces, and was almost furless. 'The instant I saw it, like an eagle I pounced and ate it, living, raw, dying–fur, skin, bones, skull and all. The delicious taste of that creature I shall never forget'.

[52] *The Tyranny of Distance.*

[53] *The Land of Promise* by William Shaw, London, 1854.

[54] *Australia and New Zealand.*

[55] *Banking Under Difficulties: or Life on the Goldfields of Victoria, New South Wales and New Zealand* by George Ogilvy Preshaw, Melbourne, 1888.

[56] *Op. Cit.*

[57] *Notes of a Gold Digger and Gold Digger's Guide* by James Bonwick, Melbourne, 1852.

[58] *Land, Labour and Gold: or Two Years in Victoria* by William Howitt, London, 1855.

[59] *A Lady's Visit to the Gold Diggers of Australia in 1852–53* by Mrs Charles Clacy, London, 1853.

[60] *A Short Account of the Late Dicoveries of Gold in Australia* by John Elphinstone Erskine, London, 1851.

[61] *Op. Cit.*

[62] *Practical Experiences at the Diggings of the Gold-fields of Victoria* by William Hall, London, 1852.

[63] *Kangaroo Land* by the Rev. Arthur Polehampton, London, 1862.

[64] *Lord Robert Cecil's Gold Fields Diary* edited by Ernest Scott, 1935.

[65] *Land, Labour and Gold; or Two Years in Victoria* by William Howitt, London, 1855.

[66] *An Australian Journalist. The Emigrant in Australia, or Gleanings from the Gold Fields.* The author remains anonymous.

[67] *The Tyranny of Distance.*

[68] *The History of Australia from 1606 to 1876* by Alexander and George Sutherland, Melbourne, 1878.

[69] *The Australian Legend* by R. Ward, Melbourne, 1958.

[70] *Australia's Son. The Story of Ned Kelly* by Max Brown, Melbourne, 1948.

[71] *Australian Painting* by Bernard Smith, London, 1962.

[72] *Australia's Son. The Story of Ned Kelly* by Max Brown, Melbourne, 1948.

[73] *Op. Cit.*

[74] *Op. Cit.*

[75] *The Land of Promise* by William Shaw, London, 1854.

[76] *The Walls Around Us* by Robin Boyd, Melbourne, 1962.

[77] Anzac, a code name for the Australia and New Zealand Army Corps.

[78] *Town Life in Australia* by R. E. N. Twopeny, London, 1883.

[79] *Following the Equator.*

[80] Horse-breaking on a station demands an iron nerve and is a difficult job. Good horses are needed to round up cattle and most stations have several thoroughbred stallions. These horses are allowed to run wild until they are four or five years old and when the time comes to break them they show a good deal of spirit. Gordon was a wandering horse-breaker for seven years and methods in his day were short, sharp and decisive. It was considered a waste of time if the colt was not ridden on the fourth day after he was caught and the first three or four days called for all the courage, resolution and dare-devil of men like Gordon.

[81] *Adam Lindsay Gordon* by Edith Humphries and Douglas Sladen, London, 1912.

[82] Bernard Smith tells an amusing story about Glover in his *European Vision and the South Pacific*. During the brief peace of 1814 he visited France and while at the Louvre set up his easel in the Grande Galerie between two landscapes by Poussin and Claude. There was no question of his copying one or the other. He was just painting one of his own!

[83] 'Conrad Martens' by Marjorie Barnard in the *Australian National Journal*, Autumn, 1940.

[84] *The Architecture of Victorian Sydney* by Morton Herman, Sydney, 1956.

[85] *The Sydney Opera House Affair* by Michael Baume, 1967.

[86] *Op. Cit.*

[87] 'Sydney Water Communications' by Brian Carroll, *Walkabout*, March, 1969.

[88] *Wainewright in Tasmania* by Robert Crossland, 1954.

Photographic acknowledgments

Most of the illustrations in this book were collected by the author from numerous sources during his travels in Australia. The author and publishers would like to thank in particular the following people and collections:

Allport Library, Hobart, Tasmania, 84; Art Gallery of New South Wales, Sydney, 205, 244a, 246; Art Gallery of South Australia, Adelaide, 156, 166r, 250-1, 252; Australia War Memorial, Canberra, 272t, 272b; Australian Institute of Anatomy, Canberra, 213; British Museum, 275b, (Natural History) 98a, 98b; Roderick Cameron Collection, 42-3, 46, 238-9, (Photo Roderick Cameron) 97a, 97r, 154, 161r, 171, 181, 187, 207, 214, 224, 228l, 228b, 229, 234, 263, 265b, 268, 273r, 274a; Miss Combes of Fonthill, 242b; Max Dupain, 8, 16, 17, 19, 124, 125a, 253t, 253mr, 253b, 257, 261; Kerry Dundas, 32, 45t, 47, 61a, 61r, 62, 64, 67, 69, 71b, 78, 118, 121, 217, 220, 221b, 232, 241, 242a, 254a, 254r, 255, 256, 271; Kaiser Friedrich Museum, Berlin, 39; Nan Kivell Collection, National Library of Australia, Canberra, 29, 35, 45a, 52, 126, 127, 131, 132-3, 137, 138, 142l, 145a, 150, 152, 155, 158, 193, 204, 212, 216, 221r, 222, 273a, 275a; Rudy Komon Gallery, 271; Launceston Museum, Tasmania, 27, 100; Mitchell Library, Sydney, 25, 71m, 76 (Photo K. Dundas), 88m, 88r, 99, 123, 141, 142r (Photo K. Dundas), 149, 174-5, 177fl (Photo K. Dundas), 179b (Photo K. Dundas), 182, 183, 189a, 189r, 199 (Photo K. Dundas), 218-9, 243, 249; Municipal Library, Forbes (N.S.W.), 205; Mr & Mrs Baillieu Myers Collection, 265l, National Gallery of Victoria, Melbourne, 41b, 237, 247; National Library of Australia, Canberra, 58l, 116r; National Portrait Gallery, London, 55; Public Library of New South Wales, Sydney, 227; Queen Victoria Museum, Launceston, Tasmania, 206, 240; Dr Graeme Robertson (from *Ornamental Cast Iron in Melbourne*), 223; Kenneth Ross, Melbourne, 230; Robin Smith, Kirribilli, 269; State Library of Victoria, Melbourne, 110, 191; Tasmanian Museum and Art Gallery, Hobart, 58r, 274b; Victorian Art Centre, Melbourne, 173, 197; by courtesy of *Vogue* (Australia), 270.

Index